THE CORPORATE CULTURE HANDBOOK

THE CORPORATE CULTURE HANDBOOK

How to Plan, Implement and Measure
a Successful Culture Change Programme

Gabrielle O'Donovan

The Liffey Press

Published by
The Liffey Press
Ashbrook House
10 Main Street
Raheny, Dublin 5, Ireland
www.theliffeypress.com

© 2006 Gabrielle O'Donovan

A catalogue record of this book is
available from the British Library.

ISBN 1-905785-29-1

Printed in the United Kingdom by MPG Books

Contents

LIST OF FIGURES

Glossary of Terms

These basic vocabulary terms describe concepts in this book. For optimal understanding, it is essential that readers understand each term as it is used.

Attitude: settled mode of thinking and feeling in relation to somebody or something which affects one's thoughts and behaviour; from a culture perspective we look at shared attitudes

Bankwide: HSBC Holdings Hong Kong, plus five local subsidiary companies

Behaviour: the way somebody or something acts in relation to somebody or something; from a culture perspective we look at shared behaviours

Beliefs: theories for guiding attitudes and behaviour which are accepted as true

Character: all the mental and moral qualities that make a person; the ability to ethically handle a difficult or dangerous situation

Change Agent: an individual who is predisposed to drive change, who recognises the opportunity in crisis, thrives on challenge and forges new frontiers

Cult: an extreme religious group that is not part of an established religion; a faddish belief, idea or attitude that influences people's lives

Culture Change: realigning a culture that has gone off the tracks and become maladapted, or modifying a culture to meet new business challenges

Ethics: the science of morals

HSBC Top Management: the Asia Chairman, the General Manager Hong Kong plus ten of their direct and indirect reports who created the programme Steering Committee and Advisory Committee

MfV: Managing for Value, HSBC Group corporate strategy, 1999–2003

Paradigm: lens through which we see the world to make sense of that around us

Personality: the qualities or traits of a person seen as a whole

Philosophy: i) the study of the nature and meaning of existence and reality, good and evil, etc.; ii) one of the many systems of thought that has this study as a base; iii) a rule you have in living your life, doing your job, etc.

Principles: basic general truth that underlies something, e.g. a subject or system of morality; ethical values

Spirit: the vital or animating force within living beings

Spiritual: of the human spirit or soul, not of physical things

Tradition: the process of handing down a culture's distinctive statements, beliefs, legends, customs, etc. from generation to generation, especially by word-of-mouth

Values: attitudes and behaviours that are considered useful or desirable; in the organisational context "values" often refers to core competencies; values may be ethical or unethical

About the Author

Gabrielle O'Donovan has worked with major blue-chip companies for many years on corporate culture management. Her recent change management programme for HSBC in Hong Kong (detailed in this book) won a number of awards including an ASTD Excellence in Practice Award in 2005 and her articles have been published in *Corporate Governance International*, *Banking Today* and *Best Practices Management*. Gabrielle has a Masters degree from the University of Sheffield and is a member of Mensa.

ACKNOWLEDGEMENTS

While I wrote this book myself, others contributed both directly and indirectly and I am indebted to each and every one; to David Givens and Brian Langan of The Liffey Press for their valuable insights, their care for its quality and their enthusiasm; to Nikki Scaife for exploring concepts with me and being a source of inspiration; to my sister Fran Wheeler for her guidance; to George Horsington, Simon Coombs and James Lewis for their valuable critiques; to Ricky, Nikki and Laura for the diagrams; to the Bernardo family in Hong Kong for their friendship and support; to my mother Christine, my family and friends; and to Dad, my guardian angel.

This book would never have existed without my heroes at HSBC; one cannot guard the values of an organisation and nurture the growth and development of 15,000 people, each day and every day, and simply stop caring when an official change programme ends. Thousands of wonderful people in the Bank strove to embrace change, and this is reflected in the outcomes and results of "Together, We Win!" They made the vision a reality, and this book is theirs as much as it is mine.

Also, I would like to thank those who told me I could *not* do it (either as a practitioner or as a writer), creating obstacles along the way. These experiences added to my resolve, providing me with unimaginable insights and rich learning opportunities which will benefit readers.

To Eamonn

My father
My role-model
My guardian angel

PREFACE

In the twenty-first century, the biggest requirement of CEOs is to drive change and, as the ugly chapters of corporate malfeasance are written, the biggest business issue to emerge in this new millennium is corporate culture management. Some observers suggest that recent governance scandals are isolated incidences, while others shrug them off with the depressing view that they are simply a reflection on human nature or the price of capitalism — something we must learn to live with. I do not subscribe to either viewpoint. Through my research, I have come to understand that while we can indeed expect more and more cases to come to light, the trend *can* be reversed. This can be achieved through the establishment of *a culture of ethics*.

In this new era, the other big cultural challenge facing corporations is keeping the internal environment apace with the external environment to meet market requirements. This requires that we foster the dual forces of corporate culture (tradition and innovation) to champion service or innovation. In young and nimble companies the workforce is more likely to be aggressive in their efforts to meet market demand and keep abreast with external developments. But as companies grow and mature, more and more staff collect in back-office functions and a multitude of policies and processes become institutionalised. Staff can lose touch with the world outside and, when policies and processes lose their relevancy, it can be hard for people to let go of that which has become a source of security and a way of life. As a result, the internal environment loses its dynamism, moving at a rate slower than that of the world beyond, and goods and services lose their market appeal. For organisations facing such a challenge, business leaders need to revitalise the internal environment to keep it in-sync with the world beyond. In the services industry this may well translate to creating *a service culture* while in the manufacturing industry it is more likely to mean the creation of *a culture of innovation*.

In response to these cultural issues, another trend is emerging — many multinationals are moving away from piecemeal change projects which target inert structures alone (policies, processes, technology etc.), to driving organisation-wide programmes which manage *the human landscape* also:

❖ In 2000 the CEO of General Motors rolled out the global programme "Go Fast" to keep the internal environment apace with the external environment;

❖ In 2000 the General Manager of HSBC Hong Kong rolled-out "Together, We Win!" to create a service culture in HSBC Holdings and five local subsidiary companies;

❖ In 2004 the Chief Executive of Citicorp set about creating a culture of ethics and accountability at the sprawling financial institution

While each of these companies will have used different approaches and with varying success, they all chose to tackle corporate culture at a strategic level. Perhaps they know that if an organisation does not manage its culture, it can risk atrophy or even death. Certainly, these trends stress that corporate culture is on the agenda now and clearly here to stay. Business stewards can choose to manage their culture, or be led by it.

While the concept of organisational culture has been around for at least sixty years, the analysis of the phenomenon only began almost a quarter of a century ago when an influential book, *Corporate Culture: The Rites and Rituals of Corporate Life*,[1] made

---

[1]Deal and Kennedy, *Corporate Culture: The Rites and Rituals of Corporate Life*, Perseus Publishing, 1982.

popular the idea that corporate culture is a key driver of business performance. This work was closely followed by a significant piece of research from two Harvard professors, Kotter and Heskett, who clearly defined the economic and social costs of low-performance cultures. Based on an eleven-year study, the authors demonstrated that cultures that emphasise all the key managerial constituencies and leadership from managers at all levels outperform firms that did not have those cultural traits, by a large margin. This work did much to raise the credibility of corporate culture management in the eyes of business leaders in the late twentieth century. In 1985, Professor Edgar Schein of MIT gave us his perspective on the essence of corporate culture, putting forward a model which went beyond tangible manifestations of the phenomenon to expose its deeper nature.

During the 1980s and 1990s many more academics and consultants came on board to develop widely varying definitions and models on the essence of corporate culture. Most definitions on the essence of culture reflected the ability of consultants to reinvent a concept "ad infinitum", while typologies of cultures provided more concrete dimensions to the collage. However, given the divergent views on the fundamentals, there was disagreement as to whether culture could be managed and measured. So while academics pondered the issue, some notable CEOs rolled up their sleeves and simply got on with the business of trying to manage their corporate culture, learning through trial and error. Over time, their organisational experiences became a source of insights for academics, practitioners and authors alike. Yet to this day, and despite the abundance of corporate culture books on the market, not one has yet addressed the design and implementation of a corporate culture change strategy based on primary research. This knowledge gap needs to be filled and with that realisation the seeds for this book were sown.

*   *   *

To provide readers with a contextual background for my views, I will share some of the more pertinent experiences that have shaped my outlook and career as an agent of change. My induction into change management came in 1991. Upon completion of my undergraduate studies at University of Bolton, I was hired by Rabone Chesterman of Birmingham UK, a manufacturer of spirit levels and other tools for craftsmen. After more than two hundred years in business, the company was folding in the face of economic pressures. Demonstrating ethical leadership and loyalty to the workforce, senior management hired a small team to re-position staff members in the workforce. I was on this team. The operations staff were mostly Indian immigrants. Many had worked with Rabone Chesterman for more than twenty years and had little understanding of the external work environment. Some had limited English, with no idea how to put together a resumé, let alone present themselves to prospective employers. Working in partnership with the management team, my job was to counsel staff, identify the skill-sets of individuals, prepare resumés, match individuals' skills with openings in the job market, call prospective employers and coach staff on interview techniques. In a recessionary environment, placing them would be a challenge.

Over time, I had the opportunity to get to know the workforce quite well. Most were welcoming and liked to pop in for a chat each day, while a few treated us with suspicion. Over time we were able to gain the trust of the workforce as, one-by-one, my colleagues and I placed staff members in new jobs. I remember one fellow Irishman particularly. He would come into the "job centre" we had established to review posts available, but he didn't talk to us much and often left in a cloud of gloom. Time was starting to run out and the factory would soon close. Imagine the rush of satisfaction I felt the day he came into the job-centre after an interview which I had arranged for him. Beaming widely, he strode up to my desk and said, "I got that job! It's a fantastic company, and I get to use machinery that I never dreamt I would have the opportunity to use. I had no idea a company like that would be interested in my skills. Thank you so much for your efforts." So he *could* smile after all! This young man and many of his colleagues had a good future to look forward to, thanks to an ethical management team who stuck with staff through good times and bad.

In 1992 I arrived in Hong Kong where the economy was booming. Within months I had set up a training consultancy and over the next few years I secured a number of major contracts with local banks and hotels. Clients included the Mandarin Oriental Hotel, the Hong Kong Chinese Bank, Hutchison Paging and the Hotel Furama Kempinski. While revenues were good, I realised over time the limitations of my fledgling business. All of my contract consultants were considerably older than me, holding masters and doctorate degrees. I had to learn how to lead them. As Hong Kong is a transient port, many were understandably not committed to Hong Kong long-term, and this could give me extra work in terms of managing client relationships. Copyright law was not enforced in those days and the intellectual property I spent a lot of time designing was not suitably protected. And finally, while I got to polish my communication skills as I interacted with top brass to sell my programmes, I recognised that my learning opportunities were considerably limited. Now in a large organisation, I would be able to learn about policies, complex processes, best practices and a whole lot more.

In 1995, I joined Cathay Pacific Airways, the Hong Kong based airline. Initially, my work in their training department was not particularly challenging (as I thrive on a big challenge) so in 1996 I enrolled in a masters degree programme. My studies helped me to better understand the macro environment and how it was impacting our internal environment. A turning point for my career came in early 1997 when our team was gathered together by our line manager. Given the impact of the Asian crisis on the airline industry, we were advised that there would be no promotions in the next couple of years, and all new hires would go through the Managing Director. However, we would have the opportunity to learn a lot as our jobs broadened. Those who were not up to the challenge were welcome to leave. I can't remember feeling particularly excited about this message. It would be bad for my career if I stayed at the same level for too long, as it might communicate a lack of ability and performance on my part. But on the other hand, my role might be getting more exciting and would provide me with a bigger challenge. Now that was an attractive proposition!

Later I would find that my new responsibilities would take me from Tokyo to Johannesburg, Dallas to Mumbai, Anchorage to Paris and many other locations, as I helped implement different change management initiatives. Projects included the global OneWorld communications plan for stakeholders facing major change as a handful of major airlines formed an alliance; service recovery simulation workshops to facilitate customer retention and loyalty; and the huge transition from the old Kai Tak airport to the a new state-of-the-art facility — Chek Lap Kok. Also, I worked extensively on the service culture change programme for front-line staff, working alongside external consultants to facilitate the indoor workshops and outdoor activities. My M.Ed. helped me to understand the strategic picture and make a bigger contribution as I wrote papers addressing company issues, for example, a critique on the culture change programme, and also my thesis, "Training as a Change Agent". This research identified some of the obvious strengths and weakness of the airline's culture change programme "Service Straight from the Heart" (SSFTH):

❖ *Strengths*: use of external consultants who had outsiders' perspective and who could share external best practices, culture analysis was conducted alongside strategic planning sessions, creation of service culture would address business need, good use of cultural embedding mechanisms on the operational front, use of experiential learning to open minds to new ways of doing things.

❖ *Weaknesses*: no assessment of internal beliefs and assumptions, no change management team to implement the programme (it was done through line management), programme was for front-line staff and there was no leadership involvement in workshops that service staff attended, the culture change was promised in TV advertisements long before any results came through.

In hindsight, my six years' service with the airline provided me with an excellent opportunity to learn a wide range of skills and this, together with my postgraduate studies, would prime me for my role in HSBC.

My change management skills would also be in demand on the personal frontier. A major event which shaped my adult life came on 26 June 1999, not long after my thirtieth birthday. Routine surgery resulted in pulmonary embolism, cardiac arrest and, over the next six months, a host of debilitating side-effects. For the latter part of 1999 I was largely immobilised, due to a rare reaction to my medication. It was a dark period, but I did manage to utilise the few hours I was alert each day to complete my masters thesis from home. Gifts come in strange packages. The near-fatal experience provided me with an opportunity to reflect on my experiences, consolidate my learning and take stock of my life. After intensive physiotherapy I came out of this experience incredibly focused, with enhanced clarity and self-awareness. Something inside me had changed. Oddly, on my list of "things-to-do" in January 2000 was *"Join* MENSA". Not *try to* join. Prior to my illness, the possibility would not have even entered the realm of my thoughts. Joining the society gave me a much-needed boost of confidence to face the world again, together with a new circle of friends, each one a character. Thankfully, my trademark high energy was well intact and was now married with a new passion for life. The new millennium dawned. As the next stage of my life unfolded, I would find that building my spiritual intelligence and contributing to the community have become increasingly important to me.

In February 2000, I started looking around for my next career move, keen to reposition myself correctly. With my studies and the health scare behind me, all my energies would now go into my career. If I could beat the "man with the sickle", anything was possible. In May 2000, I joined HSBC Hong Kong.

As programme manager for the HSBC initiative, I worked closely with the programme director to create "Together, We Win!". Between us, we used a combination of formal theory, business experience, gut instinct and common sense to develop the programme and navigate its twists and turns. While I had my own ideas on the essence of culture and how it could be measured, John Kotter's framework for implementing change ("Eight Steps to Transforming Your Organisation") became a useful guide and this I adapted to suit culture change specifically.

As we were driving the HSBC culture change programme, there was an explosion of high-profile corporate governance scandals. I reflected on these cases and came to realise that corporate culture management should not be limited as the domain of the CEO and workforce. Rather, systematic corporate culture management should be taken to board level, to facilitate sound corporate governance. A *board culture of corporate governance*, led by the Chairman, will ensure that the CEO has the best foundation for driving culture change with the workforce.

After "Together, We Win!" I wrote a number of change management articles for business publications, addressing corporate culture management at CEO level and also at board level. But 3,000-word articles did not provide me with the broad canvas I needed to paint a holistic picture that would provide readers with enduring value. Before I knew it, I was writing this book. My initial intention was to share a winning formula, based on best practices and lessons learnt over the course of my experiences. This would facilitate a more constructive working environment across a range of industries, for the benefit of all major stakeholders. But as I wrote, what I already knew became just my starting point. I found myself challenging established thought, based on insights that I had gained as a practitioner.

It was exciting to realise that there was a gap to be filled, and that I could contribute to this relatively new field of business by translating everyday practices into theoretical frameworks. This would create new frames of reference and demystify corporate culture. While esteemed definitions and models have been put forward over the past half century, business leaders need models which incorporate:

1. *A systems perspective*, highlighting how the harmonious co-existence of tradition and innovation is integral to the effectiveness of any culture; and

2. *A moral perspective* to meet the needs of an increasingly discerning public and other marginalised stakeholders.

My new definition and typology of corporate cultures reflect this paradigm shift. Also, while the creation of an inventory of beliefs and assumptions is critical to our understanding of any culture, preparing such a profile is an extremely difficult task. Therefore, I have prepared a general inventory for leaders and culture analysts alike to refer to as they try to pin down the more elusive aspects of their own corporate culture. Finally, I present new material on the measurement of a culture change programme.

For a culture change programme to reach its full potential it is necessary to bring three disciplines into play — *corporate culture analysis*, *programme management* and *change management*. The sound analysis of a corporate culture will identify any problematic symptoms together with their impact and this is the first step towards a cure. Programme management deals with the implementation logistics of the solution to the problem, while change management deals with the dynamics that unfold on the human landscape and risk management. In this book I have integrated all three disciplines to create one single implementation methodology (see Figure 1).

Figure 1: Culture Change — From Vision to Reality

1. **Strategic Planning and Design**	• Back to the Drawing Board • Form the Strategic Management Team • Create Programme Vision and Define Strategy • Organise the Workforce • Design Core Programme and Embedding Mechanisms
2. **Strategy Implementation**	• Communicate Vision and Programme Roll-out • Manage the Human Landscape • Maintain the Momentum and Solidify Ground Made
3. **Evaluation and Readjustment**	• Measure Results and Plan for the Future

© O'Donovan, 2006

The Corporate Culture Handbook is divided into two parts. In **Part One**, I present an overview of a major company using corporate culture management to add value to key stakeholders. I then establish the basic theoretical premises for the action-based strategy I will share in Part Two, because only by challenging established thought is any extended argument possible. While business leaders need a sound theoretical framework on the essence and nature of culture, I don't think they need a detailed historical account on all perspectives to date, so I have chosen to focus on the most cited and influential works before sharing my new perspective. Moving on, we will consider the case for and against corporate culture management, to instil, hopefully, a healthy respect for this vitally important business issue. In addition, we will consider different viewpoints on the role of the organisation, and how the main model employed in the twentieth century set the ground for the recent corporate governance scandals. For the twenty-first century, industry needs to embrace the new mindset that organisations are economic *and social* entities and commit to the responsible provision of goods and services. Finally, we will consider some of the myths surrounding the field of corporate culture before learning how to implement a successful culture change programme.

In **Part Two**, I follow the framework in Figure 1 — each bullet point in the Figure forming a Chapter title — to show leaders how they can implement a culture change programme. While this is transferable to all industries, no step can be omitted without serious repercussions.

Using this guide, one can tailor the strategic implementation plan in this book to suit the unique business needs of any organisation; for example:

❖ Facilitate the creation of a *culture of ethics* by weaving ethical principles and good values into the very fabric of an organisation's day-to-day activities;

❖ Facilitate the creation of a *service culture* and an outward-looking perspective;

❖ Facilitate the creation of a *culture of innovation*, while giving due respect to tradition to keep the company grounded.

These challenges are not mutually exclusive and are not a definitive list of all the cultural challenges that an organisation will face. But the issues of ethics, service and innovation do represent those major challenges common to organisations in this new era. Of course, if the corporate culture is operating well on all fronts then no intervention is required. But if a business need is established then it must be addressed. To make the vision a reality, it is essential that internal creativity is tapped and staff take ownership of the programme, devising their own tools and techniques. While the overall approach will remain constant, the tactics employed at the operational level will vary greatly to suit unique organisational needs.

Five key outcomes which I hope emerge from this book are that business stewards:

1. Collectively embrace a paradigm shift on the role of the organisation in the twenty-first century;

2. Develop a healthy respect for corporate culture as a potentially creative or destructive force;

3. Develop the knowledge, skills and desire to nurture their own corporate culture;

4. Cultivate the creation of a healthy corporate culture to minimise risk and maximise on corporate philosophy and strategies;

5. Where necessary, implement a culture change programme to address specific business issues.

My work on corporate culture is largely compatible with that of Professor Edgar Schein of MIT, considered by many to be the founding father of organisational psychology. Other major influences include Kurt Lewin, John Kotter, Marvin Bower, Stephen Covey, Jim Stewart, Neely Gardner and Jack Philips. I am not one for reinventing the wheel and am quick to borrow a good idea, so I am most grateful to all other thinkers and practitioners who have contributed to the field, affording me with the knowledge and tools to start out on my journey. Particularly, I am grateful to those who have inspired me and who have permitted me to refer to their models and insights in my book. Corporate culture does not exist in a vacuum so for this work I have also drawn on learning accumulated over the years via my personal interests (philosophy, current affairs, psychology and anthropology), in order to gain a fresh perspective.

It is my belief that for any field to evolve, and in the spirit of continuous improvement, all serious contributors must demonstrate:

❖ Courage — by challenging established thought to present new paradigms and by being open to constructive criticism and

❖ Integrity — by recognising the truths in others' works.

These principles I have endeavoured to embrace. While I believe that this work represents a significant contribution to the field of corporate culture management, it is by no means the definitive work. I hope that readers discuss both what they agree with and disagree with to stimulate a continuation and refinement of external debates. Feedback on this handbook would be much appreciated for a later revised edition, and can be sent to *corporateculturehandbook@gmail.com*.

"I would like to record our appreciation for what you have done for HSBC. There is little doubt in my mind that 'Together, We Win!' is a big success and you will always be remembered when we talk about 'Together, We Win!'"

— Mr Raymond Or,
General Manager Hong Kong,
HSBC Group

"Many thanks for your efforts and endurance in pulling off this tremendous catalyst of changes in a traditional bank like HSBC."

— Mr Dicky Yip,
Chief Executive China Business,
HSBC Group

PART ONE

PRACTICE INTO THEORY

1

HSBC AND THE NEW MILLENNIUM

*"In HSBC we believe that behavioural values shape
monetary values, and behavioural values need to be
reinforced constantly by leadership example"*
— *Sir John Bond, HSBC Group Chairman*

1.1 Background

The Hong Kong and Shanghai Banking Corporation was established in 1865 to finance the growing trade between China and Europe. Now headquartered in London, HSBC is the second largest financial institution in the world. The Bank's international network comprises nearly 10,000 offices in 77 territories and countries.

1.1.1 Core Principles and Managing for Value

In 1998, the HSBC Group was rated among the top ten banks in the world by market capitalisation. To enable the Bank to retain this position in the years to come, management and the Board developed a five-year strategy, "Managing for Value" (MfV), for the years 1999–2003. This strategy would lead the Bank into the twenty-first century. When unveiling MfV, and in response to increased public scrutiny of multinational companies, the Group Chairman Sir John Bond made explicit five principles and values integral to Group philosophy and all strategies:

- ❖ Long-term, ethical client relationships
- ❖ High productivity through teamwork
- ❖ A confident and ambitious sense of excellence
- ❖ International in outlook and character
- ❖ Prudence, creativity and strong marketing.

To reinforce HSBC's commitment to internationally accepted standards of conduct the Bank endorsed the *Global Sullivan Principles*[1] and the *UN Global Compact*[2] initiative in 2000.

The Hong Kong and Shanghai Bank is the founding member of the HSBC Group. Now using the HSBC brand name, it is the largest bank incorporated in the Hong Kong Special Administrative Region. At the turn of the century HSBC Hong Kong was successful in financial terms but daunting challenges lay ahead. The local economy had been in recession since the late 1990s, the business environment was increasingly competitive and consumer behaviour was changing. As time moved on interest rates fell progressively, the equities market fell, turnover dropped and property prices plunged from the record highs of the 1990s. By 2001 the main challenge in the industry would be coping with the deregulation of interest rates. Other activities would be regulated.

In early 2000, external change was pushing for internal change. Members of the Bank's top management team gathered together to conduct strategic planning sessions. The management team recognised the need to diversify sources of income, increase the Bank's wallet share of existing customers, improve service delivery and control costs. The centralisation and automation of processing functions would streamline service delivery, free people from back-office work and allow them more time to focus on the customer. As a result, most roles in the Bank would need to change in the years ahead.

---

[1] Global Sullivan Principles, www.globalsullivanprinciples.org

[2] United Nations Global Compact, www.unglobalcompact.org

1.1.2 The Birth of "Together, We Win!"

I joined HSBC Hong Kong in May 2000 and briefly held management development responsibilities. Having recently completed my postgraduate studies I was all fired up and ready for a big challenge. However, to my dismay, my job was smaller than the job advertisement had implied and the internal environment felt stagnant. I began to worry I had made the wrong choice of employer and remember likening the lack of energy to how my previous employer (Cathay Pacific Airways) had felt before it went into the red in 1997. But as the weeks progressed, and in response to my rising awareness of a critical issue which needed to be addressed, I proceeded to conduct an unsolicited assessment within the Bank. I wanted to learn about Group philosophy and strategies, staff understanding of these, their everyday way of doing things and their attitudes and responses to a changing business environment. Each evening I consolidated my experiences and impressions of the day. From this data I was able to glean valuable insights into both the espoused culture and the prevailing culture. These were not aligned. It quickly became apparent to me that HSBC needed a people-focused change management programme to bridge the gap. This would empower staff to meet new challenges as their roles evolved in a changing business environment. The story below illustrates how a change advocate can become an official change agent when given the authority and resources to facilitate and implement a good idea and make change happen.

During my research, I found that external pressures in the macro-environment were being felt by the workforce. Morale was very low, with a pay freeze and rumours of impending redundancies further dampening spirits. Yet, conversely, job security was taken as a given in some quarters where a job for life was taken for granted, even for mediocre performers. Executives attending management development courses I facilitated expressed little understanding of MfV and how they could personally contribute to the corporation. Also, this forum was used as a platform for airing grievances and discontent. Unlike the

Cathay Pacific Airways workforce, who had been galvanised into action to meet their challenges in 1997, the HSBC workforce expressed little understanding of the external environment and how it would impact them. The main reason for this, I believed, was that the Bank had continued to prosper during the Asian crisis, so there was no impetus for changing work attitudes and behaviours. Cumbersome processes and outmoded bureaucracy created a social environment that was stifling to empowerment, innovation, flexibility and customer service. Profitability had bred complacency and a sense of immunity to the winds of change.

It became increasingly clear that the very culture that had been a foundation stone for earlier success had gone off track because it had not adapted to the world beyond, and a major intervention was needed to re-align the workforce with corporate philosophy and strategy. As part of my research I referred to the Group Chairman's address that would lead us through the years 1999–2003. In a presentation where he personally communicated the strategy to executives from across the globe, Sir John Bond punctuated the end of his talk by telling his audience: "Those of you who return to your countries and do not communicate this message to your staff — fail HSBC!" This powerful statement motivated me to continue on my investigation.

By a happy coincidence it emerged that the corporate culture gap analysis that I was conducting complemented the local strategic planning sessions. A colleague directed me to the Head of Personal Financial Services (the retail bank), Paul Thurston, and the Head of Corporate and Institutional Banking, Brian Robertson. These two key members of the top management team had arrived from Group headquarters at the beginning of the year. In July 2000 I wrote directly to both of them, asking for a meeting to discuss how the organisation was supporting staff in the workplace to achieve the corporate vision. My impression was that:

❖ A very solid initiative was needed to address staff attitude to change;

- ❖ The daily and practical application of the Group Strategy (MfV) needed to be brought home to each employee;

- ❖ Staff needed to be educated on the progress to date implementing the strategic imperatives in Asia;

- ❖ For real change to occur, people needed to be motivated to make the change happen, see its value and take responsibility for it.

I was granted audience by Paul Thurston and Brian Robertson to discuss the topic further. During these meetings I made my point on the importance of addressing the "people part" of the change management equation by sharing the following storyline from a work of fiction:

New York was facing a terrorist threat of unprecedented proportions. In just a few hours, a bomb would level the whole city. To deal with the impending calamity, authorities brought in a recognised crisis management expert to put forward a proposal for eliminating the threat. This man had devoted some thirty years work to preparing for this day. When summoned for feedback on his strategy, he was advised that the proposal, though considered excellent in many respects, had been rejected as it stood. When the devastated man asked why, he was told, "You have correctly identified the subway as the best way to evacuate the city. However — who will drive the trains?" He had forgotten the human factor which would support his policy and process plans.

The head of the retail bank advised me that the people part of the change management equation had indeed been considered, with a teamwork event being proposed for retail staff, who represented fifty per cent of the workforce. Also, discussions were being held on the possibility of running an MfV strategy awareness workshop but no decision had been taken on this. Having already received endorsement from the Head of Training to redesign the seldom-used change management training course and align it with strategy, I expressed keenness for all staff to go to this new course. Both expressed support and agreed to provide senior staff for the pilot run of "Leading Change in the Twenty-first Century". However, it was clear that the proposed teamwork event for retail staff was a priority. I was not convinced this was the right way forward and believed that change management had to be the central focus. Only by providing both front-office and back-office staff with tools to embrace change in unison could business challenges be met.

After these meetings, my excitement quickly turned to disappointment when I heard nothing back. For the next two weeks I pondered the issue and came to realise two things. Firstly, that to get all staff to attend "Leading Change in the 21st Century", and soon, I needed a top management Executive Sponsor. Secondly, the head of the retail bank needed someone to design and implement the planned team-building event. No one had been identified. I requested another meeting with Paul Thurston. During this second meeting I endeavoured to convince him that a bank-wide culture change programme would align the whole workforce with the strategic vision. Staff needed to be able to articulate the corporate mission in their own words and explain how they could deliver on it in their own workplace. They needed the knowledge and tools to enable them to form a healthier relationship with change. Front-line service providers needed their team members up and down the service chain to be aligned with the same vision and values. As front-line staff are closer to their customers and are closer to the real world, we needed to get back office staff on board to embrace change.

As a result of these discussions, I was assigned to work on designing and developing the proposed initiative for retail staff but using "change management" as the central theme. The scope of the programme now included all of HSBC Holdings Hong Kong plus five local subsidiary companies. The General Manager, Raymond C.F. Or, would co-sponsor the programme with the head of the retail bank. The former would oversee our communication activities while the latter would chair our steering committee and serve as programme director. I became programme manager for this ambitious initiative and my team (Corporate Strategy Programmes Hong Kong) was given responsibility for designing and implementing an innovative culture change programme.

1.2 Culture Change Programme Overview

"Together, We Win!" (aka *Chung Chi Sing Sing*) was a bank-wide strategic culture change programme. Chinese and English translations of the name reflect the importance HSBC puts on a core value, "teamwork". For brevity, I shall use TWW! from this point forward.

1.2.1 Scope and Timeframe

Scope

❖ HSBC Holdings Hong Kong plus five subsidiary companies: HSBC Trinkaus Investment Management Ltd., HSBC Insurance, HSBC Precision Printing, HSBC Trustee (Hong Kong) Ltd and EPSCO (a consortium of 22 major banks whose mission is to provide greater convenience for customers and merchants via wider use of electronic fund transfer).

Timeframe

❖ September 2000 to July 2001 (roll-out November 2000)

❖ February 2001 to April 2003 (roll-out November 2001)

1.2.2 Core Purpose, Strategic Goals, Core Values

Core Purpose

❖ "To work together to embrace change and allow HSBC continuing success in the twenty-first century"

Strategic Goals

❖ To heighten levels of **customer satisfaction**

❖ To build **shareholder value**

❖ To improve **staff satisfaction.**

Core Values

Linked to the business needs identified by top management of the Bank, six core values were identified to reflect Group principles and values while embracing local needs.

Together, We....

1. *Achieve More!*

2. *Embrace Change!*

3. *Delight Customers!*

4. *Take Personal Responsibility!*

5. *Continuously Learn!*

6. *Continuously Improve!*

To highlight the importance of "communication" we threaded material on this issue through all activities and modules.

1.2.3 Strategic Management

At the request of the Executive Sponsors, a Steering Committee was formed to provide strategic direction to the programme. It was chaired by the Head of Personal Financial Services and included the Head of Corporate and Institutional Banking, the Head of Human Resources and the presiding Head of Training (three individuals would hold this post for the duration of the culture change programme). As programme manager I reported to the Steering Committee and received direction from the Chair. We would convene as a group every six weeks for the duration of the programme.

1.2.4 A Snapshot of "Together, We Win!"

The *core programme* was learning- and development-centred, as our success or failure in changing the culture would be determined by the workforce's ability to learn a new way of doing things. *Support activities and projects* facilitated programme implementation, while *culture embedding mechanisms* anchored the new way of doing things into everyday business.

Figure 2: TWW! Projects and Activities Map

Core Programme	**Phase 1:** **A Centralised Event**	**Phase 2:** **Workplace Localised**
Learning and Development Centred	Experiential Learning Activities Live Q&A with Top Management	Self-Directed Learning Interdependent Team Learning
Structured Support Activities and Projects[3]	Event Hall Development Steering Committee Meetings Materials Design and Development Facilitator Recruitment and Training Pilot Run Management Event Management Stakeholder Management Communications	Workforce Alignment Steering Committee Meetings Advisory Committee Meetings Materials Design and Delivery Materials Distribution Pilot Teams Management Event Management Stakeholder Management Communications
Culture Embedding Mechanisms	Leadership Focus Allocation of Resources Rites and Rituals Formal Statements of Values	Role-modelling, Teaching and Coaching Rewards and Status Recruit, Select and Promote Organisational Systems and Procedures

[3] To learn more about a selection of these projects and activities turn to Appendix 1.

1.2.5 Core Programme Description

The aim of the piloted "Leading Change in the 21st Century" was incorporated into the new programme "Together, We Win!". Borrowing on best practices we combined the logistics of a Group headquarters team-building initiative, and the experiential learning approach of the Cathay Pacific Airways service culture programme to create the Phase One event.[4] This was centralised in a custom-built event hall on HSBC premises and was attended by over 15,000 staff from across the Bank in groups of 120 each day over a seven-month period. Activities were facilitated by 56 line managers under the direction of the programme team.

In Phase One we established a common language for change using the six core values and addressed attitudes to change by creating awareness, facilitating cross-functional dialogue and using the experiential learning approach. Phase Two took eighteen months and ran from the fourth quarter of 2001 to early 2003. This phase was aimed at transferring the learning from Phase One into actions in the workplace. It was localised in the workplace with line managers and staff taking up ownership for the success or failure of the initiative. A total of 1,400 line managers were trained to deliver the modules and everybody in the Bank was involved either as a Team Leader or Team Member. Over the eighteen-month period, every team in the Bank spent approximately three months focused on each of the six core values in turn. This was achieved through a series of six modules which were delivered by line managers in the workplace to their own teams. The customised materials were designed and provided by the programme team. Line managers delivered each module through two or three team meetings over the lifespan of the particular module. Staff were allowed time out from normal duties to engage in the activities, reinforc-

---

[4] Both were inspired by the British Airways motivational event, "Putting People First".

ing the message that the programme was not additional to but "part and parcel" of everyday work.

Figure 3: TWW! Core Programme Design

PHASE 1: THE CENTRALISED EVENT
Cross-functional teams explored six core values during a one-day event, covering the first three steps of the experiential learning cycle ("do", "reflect" and "connect")

↓

PHASE 2: WORKPLACE LOCALISED					
Local teams action-planned on six core values in their own workplace, covering the last step of the experiential learning cycle ("apply")					
Module One	Module Two	Module Three	Module Four	Module Five	Module Six
Teamwork	*Embrace Change*	*Delight Customers*	*Take Personal Responsibility*	*Continuous Learning*	*Continuous Improvement*
Three months	Three months	Three months	Two months	Three months	Four months

Note: The diagram above expands upon the first row of Figure 2.

Phase One

The Centralised Event

An area of 10,500 square feet was given over to the programme team and the HSBC property division to transform into a purpose-built event hall. In an ultra-conservative environment, we knew that a dramatic and colourful theme would do much to communicate change so we hired external contractors to create a powerful sensory experience which would communicate change. A long corridor which we called "The Enchanted Forest" greeted people as they came into the venue. The walls and ceiling of this were covered in foliage weaved into a lattice frame, and adorned with decorative butterflies and dragonflies. Jungle sounds played in the background. This darkened and mysterious walkway created an element of intrigue and opened out into a large, bright "Fairground" area. This was home to the "Gift Shop", snack bars and ten "Breakout Rooms" where teams of twelve would engage in experiential activities. The doors to these rooms had huge motifs of theme-related images and these elicited curiosity each morning as to what was behind the closed doors. Moving through the Fairground area, a large red and yellow striped curtain veiled the entrance to the "Big Top"'. This huge seating area was home to a central stage fitted out with state-of-the-art audio-visual equipment and purpose-built circus ring seating. It catered for all 120 staff guests plus the 60 members of the programme team. Each morning, we would arrive early so as to personally greet our customers as they came through our door and I remember anxiously awaiting the reaction of one international manager. His initial cynicism turned to wonder as he gazed around before exclaiming, "I have never seen anything like this in thirty years with the Bank! HSBC *is* changing!" For me, this served to validate our festive theme.

The Participants

Over 15,000 staff from HSBC Hong Kong plus five subsidiary companies attended the one-day event. Each day between November 2000 and July 2001 the event received 120 participants. The programme team co-ordinated closely with line managers to invite a cross-section of staff from across the Bank without disrupting line operations. Any one team of twelve staff would contain a mixture of junior and senior staff from cross-functional areas. We arranged for staff with hearing and speech impairments to attend, integrating them into regular groups and hiring consultants versed in sign-language to co-facilitate event activities. Even colleagues visiting from overseas joined in to learn best practices, and bring ideas back to their own countries.

The Rundown

In an opening session held in the Big Top we welcomed our internal customers and provided the run-down and logistics for the day. Then, the large group was divided up into ten teams of

twelve who were invited to "Break-out Rooms" by their ten programme facilitators. Each team would participate in six experiential activities during the course of the day, each one focusing
on a specific core value. These activities provided a forum for
discussions on change in the internal and external environment.
Every afternoon, we brought all ten teams back to the Big Top to
engage in a live "Q&A" session hosted by a member of the top
team. As the programme matured, staff expressed more and
more confidence in giving upward feedback by posing difficult
questions and even debating topics with the top management
speaker. This made for some very lively and amusing sessions.
After the Q&A session all 120 staff would go back to the small
rooms and engage in a final experiential activity before returning to the Big Top. During the high-energy closing session learning was consolidated and core values reinforced.

Apart from the formal programme, there were lunchtime
games and lucky draws, specially designed entertainment videos, gifts and cooked food provided by Bank catering staff. We
even had a magician entertain staff over lunch to encourage
"out-of-the-box" thinking. Everyone received a photograph of
their team at the end of the day together with a gift, and many of
these groups maintained contact after the event, facilitating
cross-functional relationships. Walking around the Bank, one
could see desks and walls adorned with photos taken at the
event. Needless to say, those junior staff members who spent
the day with a top manager were most proud to display their
snapshots, and top management appreciated the opportunity to
hear staff views first-hand during event activities.

The Materials

As an objective of Phase One of the programme was to raise
awareness of the Bank's need to embrace change, we used
experiential learning activities. Unlike traditional training materials, experiential learning activities engage people emotionally and open their minds and hearts to new possibilities. These
activities are centred on the learners' own insights, knowledge,

experiences and ideas. In the debriefing session following an activity, a trained facilitator would tap on this resource by eliciting insights from participants and relating learning points directly to workplace issues.

The Event Facilitators

All 56 event facilitators were line staff who had been recruited from a pool of over 300 nominees put forward by the line. Every six-week period, twelve facilitators plus a couple of support staff would report for duty at the TWW! Event Hall, and work under our supervision. We recruited line managers to:

1. Provide the workforce with positive role models from their own work environment; and

2. Create a group of "champions" who would bring the programme principles back to the workplace upon completion of their TWW! event duties.

These facilitators knew the business intimately better than any trainer ever would and had a lot of credibility in the eyes of our internal customers. We supervised and coached the facilitators daily, providing feedback for their continuous development.

Top Management Support

❖ Top management approved and signed off the proposal for Phase One, creating the dedicated programme team and providing us with our budget and all other resources required.

❖ As noted earlier, a Steering Committee was established to guide the programme strategy as the environment evolved.

❖ Each afternoon for seven months, a member of the top management team took central stage in the Big Top to discuss current business issues, reinforce the core values and take questions from the floor.

❖ Members of the top team took every opportunity to reinforce the core values in their presentations to line staff.

Successes and Challenges

❖ At the end of each day the event was reviewed by the core
team members and event facilitators, with customer feedback actioned and the programme modified where appropriate to demonstrate customer-centricity and continuous
improvement.

❖ Staff were so excited with the programme that within weeks
they had created a number of web pages on an internet chat
room to discuss TWW! amongst themselves. My team reviewed this feedback regularly, using input to further modify the programme where appropriate. I realised, however,
that we would need to get them off the internet and provide
them with internal communication channels which they
would be happy to utilise.

❖ Keeping the solutions to event activities promised to be a
challenge so at the end of each day we asked participants to
keep this information to themselves so as not to undermine
the learning experiences of their colleagues. Staff were extremely co-operative and this in turn created an element of
intrigue amongst those who had yet to attend the event. We
would joke that the solutions to event activities became
"HSBC's best-kept secret".

❖ Given the size of the workforce, it would take us seven
whole months before we got through them all, so we did
fear that we would lose the interest of the earlier participants. However, what we found instead was that as 120 re-
turned to the workplace each day this created a wave effect
which cascaded throughout the organisation and built in
momentum. New returnees were keen to share their experiences who those who had already attended, and many
enjoyed discussing their own particular approach to problem-solving activities.

Phase Two

Phase Two was unprecedented in that it went beyond typical centralised activities that are geared to change mindsets, by transferring event learning to the multi-faceted local workplace of 15,000+ staff, providing customised learning tools to help staff embrace change in their local workplace. This would pass the baton of leadership to line managers and give the line ownership for learning. Over an eighteen-month period, and at any one time, every staff member of the Bank had a clearly defined role in the culture change programme and was focused on implementing the six core values in the workplace. Team action planning, which was carefully tuned on a strategic level, was open-ended at a tactical level to allow staff to tailor their efforts to suit local workplace demands.

The Localised Setting

For Phase Two, we implemented the programme in the workplace. This meant that, during their normal work duties, teams would action the programme core values with support and reinforcement from their Team Leaders and identified Line Champions.

The Materials and Rundown

As the objective of Phase Two of the programme was to transfer learning to the workplace, we used a combination of self-directed learning and interdependent team learning.

❖ The bilingual **TWW! Booklet** was penned by the Executive Sponsors and circulated to every staff member. This booklet explained the linkage between the TWW! core values and the HSBC Group's strategic imperatives. It set the foundation stone for articulating to staff how each individual could contribute to the Group Strategy in their own role. This type of knowledge sharing is recognised internationally as a key motivator for staff ownership in the business.

"The MfV strategy sets a business direction that enables us to confront the challenges in our environment and to build on our strengths. TWW! helps us all to focus our energies on the actions that we can take personally and with our colleagues at work, to contribute to building value."[5]

The TWW! booklet also provided an update on local progress in Asia implementing the MfV strategy, mapping core values to results.

❖ **The Six Modules** delivered to Team Leaders were based around the 6 core values. The modules continued on the fun and excitement of Phase One, but now there was a strong focus on the actions teams needed to take for their internal and external customers. Each of the 6 modules focused on a particular value and consisted of 3 key activities:

i) **An Introductory Activity**: Having met with each department head and reviewed the results of the recent Employee Attitude Survey, it was clear to me that we would need an introductory activity which would help teams to explore difficult issues in a safe environment, before proceeding to work on them with their own team. Functional heads were very keen for this approach. For three modules we used in-house designed "learning maps" with images of excellent teamwork, change and customer service to steer discussions around the core principles. Our inspiration for images came from the local Mandarin Oriental hotel (which has a world-renowned reputation for excellent customer service), a cruise-liner manned by HSBC staff taking customers through the winds of change to Treasure Island and beyond, and a theatre performance to illustrate the importance of seamless front-of-house and back-office teamwork. Staff would explore these images under the guidance of their Team Leaders. We also used videos and

---

[5] *TWW! Booklet*, 2001, p. 7.

even balloon sculpting activities for later modules. The latter proved a huge hit!

ii) **Our Team Score**: Based on the learning points elicited in the fun introductory activity, each team then assessed how well they currently demonstrated the key value under scrutiny, based on a number of identified "team behavioural outcomes" (TBOs) which articulated what each value meant. Generally, staff used a "secret ballot" to assess their team and derived a score for each TBO. The lowest-scoring TBOs showed those areas that needed most improvement. Every team was encouraged to work on three of these TBOs for the following months and to assess their progress at the end of the module.

iii) **Team Action Planning**: Each team would then generate an action plan to help them improve upon the lowest-scoring areas and agree methods of monitoring and responsibility. They would action these commitments over a three-month period. We provided a selection of Continuous Quality Improvement (CQI) tools to assist teams with their planning and implementation activities as they brought their action plans to life. Staff were encouraged to choose their own tools and tactics if they wished, and all were expected to measure their performance. Blank, poster-sized templates of action plans were provided to all. Teams would fill these in and post them in their work areas across the whole Bank.

iv) **Team Self-Assessment**: At the end of each module, teams gathered together with their line manager to assess their performance implementing their action plan using quantitative and qualitative data. Many shared their successes with the programme team who posted their results on the programme website, to share knowledge and best practices across the bank. At the end of TWW! all results would be consolidated into two types; that for which a direct dollar value could be assigned (this would amount to HK\$40m) and more qualitative data for which a monetary value could not be assigned.

To support the learning process, all staff received packages of learning resources. Team Leader packages consisted of a Team Leader Guide plus materials for team meetings. Team Member packages included initial "focus" activities for each module, and other support materials. For each package we inserted small gifts related to the particular value; e.g. key rings, computer mats and calendars. Also, we included books which reinforced core values, e.g. *Who Moved My Cheese?* for the module on "Embracing Change" and *Jonathan Livingston Seagull* for the module on "Continuous Learning". Books were provided in both English and Chinese, according to line requirements. Each team also received a set of "Tools and Techniques" to support their action planning. By outsourcing production to mainland China, we were able to keep costs down and still provide high-quality products.

Team Leaders, Team Members and Helpers

Senior management across the business identified some 1,400 line managers as Team Leaders; almost half of these were non-executives. The 13,000+ staff who reported into these line managers became programme Team Members. Every Department Head was responsible for taking ownership to drive the programme successfully in their own area of the business, 40 TWW! Champions were recruited by Department Heads to help them drive the programme in their part of the business and 290 Line Materials Co-ordinators were recruited for materials distribution.

Top Management Support

Based on the success of Phase One, top management approved and signed off our Phase Two proposal. The General Manager became TWW! Team Leader for his executive management team. To assist the strategic management team, an Advisory

Committee was established. For each of the six modules, individual members of these committees were encouraged to sponsor a particular module. Module sponsors would take personal responsibility to oversee the design of module materials and drive the modules' success across the Bank. Senior management from diverse areas of the organisation were responsible for drafting responses to questions posed on the "Ask Top Management" intranet communication vehicle. These responses were finalised and endorsed by top management who drove policy and process changes where necessary. As with the TWW! Event's Q&A sessions, most questions related to Human Resources issues rather than business issues.

Successes and Challenges

❖ For Phase Two many staff wanted another fun event away from the office. It would be a challenge to integrate programme learning and action-planning into the busy work environment.

❖ Bringing all line managers up-to-speed in terms of facilitating team activities was necessary to ensure successful implementation of Phase Two. During the leadership workshops we had the opportunity to see who had the skills required to lead their teams, and who needed further support and coaching.

❖ While for earlier modules we kept to the same format to support Team Leaders in the learning mode, we realised that it was necessary to introduce different "Introductory Activities" to keep staff interest and maintain the momentum.

❖ A common excuse for not embracing change is to claim to be too busy. Our programme was no different to any other in that we had to overcome this challenge. Stakeholder management and communications played a key role in securing buy-in.

❖ On the front-line, resistance to change gained momentum in the face of line ownership for embracing change together with the empowerment of team members, but it was diluted as line wins came through.

❖ As TWW! was the first culture change programme in the history of the bank, insiders who had not experienced a culture change initiative with previous employers had no benchmark to refer to.

❖ Once the Head of Training retired in the spring of 2001, a second and then a third individual from the retail bank took up the post. This means that over the lifespan of the culture change programme no fewer than three individuals were Head of Training and went through the usual handover periods. None were training and development professionals so as time wore on the lack of continuity and expertise would create an additional series of challenges; e.g. being allocated technical trainers to facilitate leadership workshops in the strong belief that it would be a valid developmental opportunity for them.

❖ For our "Delight Your Customer" competition, which was designed to reward the right behaviours, 317 team entries were received. This provided the business with solid proof of successes teams achieved by actioning the core values in the workplace. Significantly, the evidence came directly from customers and not the staff themselves.

❖ Staff bankwide agreed that key benefits of the programme were that:

a) it gave teams a safe forum and a common language for discussing difficult issues in times of major change; and

b) it gave teams tools and official backing for making local changes as they saw necessary.

As momentum built we received a number of requests from colleagues overseas to run the programme in other countries but decided to ensure that it delivered solid business results in Hong Kong first before taking it elsewhere.

Key features of the programme were that it:

❖ *Aligned the internal social environment with the fast-paced external environment* via strategy to set the scene for a service culture.

❖ *Gave 15,000+ staff a strong, ingrained sense of the programme's core values* — from the top layers of management right through to the most junior layers, the whole workforce action-planned in line with the six core values and programme strategy.

❖ *Cascaded the baton of leadership* from the General Manager to the most junior line managers via policy changes and leadership workshops.

❖ *Stimulated innovation, risk-taking and learning from mistakes* in an environment where staff had been expected to get it right first time.

❖ *Engaged staff bank-wide* in the process by seeking their input for materials design, development, delivery and evaluation.

❖ *Transferred responsibility for learning and development to the workplace* with training providing support courses to meet needs identified during team action-planning activities.

❖ *Empowered staff* allowing them to take responsibility for their own learning, deciding locally which tactics and tools they wished to use to convert core values into results.

1.3 Outcomes and Results for HSBC

1.3.1 Industry Awards

In 2005 TWW! won an "ASTD Excellence in Practice Award" conferred by the American Society of Training and Development. In November 2003, Best Practices Management Hong Kong awarded the programme the industry "Best Practice Award 2003" for People Training and Development. But most significantly, at the close of 2003 the retail bank won the "Customer Service Grand Award[6] for the first time in history, signifying the establishment of a new service culture and delivery on group strategy. "Together, We Delight Customers" was a core value of the culture change programme.

"HSBC believes that the 'Together, We Win' initiative is an exceptional example of a major company using corporate culture management to add value to the customers, shareholders and staff. It is particularly significant in terms of its scope, magnitude and strategic relevance. The evidence for this is seen in the following:

❖ *Senior management commitment, demonstrated through full personal involvement in every phase of the initiative and over a two-and-a-half-year period;*

❖ *A demonstrable desire to invest in people and to help them meet their current and future challenges;*

❖ *Ownership and commitment of line managers to the learning process and business outcomes;*

❖ *Creativity in the structural design of the initiative and the materials that supported learning across the whole Bank;*

❖ *Significant results at a company-wide level."[7]*

1.3.2 Internal Measures

During the programme design stage, a variety of internal measures were identified which would provide feedback from both internal and external customers. Some, for example the Employee Attitude Survey, were managed by external consultants. Others were local historic measures managed by the line. All tools would provide a benchmark in terms of key performance indicators, both before and after the culture change programme, and reflected the unique needs of the Bank. Below are

---

[6] Hong Kong Retail Management Association.

[7] HSBC "Together, We Win!" Best Practice Award Proposal, July 2003.

the outcomes and results of the HSBC programme from a culture perspective.

Return on Investment (ROI)

ROI was 634 per cent[8] i.e. for every HK$ invested in the programme, there was a direct return of HK$6.34 in net benefits. The costs were as follows: 43,082 delegate days delivered at HK$146 per day. The total external cost of both phases of the initiative was HK$6.3 million over two and a half years. The total number of delegate days delivered was 43,082. This equates to HK$146 per delegate day or HK$450 per person over two-and-a-half years.

Results

Shareholders

HK$40 million in increased revenue plus significant cost savings through line teams applying all six values in the workplace via action planning. The bank's profit performance would remain strong despite the difficult economy and market conditions, supporting the belief that a more satisfied team and more satisfied customers lead to an improved profit.

Continuous Improvement

The Bank operates a staff suggestion scheme for improvements in work practices. The value of suggestions implemented was HK$16.1 million. During the period of the TWW! initiative, the scheme evidenced an increase in the number of suggestions and the value of bottom-line improvements gained from those suggestions was as follows:

---

[8] These figures represent direct return and benefits from team action-planning, and exclude indirect HK$ benefits from staff suggestion scheme (HK$16.1 million)

Year	No. of Suggestions	Implementation Value
2001	2,202	HK$6.7 million
2002	7,359	HK$9.4 million

Brand Image

The brand image of HSBC benefited when the programme won a number of industry awards.

Customers

Every measure of customer satisfaction increased. Customer satisfaction was measured by telephone surveys and question-naires to existing customers. Over 7,000 customers are con-tacted each year to gain their views against eleven key service categories. The Bank also runs a "mystery shopper" pro-gramme to assess the reception given to an anonymous cus-tomer. They are therefore able to provide regular feedback to every branch and the call centre on the quality of their service. Over the two-and-a-half years of the TWW! initiative there was consistent improvement on all historical measures. The highest level of improvement was 27 per cent.

Host Community

Module activities included community service components in team action-planning activities. Many teams gave up their own time to help those in need including the physically impaired and children in foster homes. Also the Phase One event hall seating was donated to a boys' school in China.

Staff

A total of 1,400 teams bank-wide generated 100,800 completed action plans over the course of Phase Two. Below are some ex-amples of the type of results achieved by line teams:

❖ Through their efforts to improve "Teamwork" a Premier Centre team achieved a 32 per cent reduction in the amount of overtime required. They also maintained their standard delivery lead-time at four minutes despite a five per cent increase in counter traffic, and won the first ranking in the Credit Card Sales Programme within their divisions.

❖ In their efforts to "Delight their Customers", another branch team enhanced their service standards by revisiting branch service standards through videos, briefings, experience sharing and role-plays. For the fourth quarter of 2001 this team opened 95 new accounts compared to 96 for the period January–September 2001. Customer satisfaction increased as their service approach became more informed and this was reflected in an increase in customer commendations between November and December 2001.

Artefacts

Items which would result directly from the programme activities and serve as programme artefacts included the following:

❖ **Employee Attitude Survey Results** 2000 and 2002;

❖ **TWW! Customer Feedback Focus Group Results** 2001 and **TWW! Customer Satisfaction e-Survey Results** 2002;

❖ **Phase Two Scaffolding** (the Roles and Responsibilities Map and supporting databases);

❖ **Programme communications materials** (videos, posters, bi-monthly internal articles, photographs); programme intranet plus the **Ask Top Management** e-communication forum and resulting **policy changes**;

❖ **Programme learning and development materials**;

❖ 8,400 completed **Team Action Plans** and many resulting **New Work Processes**;

❖ **Internet website pages** which staff created in the early days to discuss the programme;

❖ Eight "Delight Your Customers" competition **Gold and Silver Cups** for winning teams 2002;

❖ **Steering Committee and Advisory Committee** documentation;

❖ Trophies for **ASTD Excellence in Practice Award 2004, Best Practice Award in Training & Development 2003, Customer Service Grand Award 2003.**

Behaviour

❖ **All six core values**: on a daily basis teams across the bank carried out tasks related to their workplace action planning; department heads confirmed with the strategic management team that their staff were participating.

❖ **Continuous Learning and Embracing Change**: 22.3 per cent increased participation in training and development. During the period of the programme, the number of attendees at training courses increased by 22.3 per cent. This signifies an increased desire to develop and embrace change in the workplace as staff took personal responsibility for learning new knowledge, skills and attitudes.

❖ **Communication and Transparency**: The average number of visits to the TWW! intranet is 10,000 per month and rising. The TWW! website has proven to be a popular form of internal communication. The number of visitors to the site increased from a monthly average of 4,851 in 2001 to 7,166 in 2002 and 10,223 in 2003. The "Ask Top Management" (ATM) forum has received thousands of questions to date and is still going strong.

Attitudes

The General Manager conducted an Employee Attitude Survey before TWW! commenced, and again at the end of 2002. Every category of feedback improved. The following percentages indicate the degree of improvement for the top six categories:

❖ Company Image — +15%

❖ Quality of Supervision — +14%

❖ Empowerment — +14 %

❖ Customer Focus — +14%

❖ Working Relationships — +12%

❖ Quality — +10%

The categories that were most improved related to the areas covered by the TWW! initiative, inclusive of the leadership workshops and the bankwide use of continuous quality improvement (CQI) tools during Phase Two action planning (the EAS format should really be aligned with the programme core principles and values).

Principles, Values, Beliefs & Assumptions

For the Phase One event all 15,029 staff members attended the event and participated in six activities which introduced the six core values. Also, every staff member received a personal copy of a booklet outlining the programme core values and their relationship with Group Strategy (MfV). For Phase Two action planning every team received a toolkit to support action planning on core values in the local workplace. A total of 8,400 such action-plans were generated. Core values were integrated into the new performance measurement tool (the balanced scorecard and core values were integrated into all training and development programmes). Internal documents would reflect the bank's unique web of cultural beliefs and assumptions which acted as the primary driver of the culture and determined for the most part the outcomes and results.

Staff achieved this success over two and a half years in the face of significant redundancies, resistance to change, the removal of the guaranteed thirteenth-month pay (and the introduction of performance-related pay) and a recessionary environment where the pay freeze continued. The culture change programme clearly struck a chord with the workforce who improved their performance during challenging times. It enhanced their view of their employer and their work environment, making them ambassadors for the company. Also, many teams achieved positive outcomes from their action-planning which we could not put a direct monetary value to. For a culture-change programme, these outcomes — for example, learning to work together in line with corporate philosophy and strategy, and the creation of customer feedback centres in all departments — are more important than the quick monetary wins and set the groundwork for long-term benefits.

1.4 Chapter Summary

At the beginning of the millennium, an innovative corporate culture management programme was designed and implemented in HSBC Holdings Hong Kong plus five subsidiary companies. The strategic "Together We Win!" encompassed over 15,000 staff, and aimed to enable the workforce to embrace change to facilitate HSBC's continuing success in the twenty-first century. This would be achieved by supporting the building of staff satisfaction, customer satisfaction and shareholder value. Home-grown in Hong Kong, the programme struck a chord with the local workforce who enhanced performance and productivity during challenging times; and by allocating considerable resources during times of scarcity, the General Manager communicated to the organisation the importance of corporate culture management.

Phase One took the form of a centralised event, where six core values were explored by the entire workforce, over a period of seven months. Phase Two was localised in the workplace with line staff taking ownership for the success or failure of the initiative. Over an eighteen-month period every staff member, from the most senior to the most junior levels, spent approximately three months focused on one of the six core values in turn, using custom-made learning materials to embrace change in the workplace. A host of projects ran in parallel to the core activities to support implementation and embed the new culture. "TWW!" went on to win an industry Best Practice Award in

2003 and the retail bank won the "Customer Service Grand Award 2003" for the first time, confirming the establishment of a new service culture. In 2005, the programme won the ASTD Excellence in Practice Award conferred by the American Society of Training and Development.

The programme served to create a service culture which was based on continuous learning in the workplace and would come to represent a major entrepreneurial initiative in a traditional organisation. The innovative "TWW!" has been planned for roll-out in HSBC offices in China, Malaysia, Taiwan, India and Singapore. With increases in shareholder value, customer satisfaction and staff satisfaction recorded, and during tough times, this strategically driven approach to corporate culture management has proven a successful formula.

HSBC would not claim to have carried out a culture change programme that was a success in all departments; in hindsight one can see how certain aspects could have been dealt with better. Winning practices and lessons learnt will be incorporated into the strategic implementation plan put forward as Part Two of this book.

2

CORPORATE CULTURE DEFINED

Having reviewed a practical example of a major culture change programme recently undertaken to demonstrate that the "impossible" is indeed possible, we will now address corporate culture from a more theoretical perspective to divine the essence of the phenomenon. Given the huge impact corporate culture has on organisational performance and credibility (see the business case in Chapter 3), it is imperative that senior leaders understand its form so they can harness this powerful resource for the good of the business. In addition, leaders need to understand the benefits of a healthy culture and the risks associated with a toxic culture. Below is a look at the most influential models to date.

2.1 A Historical Perspective

2.1.1 The Way We Do Things Round Here

In 1966, Marvin Bower (Managing Director of McKinsey and Company, 1950–1967) gave us some of our first building blocks for understanding organisational culture in his book *The Will to Manage*.[1] Having noticed that top management executives in the most successful companies often referred to "our philosophy" and assumed that everyone knew what they are referring to, he defined this philosophy as "the way we do things around here" or the basic beliefs that people in the business are expected to hold and be guided by as they perform and conduct

---

[1] Marvin Bower, *The Will to Manage*, McGraw Hill, 1966.

themselves (this reflects the view that "the way we do things around here" and "the way we *are expected to* do things around here" are one and the same). Bower identified five basic beliefs which he found recurring frequently and noted that once a company philosophy crystallises, it becomes a powerful force indeed. These five beliefs are:

1. High ethical standards

2. Fact-founded decision-making

3. Responsiveness to internal and external environmental forces

4. Judging people on performance not personality

5. A sense of competitive urgency.

2.1.2 Rites, Rituals and Ceremonies

In the early 1980s, Dr Terrence Deal of Harvard and consultant Allan A. Kennedy of McKinsey took up the baton to explore this force further, tagging it "corporate culture" and listing the key elements as "company values, heroes, rites, rituals and ceremonies, the cultural network and the business environment" (see Figure 4).

Figure 4: Rites, Rituals and Ceremonies

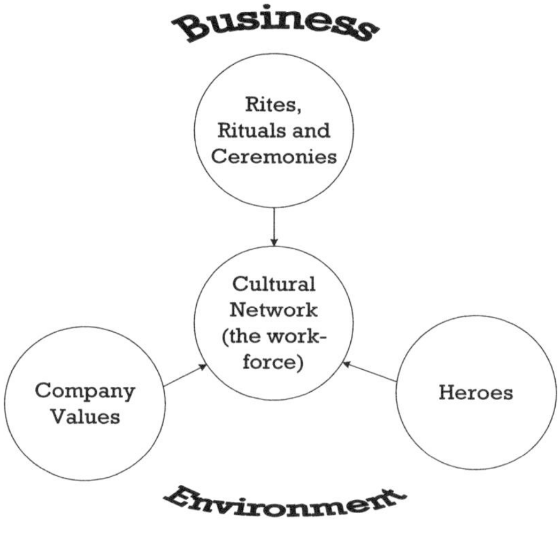

❖ **External**: Business environment.

❖ **Internal**: Company values (official concepts and beliefs); heroes (both authentic and manufactured, who personify company values); rites, rituals, ceremonies (programmed mechanisms which show employees what routine behavioural rituals are expected of them).

❖ **The Cultural Network:** Story-tellers, gossips, spies, whisperers and so on.

This model was inspired by the methods of anthropologists in the late twentieth century where research focused on the study of tangible manifestations left behind in the form of ritual ceremonies and artefacts. The transfer of language terms familiar to us made it easy for us to grasp the new concept being put forward. However, in the twentieth century, where the main metaphor of business was that of a machine, humans were often viewed as responding mechanisms and the model above reflects this stance. Corporate culture was primarily a one-way street and, apart from their oral contributions via the informal network, the role of the workforce was to bend themselves to management controls. Deal and Kennedy would reflect this mindset again when commenting on how managers can influence the workforce through explicit instructions. "Much management time is left to the whim of the manager. We see nothing wrong in a more heavy-handed approach. Middle management should be told exactly what to do. After all, blue collar workers are told what to do; why shouldn't managers?"[2]

In the field of anthropology, the advent of DNA analysis revolutionised methodologies and has added a further dimension to our understanding of ancient peoples. The basic premises on the essence of corporate culture needed to evolve too. The ultimate quest of those studying ancient civilisations is to get into the *minds and hearts* of ancient peoples to understand their cul-

---

[2] Deal, T. and Kennedy, A., *The Rites and Rituals of Corporate Life*, Perseus Publishing, 1982, p. 78.

tures. Researchers will use whatever tools and techniques are available to them as they piece together their puzzle. With organisational cultures we are dealing with the diagnosis and management of *living* cultures, and the ultimate resource is available to us — the workforce! That is not to say that the more tangible *vehicles of culture* have no place. But when our understanding of the phenomenon is largely limited to mechanisms external to the individuals who make up corporate communities, we can neither manage nor change corporate culture in any meaningful way. Besides, corporate culture and national culture are two different phenomena, just as family culture and national culture are. They are parallel in some regards — for example, rites, rituals and ceremonies *do* figure in all types of cultures — but one size does not fit all. Each type of culture has its own distinctive features, and these are outlined below.

Primary Role

National and family cultures are primarily social entities, whereas corporate cultures are primarily economic entities. A national culture protects the way of life of its community; a family culture continues on the family's genetic line and its main role is to provide children with a safe environment to grow; whereas corporate cultures most often focus first and foremost on making a profit. National culture can be seen as an extension of family culture, where one might go off to battle and lay down one's life for the good of one's nation. In a nation, a member's rights (whether as a child, a worker, etc.) are protected by a written constitution and legislation. This is not the case with organisations, which are regulated by external drivers (national laws) to respect the rights of workers and local communities. The failure of organisations to meet these standards led to the advent of staff unions.

Governance

In western nations cultures are generally democratic, whereas most corporate cultures tend to be autocratic. In the family situation, it can go either way. The mindset from which a community leader operates will be reflected in how they relate to others and the world around them. For example, in terms of a mode of enquiry and dissent, parents will often guide a child's inquisitive and spirited behaviour with love and understanding, realising that this behaviour is a natural and critical part of the natural learning process. In the corporate environment such behaviour will often be met with intolerance by line managers who do not share blood ties with their team members. Yet staff are often expected to be compliant and "get it right first time". It is a truism that there cannot be good governance without democracy.

Leaders

National leaders are voted in by their communities. We don't get any vote on who our parents are; nor do we get to vote on who our corporate leaders will be.

Love

Love in this context refers to acts of kindness towards others. In the family setting, love is unconditional. To be treated in a loving way by society depends on how well we integrate and contribute to community life and is often subject to our social status (as defined by our community). In the corporate sphere to be treated in a loving way is completely conditional, and the conditions vary from one corporate culture to another; for example, one may be rewarded for toeing the line *or* for taking risks. Particularly during times of major change, one might be rewarded and punished for both toeing the line *and* taking risks. This happens when there are sharp divisions on the leadership team.

Membership

At birth, we automatically become members of our family and national cultures, whereas our membership of a corporate culture is a contractual obligation which can usually be severed at any time by either party. This ability to detach from the organisation as one pleases allows individuals to pursue better and more rewarding work environments which are more congruent with their own values and expectations. Parents work on the assumption that their children will fly the nest to further their growth and development, only to return in a different capacity as fully fledged adults; while to sever the corporate contract can be looked upon as betrayal and ungratefulness in a clannish culture. It is not common for a worker to return once they leave a corporation.

Knowledge Transfer

Parents pass on their knowledge of the world to their young; however, managers often hoard knowledge and information to protect their own power bases. Both tactics are survival-based.

The Sharing of Resources

In the family setting and when food is limited parents will normally feed their children first. When resources are short in the corporate environment the more senior staff will take care of themselves, first and foremost, and either hoard or jump ship.

Stories and Legends

In ancient times, legends acted as metaphors for those who had a limited understanding of the world. Communities would appoint elders and priests as keepers of key lessons and, in traditional societies, their position was revered and upheld. These guardians knew to protect the integrity of core values and important lessons, and used story-telling to help guide successive generations to deal with life's challenges. For example, when an elder of the indigenous Mocan tribe in Thailand watched the shoreline recede in an unusual way on 26 December 2004, he recollected their ancient "Seven Waves" legend. It spoke of the shoreline receding far into the distance before returning in giant waves to eat people up and make way for new beginnings. Alerted to the impending calamity, the elder ran around the beach warning locals and tourists alike. Together, they all headed for the hills, safely avoiding the incoming *tsunami*. Unfortunately, key lessons are not preserved in the same way in the corporate domain, so we do not have this important resource to fall back on when things get tough. Authorities on the culture (those who have worked with the company for a long time and know its roots, and also corporate culture professionals) are usually given no official recognition and are just as susceptible to redundancy, outsourcing and even excommunication. This means that important values and lessons get corrupted or even lost over time. As a result, stories passed on orally are no accurate guide to a culture.

Rites, Rituals and Artefacts

Ancient peoples have left behind them an abundance of artefacts which demonstrate the importance of rites and rituals in the development of all cultures. These artefacts could take the form of buildings ruins, murals, jewellery, sculptures or ornaments, and while some were traced back to a national/ethnic culture, others originated with religious cultures. Through the use of simple imagery and phrases these peoples managed to retain the essence of key messages and learning points. To this day, rites and rituals continue to give meaning to our existence, provide us with moments of reflection and mark transitional periods of our lives. On the personal front, most are enacted with care and reverence, and the related artefacts are treasured for their symbolic meaning. However, as the corporation is largely a new phenomenon, and as the practice of corporate culture management has yet to become the norm, the same cannot be said of *formal* corporate rites and rituals and their related artefacts. Ceremonies rattle hollow with symbols devoid of congruency with espoused philosophies. That said, *informal* rites and rituals are quite a different story because they dicate "how we do things around here". These are integral to the culture and any related artefacts can share a wealth of information.

First Impressions

When we consider any given national culture, we can conjure up images of their distinctive national dress, language and cuisine — all of which are creations of that particular community. These images serve as indicators to the general set of beliefs held by that distinctive group. They also serve as guidelines to how we should behave when immersed in these cultures and we will adjust our behaviour accordingly, for example, a little bow from the waist when greeting a native Japanese. This type of mental map also applies to religious cultures; when we think of any of the major organised religions (Hinduism, Christianity, Islam, etc.) we can immediately imagine the traditional garb worn by followers, priests, nuns, imams, etc., and some of the distinguishing beliefs held by any of the particular communities.

Alas, when we turn our attention to the recently identified phenomenon of "corporate culture" we are on altogether more difficult terrain and all the more so when the organisation is a global entity. "Western dress" is now the norm on the international scene, cuisine does not come into the equation (unless the company is in the catering industry and known for particularly wonderful/terrible food) and any turn of phrase particular to a given culture is decipherable only to insiders. To compound matters, corporate images are often manufactured. This means that, in the past, it has been exceedingly difficult for outsiders to decipher the personality and character of any particular organisation. To get past the public image of a corporate culture, we need to focus on:

a) The outcomes and results achieved by the organisation in terms of major stakeholders; and

b) The means used to achieve those ends.

2.1.3 A Pattern of Basic Assumptions

In 1985, Edgar Schein (senior lecturer at the MIT Sloan School of Management) shared with us his perspective on the essence of organisational culture. According to Schein, organisational culture is:

> a pattern of basic assumptions — invented, discovered, or developed by a given group as it learns to cope with its problems of external adaptation and internal integration — that has worked well enough to be considered valid, and therefore, to be taught to new members as the correct way to perceive, think and feel in relation to these problems.

Like Bower, Schein considered shared beliefs as central to culture. He taught us that culture is a learned group experience resulting from the problem-solving process of a given group, and that a pattern of basic assumptions are the ultimate source of values in action. However, a limitation of this definition is that it does not consider the unique contribution of newcomers to a group. Their ideas and practices are a vital source of nourishment for any corporate culture because, by virtue of the fact that they are not privy to the internal way of doing things, newcomers will, quite innocently, challenge established traditions. When this happens, it can encourage more reflective insiders to think about *why* things are done a certain way and even to adapt internal practices if necessary. As a result, the culture is invigorated, inclusive and more at one with the world beyond the confines of its social boundaries.

Schein layered the elements of culture as he saw them:

❖ **Artefacts**: visible organisation structures and process, including rites, rituals, etc.

❖ **Espoused values**: strategies, goals and philosophies

❖ **Assumptions**: unconscious, taken-for-granted beliefs, perceptions, thoughts and feelings.

At this point it is worth taking a step back to distinguish between *espoused* culture and *prevailing* culture because, more often than not, there can be a world of a difference between the

two. Indeed, if this is the case with a given organisation the espoused values will not be supported by a network of complementary assumptions because the real assumptions that guide
behaviour will differ from them, and those artefacts that reflect
the espoused culture will be insignificant because they will be
swamped by the artefacts of the prevailing culture:

Prevailing Culture		*Espoused* Culture
Artefacts		Artefacts
Actual Values	vs	*Espoused Values*
Actual Assumptions		(no foundation)

A Comparative Study

While there are a great many more definitions of culture out
there, I have cited these particular models not only because of
their far-reaching influence, but because they differ in significant ways. For example, the second and third models reflect
polar assumptions on an individual's locus of control. Deal and
Kennedy's model reflects the view that people are externally
directed, responding to forces around them, while Schein's
model reflects the view that the members of any given community (or current employees anyway) are internally directed. I
agree with the latter view and believe that people have a need
to control their own destinies. The basic assumptions held by
management on this "locus of control" issue will make for a
world of difference in the results an organisation achieves. The
second point to take into consideration is the fact that Deal and
Kennedy's model completely omits the influence management
assumptions will have on business outcomes and results. When,
for example, a management body drives their organisation's
culture from their own negative assumptions about people,
places and things, this can yield very destructive results. The
case below illustrates the point.

Arthur Andersen

Long before the term "corporate culture" was coined, and following trends in professional services firms, the AA business model was to charge high fees while passing the majority of work to inexpensive junior staff. To protect the business model from collapsing through either inconsistent standards or the loss of an outstanding performer who took their knowledge and skills with them on departure, Arthur Andersen deliberately created a team that was interchangeable — clones — so that, should a staff member leave, they could be replaced by any one of ten others who could provide the same service. To achieve this objective, and apart from normal socialisation activities like sharing the firm's history, goals and values, the management team purposely indoctrinated new recruits into the ways of AA using a variety of indoctrination mechanisms:

❖ Deliberately hiring fresh graduates because they were young and impressionable;

❖ Choosing staff for their ability to adapt to and comply with the established way of doing things;

❖ Telling new recruits there is "only one way — the AA way";

❖ Requiring obedience and making it completely unacceptable for a staff member to question "superiors"; as a result, creativity and independent thought were quashed;

❖ Encouraging staff to socialise primarily with colleagues; this would undermine critical thinking;

❖ Placing demands on new recruits regarding how they spent their personal time; they had no time to regroup or collect their thoughts;

❖ Leaning heavily on all new recruits to engage in group-oriented athletics regardless of whether or not individuals were willing or able.

The AA approach to training did not utilise the experiential learning approach (where learning is delegate-centred to facilitate empowerment), nor was it the more traditional trainer-centred approach (where the professional trainers set themselves up as experts to "fill empty vessels"). Rather, it was the policy of Mr Arthur Andersen himself to reject outside help. Instead, partners and even juniors would inculcate new recruits in the values and norms of AA. Clearly, training was used as a platform for brainwashing and was not really about people development — it was about mind control. Over time, the workforce even learned to *proudly* call themselves "Androids"!

Professional headhunters recognised that the survival of the insular firm was dependent on its ability to evolve with marketplace demands and this in turn was dependent, in part, on the integration of external seasoned professionals into Arthur Andersen. But while the firm could attract the right people, based on its brand image and its message pertaining to the espoused culture of the company, it was unable to motivate and retain such employees. Even the head of ethics was forced out. It is ironic that although "integrity" was said to be a cornerstone of the AA recruitment process, the systematic use of management mechanisms to inculcate "groupthink" negated out morality. Also, by treating people as passive responders to management-controlled mechanisms they failed to create a healthy corporate culture. Rather, they created a soulless cult.

It is normal and acceptable for organisations to use mechanisms such as induction programmes to introduce new staff to their jobs and *socialise* new members to their group, as this promotes harmony. But it is dysfunctional, immoral and an abuse of power to *indoctrinate* staff.

Let's take a comparative look at IBM.

IBM

Much has been written about the culture of the "Big Blue". For example, in *The Leadership Engine* Noel Tichy[3] described IBM's "button-down culture" and its inward-looking management team that perpetuated a culture of conformity in the early 1990s, which in turn failed to reinvent the tremendous legacy left behind by founder Tom Watson Sr. Certainly the use of the military metaphor and the word "conformity" would have one assume that the workforce was recruited and groomed to simply follow established rules — that they were not allowed freedom of thought and expression. But IBM staff were recruited for their compatibility with the service-oriented culture, not for their ability to conform. Also, since the early 1930s the front door of the IBM training centre had the motto "THINK" written over it in two-foot high letters to encourage a mode of enquiry; in later years, the word "THINK" was placed on signs all over the company. In addition, in 1962 founder Tom Watson publicly articulated the core value: "respect for the individual". These are not the practices of a management body seeking to perpetuate a culture of conformity. That IBM should find itself in a cultural quagmire in the early 1990s is more a reflection of the complacency early success had bred.

2.2 A Paradigm Shift

Corporate culture can be defined as:

> An organic group phenomenon whereby tradition passes on acquired learning to successive generations while innovation builds capacity to evolve with the environment. The interplay between these complementary forces manifests in the shared beliefs and assumptions of the workforce. It is visible in attitudes, behaviours and artefacts, and determines the quality of business outcomes and results. (© *O'Donovan 2006*)

---

[3] Noel M. Tichy, *The Leadership Engine*, Harper Business, 1997.

Given the complexity of the phenomenon, no single image could possibly encapsulate all of its subtleties. In Figure 5 the focus is on the dual nature of culture as this will provide those seeking to create a *service culture* or a *culture of innovation* with a useful frame of reference. CEOs seeking to create a *culture of ethics* face a different set of challenges and need another frame of reference and this will be illustrated in Figure 6. But for now, let's focus on the relationship between the dual forces, and the implications of this model for the organisation.

2.2.1 A Systems Perspective

Culture has a dual nature. It is constant, yet it is also inventive. This is because the function of any group culture is to enable a distinctive group to *survive and thrive* in an evolving environment. So on the one hand, the reinforcement of tradition shows "young ones" the ropes and provides any given community with a sense of identity, belonging and continuity. On the other hand, culture gains much of its form when each new generation questions established beliefs to put forward new ideas in an effort to make attitudes and behaviour more relevant to their new world.

For example, while the Irish culture continues to be very distinctive from any other national culture, the beliefs and norms of behaviour which prevailed in the 1970s and 1980s have, to a large extent, shifted for the new generations. Divorce is now legal and traditional institutions have lost much of their power. As social values have changed, smoking has been banned in pubs and drinking on the street outlawed. These trends show that national cultures are constantly shifting, thanks — in no small part — to that spirited, inquisitive force which is our youth. Anyone who has raised a child will testify to a small child's great propensity to ask questions, and an adolescent's insistence on doing things their own way — *just because*. Perhaps these are nature's mechanisms for invigorating cultures and facilitating their self-renewal. Also, environmental pressures have a major role to play *in the shaping of* cultures (though they are not *elements* of culture), because when resources in our environment are depleted or become redundant, necessity becomes the mother of invention. To continue our example, to survive and thrive, Ireland has transformed herself from a nation in decline to a model of economic success.

Therefore, corporate culture has a dual nature, whereby equilibrium is a steady-state-balance between opposite, but complementary, forces. The kinetic forces drive inventiveness while the static forces restrain it to reinforce tradition — that is, tradition preserves the group's distinct identity and way of life while ongoing innovation invigorates the culture and optimises problem-solving abilities in the face of change. This constant interplay gives the impression of homeostasis and governs system activity.

Figure 5: Culture Stabilises — and Invigorates!

© *O'Donovan, 2006*

In a healthy system, both tradition and innovation will strive towards a state of equilibrium. In their maladapted cousins, either tradition *or* innovation will undermine its opposite force. Therefore, the *statis* can reflect three different scenarios and the implications for the organisation are as follows:

1. When **tradition is overwhelmed by innovation** the company loses touch with its roots. Enron had an aggressive culture geared primarily towards innovation, Digital Equipment Corporation (DEC) was built on a set of values primarily

geared towards innovation and, in terms of problem-solving capabilities, the dot.coms are said to have been heavy on "Innovators" but light on "Adaptors" (turn to Chapter 6 for more on Innovators and Adaptors).

2. When *innovation is suppressed under the weight of tradition*, the ability of the corporation to solve problems and adapt to a changing environment and customer requirements is undermined. Cultures that ignore environmental drivers for change and inhibit a healthy mode of enquiry and dissent will initially stagnate and ultimately fossilise under the burden of tradition.

3. When *tradition and innovation are in harmony* the organisation is true to itself, staff have a sense of identity and belonging, a mode of enquiry and dissent is encouraged (to stimulate creativity and respect human dignity) and innovation is ongoing. This enables the workforce to continuously generate a broad range of solutions to problems.[4]

Note that growth-retarding situations occur when a growth-reinforcing propeller (a culture change programme) is overpowered by a restraining force (resistance).

2.2.2 A Moral Perspective

Given that the twenty-first-century business environment demands that organisations have a reputation for integrity, let us now consider the role of principles and values in corporate cultures.

In the late twentieth century it became common for organisations to communicate principles and values as a key component of their company philosophy, and increasingly this has

---

[4] While the *process* of inventiveness should become part of the fabric of the organisation, and retain its integrity as a stimulator of progress, the *output* it generates (ideas, methods and innovations) which is retained by the organisation will eventually become part of established tradition. Some of this output will endure, while the rest will be replaced over time by new approaches.

been reflected in company websites and annual reports. This would indicate that business leaders came to realise that their organisation's success was inextricably linked to good standing in the external community. The trend was driven by external forces, but unfortunately it often accounts for little more than window-dressing. Stephen Covey distinguishes between "principles" and "values", commenting that a gang of thieves will have shared values but will not be ethical. This distinction needs to be reinforced given the massive implications it can have for the organisation and society. For example, an organisation may well officially trumpet "integrity" as a core principle but in the day-to-day business may value collusion, intimidation and injustice. And in this era of global terrorism, we are only too familiar with the war crimes of those who are "values-driven" — yet even children and innocent holiday-makers are considered viable and expendable collateral damage.

There are good and bad values. Also good values that are not underpinned by ethical principles can become corrupted and will need to be managed. For example, at IBM Lou Gerstner found that "respect for the individual" had devolved into a pervasive institutional system for non-action where one individual could block the efforts of the majority. Ethical principles, on the other hand, are universal laws like "integrity" and "justice". They are non-sectarian and common to all socially responsible cultures. It has been said that we cannot break such principles; we can only break ourselves against them. Such laws exist to maintain balance in the universe and can be evidenced in moral, ecological and biological spheres.

Typology of Cultures

As reputational risk (the cost factor relating to possible damage incurred on the image and goodwill of a given organisation as a result of any internal malpractice) represents the greatest threat to organisations in this new millennium, a moral perspective is employed as the primary focus of a new typology of cultures shown below.

Figure 6: The Backbone of Corporate Cultures

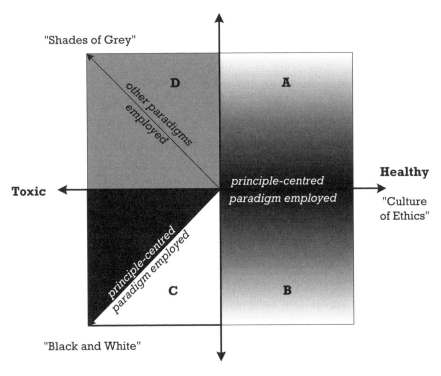

© *O'Donovan, 2006*

❖ **In Quadrants A and B** the *culture of ethics* is principle-centred with the formal central purpose of the organisation aligned with each individual's internal moral compass via ethical principles. Flexibility is employed to respect the spirit intended behind the law and the spirit of the workforce. Staff are able to appreciate paradoxes, complexity and alternative views without losing sight of their own authenticity and values. Creativity flourishes. Marketing communications reflect the authentic character of the organisation.

❖ **In Quadrant C** principles still govern; however rigidity overrules flexibility with the law quashing the spirit intended behind the law and the spirit of the workforce. This creates a "black-and-white" view of the world. Staff have an "either/or" mentality" and have a low tolerance for ambiguity or diversity. This closes minds to new possibilities and blocks creativity. On a moral level, the community is misguided.

❖ **In Quadrant D** flexibility overrules principles, and other paradigms like money and self-interest are employed to create a toxic "shades-of-grey" culture. The integrity of the individual is systematically undermined and the public image glosses over the truth about the real nature of the corporate psyche. Power is centralised and the general workforce is disenfranchised. Consciousness and conscience are undermined on a community, team and individual level. On a moral level, the community is on a downward spiral towards utter corruption.

Basically, each type of culture operates from a different set of beliefs and assumptions which constitute the unspoken rules of the game.[5] Any one of these culture types can be considered strong when the majority of staff behave in accordance with the respective established norms. The implication is that a strong culture is not necessarily a healthy culture.

A Healthy Profile

Culture of Ethics

Moral principles are the backbone of a **culture of ethics**, with respect for oneself, for others and for the environment being of paramount importance. This balanced and ethical perspective encourages the safeguarding of beliefs and values that are constructive in nature, and the pruning of those that are not. Flexibility is engaged to respect the spirit intended behind the law and the spirit of the workforce. There is a clear corporate philosophy which guides strategy, and the workforce is aligned with both. Leaders demonstrate congruency by role-modelling

---

[5] For the ground rules of a healthy culture, see Chapter Five; for basic ground rules of a "shades-of-grey" culture refer to Appendix 3; and for the ground rules of a "black-and-white" culture refer to Appendix 4.

the corporate principles and values to set the right tone for the workforce. They operate from the assumption that the organisation is an economic *and* social entity. Espoused principles and values are an honest reflection of the prevailing culture and the authentic character of the organisation, and so will attract and retain those who reinforce the culture. Staff understand the organisation's place in, and contribution to, the world and their own place in this scheme. They are respected and empowered by their leaders, and this stokes the flames of passion, creativity and ownership. Tradition preserves the past while the process of inventiveness facilitates adaptability to change and this balance enables the organisation to survive and thrive.

A *culture of ethics* will benefit the business in a number of ways:[6]

1. By building *staff trust, commitment and passion*: Staff will have a genuine sense of belonging; they will know that they can do the right thing in confidence and when there is any doubt about what action to take, they can rely on the wisdom of their moral sensibilities to guide them as they navigate unfamiliar territory. This develops staff confidence in their leaders as they know that ethical behaviour will be rewarded. Employees can count on leaders to safeguard their interests in difficult and dangerous situations.

2. By building *customer trust and loyalty*: The company can be counted on by customers to a) provide goods and services in a socially responsible manner and b) take care of customer interests in difficult and dangerous situations. This enhances customer confidence in the organisation and reduces the likelihood that they will defect to the competition.

3. By building *shareholder value*: Through the character of its actions, it builds a favourable image and strong brand. Company image is based on long-term goodwill which results from a history of ethical conduct.

---

[6] Adapted from *The Will To Manage*, Marvin Bower, McGraw-Hill, 1966.

4. By building *relations with host communities*: When a corporation gains the goodwill of its host communities and enhances the local quality of life, this enhances its ability to do business locally.

A Toxic Profile

A toxic culture harms employees and threatens the survival of the organisation. It manifests when moral principles are undermined through "shades-of-grey" thinking or "black-and-white" thinking.

Shades of Grey

Shades-of-grey thinking takes hold when flexibility overshadows principles to become overly dominant; principles in turn become subordinate and are subject to erosion. In a *shades-of-grey* environment, it matters little whether there is a corporate philosophy, or if the correct policies and processes are in place, because espoused corporate principles will not determine the internal way of doing things. Policies and processes will be open to exploitation to suit self-serving individuals and cliques. With *shades-of-grey* thinking, how individuals and groups perceive a situation is not driven by any espoused company principles and values. Rather, people will learn to assess any given situation in terms of what outcomes are of benefit to themselves, and will work backwards from the external environment to decide on their response to a situation. As the external environment changes the double-minded will change their stance and alliances — a foot in every camp. Ultimately, it is "every man for himself". When the chips are down in a difficult situation, protecting self-interest will be more important than doing the right thing and demonstrating good moral conduct. In this process, an individual's moral sensibilities are not only subordinate to a toxic culture but are eventually eroded. People become unwittingly institutionalised through ongoing pressure to suppress their basic instinct on what is right and wrong. On a personal level, the price each individual pays for subscribing to this type of culture is very high.

Shades-of-grey thinking will thrive where the cult of the shareholder prevails, as it creates many possibilities and opportunities which would be inconceivable if the constraints of a fundamental sense of what is right and what is wrong were collectively employed. Indeed, finely tuned moral sensibilities might serve as a severe handicap for making it through the glass ceiling because those who upset the current way of doing things will be excommunicated. Any employee who gets involved in shady dealings will slide in deeper and deeper as the hold over them grows. Self-esteem suffers as their wrongdoings accumulate, and to compensate individuals may try to raise their self-image by outsmarting others.

The *shades-of-grey* corporate culture will look something like this:

❖ *Staff* are disenfranchised, uninformed and kept within the confines of a small job description so that they are easily replaceable. In times of crisis a person of integrity will not be able to trust management to support an ethical approach to decision-making; instead they will fearfully "walk on eggshells", unable to navigate the social environment because the internal rules of the game will be too foreign to their own personal mental map. Energy better spent on delivering results will be diverted trying to a) fend off pressure to conform and b) understand what is incomprehensible to them.

❖ *Customers* might stay to avail of a superior product but they will not be loyal to the company. They will be more likely to use the products and services of competitors also, and will more easily defect to the competition.

❖ *Shareholder value* can be destroyed because poor morale results in poor performance and poor results. If news of malpractice makes it to the press the company image will be tarnished and shareholder value may not only be undermined — it can be wiped out overnight.

❖ Goodwill is eroded in *host communities*, creating roadblocks to getting things done.

Black and White

A *black-and-white* culture is rigid. It demands that the letter of the law be followed, with little reflection given to the spirit intended behind the law. In a different context, organised religions all too often lose touch with the spiritual aspect of their founding principles to enforce rigid and outdated rules and regulations. This does much to control the masses but little to empower communities to embrace a changing world. This happens in the organisational context too. Over time, basic principles become submerged by bad values.

President George W. Bush has spoken more about values than any other American president in living memory and has been the focus of a critique by leading philosopher Peter Singer. In his appraisal of Bush's values and actions in office, Singer has this to say: "The Bush White House has provided us with a textbook example of what is wrong with an ethic based on rigid adherence to fixed moral principles literally interpreted." Reflecting on how Bush gave false impressions to his worldwide audience about Iraq's alleged possession of weapons of mass destruction, he goes on to say that "Bush's childishly literal notion of what is to be truthful has set the tone for his entire administration" and that is why Condoleezza Rice and Donald Rumsfeld insisted that the content of the State of the Union speech was correct in 2003.[7] Singer's example highlights the dangers of rigid black-and-white thinking. In a recent article in *Time* magazine, journalist Andrew Sullivan provides further insights on George W. Bush which reinforce Singer's observations: "He is loved for his undeniable charm, good humour and geniality. He is reviled

---

[7] Peter Singer, *The President of Good and Evil*, Granta Publications, 2004, p. 214.

for excessive rigidity, indifference to those outside his political orbit and lack of reflection and curiosity."[8]

Politics aside, while the *black-and-white* corporate culture is principle-centred, and while the head of the organisation may well be an honest individual, a lack of flexibility ensures that the law gains precedence over the spirit intended behind the law. Therefore, a corporate culture that is principle-centred in word only will not facilitate constructive beliefs. It will look like this:

❖ *Staff* are frustrated, with reflection and independent thinking discouraged. In an environment where compliance with the written word is overly enforced, the orders of an authority figure will over-rule the personal misgivings of those experiencing ethical conflict. Understanding of human circumstances and motivations is in short supply. Creativity and innovation are stifled.

❖ *Customers* are frustrated and disempowered. Those seeking flexibility to adapt to a changing environment might feel patronised and/or frustrated by the rigid mentality of product and service providers. Their feedback may not be highly regarded.

❖ *Shareholder value* is destroyed. A lack of ability to adapt to a changing world and to consider others' views will threaten the long-term survival of the organisation.

❖ Goodwill is eroded in *host communities*, creating roadblocks for getting things done locally.

Black-and-white thinking can surface in a shades-of-grey culture when it serves a purpose, particularly when those who engage in malpractice seek to claim the moral high ground to cover their tracks. Also, it is entirely possible for the workforce at large to have a reasonably healthy corporate culture at the outset, and for a toxic sub-culture to emerge amongst an increasingly remote executive management team/board of directors.

---

[8] Andrew Sullivan, *Time* magazine, 26 April 2004, p. 44.

This happens when the masses are subject to a different set of performance measures to those in the upper echelons and the minority are playing by different rules. If this is left unattended, the workforce will adjust to suit business leaders. Edgar Schein advises that if cultures become dysfunctional, it is the unique function of leadership to perceive the functional and dysfunctional elements of the existing culture and to manage cultural evolution and change in such a way that the group can survive in a changing environment.

It Takes Two to Tango

At this point it is worth considering how any management body would facilitate the development of such an unpleasant and harmful environment. In an article in the *New York Times*[9] entitled "Remaking the American CEO", Steven Prokesch wrote that corporate leaders are going through a massive rethinking process, and their response to the imperative to change has been to become more ruthless, more manipulative, more dishonest, more rigid, less creative, and less willing to take risks. Prokesch observed that all allegiances to workers, products, corporate structures, business, factories, communities and even the nation are viewed as expendable under the new rules. With survival at stake, only market leadership, strong profits and a high stock price can be allowed to matter. Given that Prokesch made these comments back in 1987 it would seem that recently, and as a result of the havoc wrecked by corporate governance scandals, this imbalance is being corrected somewhat by natural laws as white-collar criminals are brought to task.

More recently, Andy Serwer of *Fortune* magazine provided a perspective on *why* attitudes and behaviours shifted in the US during the 1980s and 1990s. According to Serwer, the expansion of Wall Street introduced an increasing number of Ameri-

---

[9] Steven Prokesch, "Remaking the American CEO", *New York Times*, 15 January 1987.

cans to the markets and to corporate America through their role as shareholders.

Before the 1980s one tenet of corporate governance was that company management served several con-stituencies: shareholders, yes, but also employees, customers, and perhaps others too, like citizens of towns in which the company did business. But the shareholder-driven crowd insisted that the only clien-tele that mattered was stockholders. If they were re-warded, then all other players would reap benefits as a by-product of an even higher stock price. This mantra of shareholder value, however, could be taken to an extreme and perverted — you can see how this bit of dogma would become a handy all-purpose justification for mass firings, shoddy products and the dumping of chemicals into rivers. In the roaring bull market of the 1990s, shareholders and their proxies — mutual funds and pension funds — flexed their muscles by placing more demands on the corporation. For instance, they and Wall Street's new superstar analysts like Jack Grubman and Henry Blodget wanted more and more information, and they wanted it now! P&G's John Smale remembers this change: "At some point the company began to provide guidance about earnings in the future — before that, the company never commented on fu-ture earnings in any public sense." Shareholders in-creasingly looked to companies that provided regular and smooth earnings. No surprises, just 15% com-pounded per year, which, as Warren Buffett and others pointed out, was unsustainable. As the markets climbed ever higher, some corporate managers (and soon-to-be-fodder for Court TV) found that the only way to sate the demand for better and better numbers was to cheat. You want incredible earnings growth? Skilling and Ebbers at Enron and Worldcom — along with their Wall Street enablers — were ready to de-

liver. But of course to do so the books must be
cooked.[10]

Commenting on the recent backlash from the rise of "the cult of
the shareholder", Serwer says that today CEOs like Howard
Schultz of Starbucks argue that employees should be prioritised
over stockholders. He points out that companies like Coke and
Gillette no longer mete out earnings guidance to Wall Street.
This allows a healthier balance to be struck, as CEOs weigh
short-term demands of impatient investors against long-term
responsibilities of other constituencies.

But the "cult of the shareholder" has spread its tenets further.
Recently, the Aspen Institute in the US surveyed 2,000 MBA stu-
dents from the class of 2001 and found that their values had altered during their studies. By the end of the course, they cared
less about customer needs and 75 per cent said that companies'
top priority should be to maximise shareholder value. Keep in
mind that many of the major business schools worldwide rely on
funding from the business sector and have, in the past, delivered
on industry *wants* as opposed to industry *needs*. The Richard Ivey
School of Business in Canada is one of a new breed of business
schools which take corporate responsibility seriously, and which
believe that nurturing people who are ethical, with a vested interest in society, is important. Ivey's vision statement commits to
developing business leaders who will act globally, think strategically and contribute to the societies in which they live.

Rather than suggesting that corruption is a necessary evil to
contend with in a capitalist environment, or a sad reflection on
the true essence of human nature, these insights suggest that
the recent spate of scandals is a result of the general adoption
of an imbalanced mindset on the role of the organisation in the
twentieth century. This led to the cult of the shareholder in the
1980s and the marginalisation of other stakeholders. But the

---

[10] Reprinted by permission of *Fortune* magazine, from "Wall Street Comes to
Main Street" by Andy Serwer, May 2004, p. 88. Copyright © 2004 by *Fortune*
magazine, all rights reserved.

trend is already being reversed by industry leaders. An alternative paradigm, that "organisations are economic *and* social entities" (Freeman, 1994) will better serve us in the twenty-first century as global corporations take on responsibilities previously reserved for nations. To act on this new philosophy and demonstrate moral leadership, organisations need to take responsibility for nurturing a healthy corporate culture.

Having thought about what drove industry leaders to facilitate toxic corporate cultures, another question worth considering is why staff would tolerate working in a maladapted corporate culture:

❖ A curious feature of how the human brain works is that we often look to the external environment for validation when we are concerned about something. If we do not receive the encouragement or validation we expect from our peers and those in a position of trust, we can question our own judgement and quash our concerns, thereby facilitating others' questionable ways of doing things.

❖ If a person was brought up in a toxic family environment, where some form of addiction and/or abuse was routinely experienced, they are more likely to find themselves in a similar environment as an adult, particularly if they have had no real experience of a healthy environment. We are most comfortable with what we know, even if it is not what is best for us. The more fortunate ones will learn to transcend harmful memories to move on to better things as they build inner strength.[11]

❖ Some who facilitate a maladapted culture might have been reared in a healthy environment but will have spent their entire working lives with the same organisation/industry which has a maladapted culture. With no other work experience against which to benchmark, they will not be able to grasp in any meaningful way that there might be a better

---

[11] Schaef, A.W. and Fassel, D., *The Addictive Organisation*, Harper Collins, 1990.

way of doing things. They may not even question why things are done the way they are, as the established way of doing things is all that they know. Much like the proverbial frog who did not notice the water it was sitting in rise to boiling point, the institutionalised will not recognise the harm the culture is causing them and will learn to suppress their internal misgivings. As they conform they become part of the problem, perpetuating toxic values and behaviours that will undermine their employer organisation.

❖ In an environment where a person's career progression is determined not by their performance but by their ability to keep their nose clean, staff will have learnt that communicating bad news and challenging unethical behaviour is career limiting.

❖ Others who facilitate a toxic corporate culture will be those who know better but who are keen to hold on to their jobs when jobs are scarce; those who are under pressure to support their families or the vices of their spouses; and those who are tied into the company through "golden handcuffs". For the latter, their lifestyle may be so tied into their employer that they have lost confidence in their ability to be successful in the external environment.

It has been said that the one who fails to conform to a toxic corporate culture is truly the lucky one.

2.2.5 Common Traits

Both healthy and toxic cultures have commonalities and learning these traits allow one a grounding in some of the basics of corporate culture analysis.

1. **Corporate culture evolves during work teams' learning and development at company start-up stage, and over time will be shaped by influences in the internal and external environment**. It is a function of group dynamics and

is created by founding leaders, current staff and new recruits. According to Tuckman and Jensen (1977)[12] all newly
established groups, and not just work teams, will go
through five stages of maturity — forming, norming, storm-
ing, performing and adjourning. As new members join:

a) They are consciously taught the established way of doing things to achieve outcomes and results desirable for
the group; and

b) They unconsciously share their own lessons learnt as
they go about their duties.

Whatever is accepted and adopted will become part of the
internal way of doing things. As the organisation matures, its
culture is shaped and reinforced by shared experiences,
traditions, history and events so it is continuously shifting
form (it can evolve and devolve) and must be steered on an
ongoing basis. As key leaders and the environment change,
the organisation is subject to new influences. Therefore
leadership, communication and staff development play a
key role in keeping organisational culture aligned with corporate philosophy and strategy. In a young company, the
culture will change many times as it goes through the shaping process. In a mature organisation, it will evolve at a
much slower rate as policies, processes and long-term employees reinforce established norms. In the latter case, it
will take the collective efforts of management over a number of years to change an entrenched toxic culture.

2. **Culture is a human system and has a dual nature.** Tradition and innovation are the dual forces of corporate culture.
These seemingly contradictory forces coexist and have done
so since the earliest human groups were formed, and the
necessary conflict inherent in this partnership is as old as the
human race. As the survival of the *homo sapiens* species has

[12] Tuckman, B.W. and Jensen, M.A.C., "Stages of Small Group Development",
Group & Organizational Studies, 2, pp. 419–427, 1977.

relied on our ability to embrace change, inventiveness and innovation have been key to problem-solving. Yet the survival of distinctive groups has also relied on the passing down of tradition — even though tradition is the antithesis of change and innovation. When these seemingly contradictory forces give-and-take to strive towards a sense of equilibrium, we have the basis for a culture which can survive and thrive. Tradition can be used to socialise new recruits to an organisation, while innovation stimulates creativity, risk-taking and adaptiveness to a changing environment.

3. **Morality and personal accountability must become part of the fabric of the organisation's culture because only through a reputation of integrity and transparency can a corporation attract funds, business and talent away from the competition**. Ethical principles act as the internal compass which navigates all towards the corporate vision and determines the means employed to achieve the ends. An effective system of accountability comes down to the business leader who upholds a code of honour. Leaders cannot turn a blind eye when individual executives consistently fail in their responsibilities, even if they are useful in maintaining the established balance of power. Ultimately, accountability comes down to the head of the organisation to implement and reinforce a *culture of ethics*.

4. **Culture is leader-facilitated and is thus a directly controllable variable.** In their formative years, all cultures are leader-led and, as a company matures, healthy cultures become leader-enabled when the baton of leadership is cascaded throughout the organisation. Unhealthy cultures remain leader-led so that an authority figure can retain control. For example, in a "black-and-white" culture the beliefs of the leader are rigidly enforced, with individual thought discouraged. Given that in a "shades-of-grey" culture ethics do not guide behaviour, staff have more latitude for engaging in unethical practices. Intimidation may be the weapon of

choice to control the leadership team and the "leader" is surrounded with "yes men". As a culture is forming, leaders have available to them cultural embedding mechanisms (policies, processes, etc.) to help them reinforce the culture. The effectiveness of such mechanisms can be undermined:

a) When the leadership team do not systematically manage the culture;

b) When the use of such mechanisms is heavy-handed and alienates the workforce; and

c) When there is a discrepancy between formal processes and informal processes; when this happens there is a gap between the prevailing culture and the espoused culture.

5. **Any given community will hold particular beliefs, attitudes and behaviours which are considered valid by the group for fulfilling needs and achieving results; the latter of which may, or may not, be constructive and business-focused.** Any collection of people will develop its own culture, or way of doing things, to achieve its group objectives, whether as a nation, an industry, an organisation, a family or an established group of friends. In the business environment, corporate culture will initially evolve in line with business survival because the fulfilment of individual and group needs will be so closely linked with the success of the fledgling business. However, in a large successful organisation, short-sighted and self-interested individuals can collude to survive and live comfortable lives for decades, even if the business is slowly losing its competitive edge. The central paradigm of any organisation is based on underlying assumptions which define shared truths, and these influence the attitudes, behaviours and results a particular community works towards. Just like parents and spouses, business stewards can inadvertently reinforce the wrong behaviours when they themselves hold harmful beliefs.

6. **It expresses itself as the personality of an organisation, and will attract or repel business.** No two people have the same personality and no two organisations have the same personality. This is why corporate culture can be a key differentiator and so a competitive advantage, given its impact on the customer experience. Tradition, artefacts and company history are a reflection of the distinctive personality of an organisation. As the organisation matures it will take on new ideas and experience new challenges which will further shape its personality. Positive experiences should be celebrated and repeated if possible. Lessons should be learnt from negative experiences so that they are not re-lived. If fundamental principles and values are established and taken on board by the workforce, the organisation will remain true to its central philosophy. If management and/or the workforce lose sight of these (or if values are not under-pinned by principles), then the culture will become increasingly maladapted and will repel business.

7. **Corporate culture is communicated through tangible and intangible media and can attract and retain talent, or drive it away.** Corporate culture conveys itself through a variety of channels. It will be experienced externally on two levels:

   a) How it is formally communicated in company reports and marketing campaigns; and

   b) How it is informally experienced by the community coming into direct contact with the organisation.

   These can be two very different experiences. Even within the organisation, disparity can be evidenced when poor morale is glossed over in internal magazines, which almost manically reflect images of "happy, happy winners". According to Attraction-Selection-Attrition theory,[13] new re-

---

[13] Schneider, B., "The People Make the Place", *Personnel Psychology*, 40, pp. 437–453, 1987.

cruits are attracted to a corporation if the values it espouses are in line with their own. If new recruits find, over time, that the prevailing culture is not supportive of the espoused principles and their personal principles, they will either:

a) Fight to change the culture;

b) Leave because their spiritual core is being undermined;

c) Stay and under-perform if the job-market is poor; or

d) Be forced out so that the status quo is maintained.

8. **Corporate culture at board level is a key driver of corporate governance and so will impact company image/ credibility and stakeholder value.** The high priest of capitalism, Adam Smith, believed that for a market economy to work participants must abide by a code of morality. The board of directors is responsible for corporate governance, and therefore determines the integrity and prosperity of the organisation. While the board will not control the means employed by directors and management to ensure that results are achieved, it must control the means employed to safeguard ethics and a healthy board culture. If the culture of an organisation is predominantly focused on the bottom line and winning, ethics and goodwill will suffer and non-shareholders will be marginalised. But if the culture is based on morally sound principles and values and top-line growth, it will encompass all major stakeholders and facilitate sound corporate governance.

9. **A useful measure of any corporate culture is quite simply, "what behaviours are rewarded, and what behaviours are punished?"** While senior leaders are not "god-like" creatures who can shape the culture alone, they do have considerable power to reward and punish and thus shape behaviour. Also, it is human nature to seek pleasure and avoid pain, so a corporate culture emerges through a learned understanding of which attitudes and behaviours will result in more pleasure and less pain. Unlike other

stakeholders, the workforce lives and breathes the corporate culture on a daily basis. As insiders they are active participants in, and direct observers of, the real way of doing things internally. Outcomes and results set the tone and staff will learn from the past to take action which will serve their own interests. But never assume that extrinsic motivators like money and status are all that drive people, because some will forfeit these to protect their personal integrity.

10. **It is in every worker's interests to understand the nature of corporate culture because it can have more influence on us than that of our national culture or even our religious culture. Indeed, it can come to dictate the most personal aspects of our lives.** In the family setting, children often do not have much exposure to the world beyond their home, school and church and in the organisation staff can live in a similar cocoon. This is certainly true for those who are workaholics or long-timers, those who experience isolation from the rest of the world (by living on company compounds, socialising primarily in company spots, shopping primarily in company outlets, banking primarily in company outlets, and so on) and those who have made it into a clannish leadership team. As exposure to new ideas gets increasingly constricted and our lives become more predictable, we can forget to take our corporate "specs" off when we get home and, as a result, our view of our private space becomes distorted. This influence is not always passive. For example, one *Fortune* magazine article detailed the role of the wife in company thinking. It surveyed executives across the US and quoted one executive as saying mournfully: "We control a man's environment in business and we lose it entirely when he crosses the threshold of his home. Management therefore has a challenge and an obligation to deliberately plan and create a favourable, constructive attitude on the part of the wife that will liberate her husband's total energies for the job." The *Fortune* reporter asked what the main traits were that corporations should look

for in a wife and reported back: "Management knows exactly what kind of wife it wants. In her simplest terms, she is a wife who is a) highly adaptable, b) highly gregarious and c) realises her husband belongs to the corporation." Also, our corporate culture can have a greater influence on us than our religious culture. Humans are built to adapt and survive and to do just this, millions of people operate from one set of beliefs and assumptions in their private life and another set of beliefs and assumptions in their work life. In effect, they compartmentalise ethics into two domains: personal and occupational. The beliefs and assumptions that operate in their private lives might be a product of their religious culture while those that take over in the workplace will emit from their corporate and industry culture. Often they fail to adequately consider the morality of their professional behaviour and people feel justified for doing things at work that they know to be wrong in other contexts. Common rationalisations for unethical conduct in the workplace include "that's business", "if it's legal, it's proper", "my boss told me to" and the false necessity trap. For more on common rationalisations, turn to Appendix 6.

The Levels of Culture

While the concept of corporate culture is intangible and subject to debate, corporate culture has a very clear "cause and effect" relationship with literally everything that goes on in an organisation. As such, its effects are manifested in an abundance of data which can be organised into categories or levels. The model below incorporates the best ideas put forward to date, and by shifting perspective on the essence of culture more is revealed.

Figure 7: The Levels of Culture

Drivers	Needs ▼	What we require as a g: productive workers; ne tions, motives and ene: tive or negative.
	Central Paradigm ▼	The network of shared beliefs (p--- - and values) and assumptions from which people derive meaning and understanding of their world.
Expressions	Attitudes ▼	Patterns of shared attitudes in relation to people, things and situations.
	Behaviour ▼	Patterns of shared conduct in different situations, including daily routines and the means deemed acceptable for achieving ends.
Reflections	Artefacts ▼	Artefacts include symbols of the past and present, and those which represent what the company aspires to.
	Results	Results reinforce or explode the beliefs and assumptions of major stakeholders on the culture in terms of ethics, service, etc.

© O'Donovan, 2006

Needs

Corporate culture is a product of group formation, and groups will be effective to the extent that they achieve goals and satisfy the needs of their individual members. At the individual level, each one of us is constantly seeking to meet a complex myriad of needs, and since we spend a great deal of time in the organisation it is in the workplace where we will seek fulfilment of these needs. In a young company staff will learn how easy or difficult it is to have their various needs met in the workplace and these shared learning experiences will influence the web of beliefs and assumptions which comes to dominate as the company matures. Needs generate emotions, motives and energy and these can be constructive or destructive depending on how strong the individual proves when coping with adversity. As the company matures, and if the experiences of the ɾce are positive on the whole, a healthy culture emerges. ɹf they are mostly negative a toxic culture emerges.

The relationship between needs and beliefs is at its most transparent in the following situations:

❖ When in the short term, and to make it from A to B, we cling on to positive beliefs about an individual or a situation in order to complete our journey or the task in hand. This barrier to critical thinking — self-deception at its best — is nature's way of protecting us from conflicting information which we might not be ready and able to cope with. Only when we have accomplished our task, completed our journey and fulfilled more pressing needs are we ready and able to stand back and cast an objective eye on data accumulated. This sets the stage for a paradigm shift.

❖ When in the long term, and to gain a sense of power and control over our lives, we subscribe to a set of beliefs which promise to fulfil starved needs. Often the lower ranks of terrorist organisations are drawn from those who are struggling with abject poverty, discrimination and low social status — those who lack a sense of power and control over their lives and their ability to have their needs met. Terrorist organisations, religious cults and some politicians know that beliefs are the pathway to power over others, and exploit the minds and hearts of the impressionable for their own ends.

❖ When staff leave much of themselves at home, do the minimum required to keep their jobs and engage in social activities which meet their neglected non-material needs. The case study below illustrates this point.

When the new CEO of a manufacturing firm realised that workforce morale and performance was rock-bottom, he enlisted the help of key personnel to find out how staff were spending their personal time. They reported back cases where staff were:

1. *Engaging in sporting activities and winning awards on a local and national level*

2. *Volunteering for local charities to help the elderly and disadvantaged children*

3. *Partaking in further studies to better themselves so that they could move on*

4. *Caring for elderly parents and handicapped children*

5. *Holding positions of responsibility in social clubs and societies.*

The CEO learnt that his workforce had developed a shared set of negative beliefs about the company based on their difficulty in having certain needs met at work, and had found their own outlets to redirect their passion and energies. To deal with the situation, he set about instigating a range of initiatives which would woo back the hearts, minds and energies of the workforce.

Given the nature of large established organisations there will be some degree of uniformity regarding the satisfaction levels that staff achieve in having their needs met. Turnover figures in different parts of the business and employee exit interviews can flag incidents (for example, a history of harassment and malpractice) while Employee Attitude Surveys can be a valuable resources for management who wish to glean insights into trends on staff perceptions of what needs are being fulfilled or left unsatisfied. More current data can be collated from regular "Q&A" forums between management and staff — be they live, electronic or otherwise. Even if these forums are intended to cover more strategy-related issues, staff tend to focus on issues "closer to home", particularly when such issues are not being addressed in any meaningful way.

Organisational needs, and how they are addressed, impact corporate culture but they are not in themselves part of the phenomenon which is culture. Examples of organisational needs include the need for more advanced technology like an e-banking facility and the strengthening of a particular aspect of the culture (for example, service style) to meet changing business requirements. In *The New Corporate Cultures* (1999), Deal and Kennedy provide us with an excellent account of how fashionable measures to address organisational needs (short-termism, downsizing and reengineering, outsourcing, mergers, computers and globalisation) have had a destructive impact on corporate cultures across the globe. Actions carried to extremes by managers obsessed with improving stock market performance have alienated employees and driven them into protective pockets of self-interest unprecedented in modern times. In the most extreme cases, employees are left so disillusioned that they go to work reluctantly and only because they need a livelihood. Short-term driven actions have fragmented traditionally strong corporate cultures and weakened their long-term performance potential.[14]

Central Paradigm

A paradigm is a unique worldview which is formed by the individual's experiences and reflections; it is made up of a network of beliefs and assumptions about people, places and things, and shapes the individual's attitude and behaviour. According to Rudinow and Barry (1994) most of these beliefs and assumptions are held without any conscious deliberation. So if we are like most people, the vast bulk of our belief structures are probably "subterranean", and function in a largely unexamined way as a set of assumptions of which we are for the most part unaware. But it is a worthwhile endeavour to take time out, reflect on our experiences and try to unearth our beliefs and assumptions because these can become outdated and start to work against us.

In his remarkable book, *The Seven Habits of Highly Effective People*, Stephen Covey affirms established thought that we each

---

[14] Deal, T. and Kennedy, A., *The New Corporate Cultures*, Perseus, 1999, p. 282.

approach our lives according to how we see the world. According to Covey's research our paradigms include:[15]

spouse	family	money
work	possessions	pleasure
a friend or friends	church	self
	principles	

Whatever is at the centre of our life will be the source of our security, guidance, wisdom and power. Covey gives clear examples of how behaviour and results are shaped by our paradigms. He demonstrates that a principle-centred paradigm is the only real winning approach to long-term success. This philosophy ties in with Aristotle's ancient teaching that the road to a happy life is through a path of virtue which requires choices to be made, and not through a path of short-term pleasure-seeking which can only achieve a temporary "fix" to problems. Of course, a principle-centred path requires more self-discipline and is the tougher path, calling on difficult decision-making as one is sometimes called upon to make hard choices. These choices will shape the life we will each look back on and measure. They will make the difference between a moral and an immoral leader. Once we have created an integrated set of beliefs and assumptions we will be comfortable with others who share the same set of beliefs and uncomfortable and vulnerable in situations where different assumptions operate because we will not understand what is going on, or worse, misperceive and misinterpret the actions of others (Douglas, 1986). This happens because we are not wearing the same pair of "specs" as the next person. Any resulting communication breakdown is a root cause of conflict in the workplace. We all have our own values and perceptions and when we im-

---

[15] Stephen R. Covey, *The Seven Habits of Highly Effective People*, Fireside, 1990, p. 111.

pose our point of view on others this creates conflict. Social harmony depends on tolerance for others' beliefs.

When our needs and world-view are reinforced, we experience comforting emotions and act on these. When our needs and worldview are challenged, this gives rise to uncomfortable emotions (e.g. fear) which can impact our attitudes, behaviours and results. A person of integrity who applies critical thought and reflection will be able to process uncomfortable emotions head on, use free will to choose their behaviour and *respond* appropriately. A person who is operating from other paradigms, and/or who simply reacts to pressure, is more likely to *react* and behave immorally. For example, many of the corporate governance scandals appear to have been driven by "esteem needs", that is, the need to gain approval from a boss who was totally focused on dollar results, giving little thought to how results were achieved, a hunger for power and a money-centred paradigm. For some, fear of being perceived as incompetent or a failure may have precipitated initial wrongdoings. Later, fear of being found out will have driven further misdeeds. Another motivator will have been greed coupled with the excitement of making extraordinary amounts of money for personal gain. Others still will have known that bowing to toxic values was a key requirement to surviving and succeeding in their organisation, and in the case of Enron, the top team is said to have gained a heightened (albeit short-lived) sense of self-esteem when they out-smarted their peers.

Organisations, as communities of people, have their collective worldview and the dominant paradigm will have a domino effect on attitudes, behaviours and results. Like our personal beliefs and assumptions, our network of organisational beliefs and assumptions are largely subterranean and function in a largely unexamined way. For the most part, we are unaware of them but they have a knock-on effect every day of our working lives. The espoused paradigm (corporate vision and values, strategies and goals) will be reflected in official statements. If this is not congruent with the actual paradigm (operating assumptions and beliefs of the organisation), the discrepancy will be reflected in the prevailing attitudes and behaviours of staff, the means used to achieve ends and actual results.

Figure 8: The Domino Effect

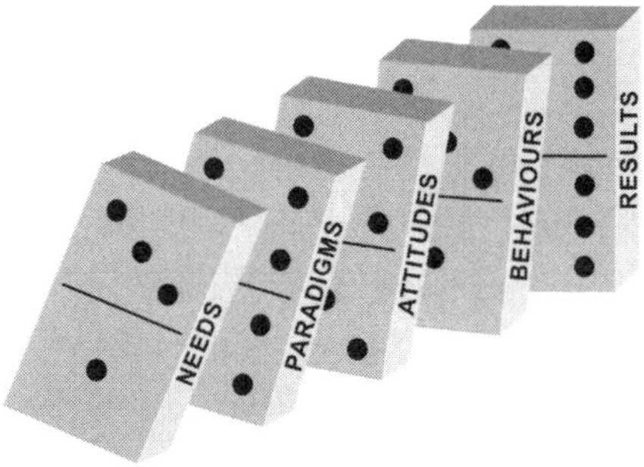

Attitudes

Attitudes do not exist in the abstract. Instead, they exist in relation to people, places and things and can be deciphered by observing behaviour. The attitudes we hold are the product of our beliefs and assumptions and any reflections we have on these. As groups develop, established norms create a shared view of the world with certain attitudes encouraged or discouraged amongst group members. We can read these attitudes by directly observing a person's tone of voice, body language, choice of words and general demeanour. We can also infer attitude through indirect observation of the workforce by studying emails, memos, reports, proposals, strategies, goals, policies and processes for not only style and content, but for also how these media are used. For example, by considering who is included or excluded on an email distribution list or in a company photograph, one can glean insights into whose star is rising or falling. As our attitudes significantly influence our behaviour they must be considered when either managing or changing corporate culture. Customers know well the value of attitude when they give feedback on service — particularly critical feedback (they refer not to the needs, beliefs and assumptions of staff, but to the *attitude* of service providers as they experi-

ence it) and the attitude of a manager towards their staff can go
a long way towards making or breaking morale and performance. Also, training departments have long valued feedback on
attitude for divining training needs with a view to enhancing
company performance.[16]

Behaviour

Behaviour in this context refers to those behaviours we share
with our social group — those that demonstrate to the world our
internal way of doing things and distinguish us from other social
groups. When we start a new job or join a club we are often appointed a buddy or mentor who will "show us the ropes". This
person is in fact sharing with us the internal way of doing things
— and if we are lucky they will advise us on those behaviours
that are socially accepted inside, and those that are not. Our
willingness and ability to follow the established order will determine, in no small part, how well we fit into our new group. If
we are transparent and authentic individuals, our behaviour
will be congruent with our underlying beliefs about people,
places and things, but if we are double-minded this will be reflected in our behaviour and it is only a matter of time before
the inconsistencies will reveal themselves.

In a strong (and toxic) culture, behaviour can be so homogeneous that colleagues of differing race, gender and generation can respond with the same quirks and mannerisms to
communicate specific emotions. It can be hard to identify
where one person stops and another starts. In a weak culture,
behaviour will differ from one sub-culture to another, so newcomers won't so obviously stick out. However, this inconsistency can make cross-functional teamwork an anxiety-ridden
experience for anyone attempting it. That is not to say that

---

[16] While social scientists agree that there is a direct relationship between attitudes and behaviour, there has been no consensus as to which comes first.
For a change management programme, we must address attitudes first to unfreeze mindsets and get buy-in for alternative beliefs. Then we must give the
workforce the tools they need to behave in a new way. We will not get the
same level of commitment and results if we impose behavioural change first.

strong cultures have an advantage with cross-functional team-work, for if an underlying belief of management is that their area of the business is their turf, intruders on that turf will be swiftly put in their place.[17]

Artefacts

Artefacts are tangible and intangible products of behaviour and are the most outward expressions of an organisation's culture. They are literally anything you experience with your senses and can refer either to a bygone era, the present or the future. Some artefacts reflect aspirations, while others reflect actual results. This makes them very difficult to analyse and interpret correctly. Examples of artefacts include:

❖ Company vision statements and strategies.

❖ Company architecture, on-site statues and gardens.

❖ Office structure, layout and design.

❖ Work attire and old uniforms.

❖ Technology.

❖ Corporate language (both style and content) and corporate communications.

❖ Safety and ethics manuals, internal surveys, ceremonies and other organisational processes which serve to rein-force/regulate behaviour.

---

[17] If we were to think more scientifically, we could take the view that the purity of data pertaining to attitude and behavioural regularities in the workforce could well be "contaminated" by situational stimuli and deemed unfit data for diagnosing culture. While this may well be true in some instances, I don't think we should throw the baby out with the bathwater. Any CEO, or any seasoned business person for the matter, will recognise that their workforce does share common ways of behaving in response to their environment, be it a common situation or a crisis. As such, this data provides us with a useful resource for diagnosing the cultural traits of our organisations. Once the underlying paradigm of beliefs and assumptions has been unearthed, it will quickly become apparent which behavioural patterns are situational and which are a true reflection of the corporation's culture.

❖ Customer feedback and how it is handled.

❖ Products and services, organisation structure plus company history and industry awards.

Some artefacts are obvious to outsiders while most are privy only to internal staff. When public artefacts (for example, company buildings) communicate power and success this influences the self-image of staff. The reverse is equally true. Speeches made by individual leaders can more accurately reflect their underlying beliefs than any formal vision statement (speech writers usually lack any knowledge of the leadership traits and expressions which indicate a healthy or toxic corporate culture). Interesting data can also be collated from official statements on core ideology, strategies and goals, Employee Attitude Surveys and daily routine emails and circulars.

Results

The results a corporation achieves in terms of all major stakeholders give outsiders insights into a) the character of an organisation and b) whether or not the espoused culture and the prevailing culture are one and the same:

❖ **Workforce**: the presence/absence of a team of people who have the experience, ability, desire and common objectives to executive vision and strategy; the presence/absence of a culture which attracts, motivates and retains high performers and persons of integrity, the integrity of recruitment communications as an honest reflection of the corporate culture and the actual working environment.

❖ **Customers**: the quality and competitiveness of products and services; the speed and quality of customer service; the integrity of marketing communications as an honest reflection of corporate philosophy and culture.

❖ **Shareholders**: the ability of executive management to secure market share and achieve sustainable revenue growth;

the quality of corporate governance; brand value; the integrity of annual reports.

❖ **Host Community**: the impact of the corporation's presence in the community on the local quality of life from a social and environmental perspective.

2.5 Chapter Summary

In 1966, Marvin Bower of McKinsey provided some of the first building blocks for understanding organisational culture. He established leaders' philosophies and values as the steer which guides "how we do things around here" in successful organisations and identified five key beliefs which are held by these companies. These beliefs have proven timeless. In the 1980s more comprehensive studies on the essence of organisational culture emerged and analysts put forward divergent views on the essence and elements of this phenomenon. Two models have been widely cited in business literature:

❖ In 1982, Deal and Kennedy's model on the essence of culture focused primarily on tangible manifestations and management controls, plus the passing on of myths and legends by the workforce. This model was inspired by the methods of anthropologists in the late twentieth century and reflects the underlying assumption that people are externally driven, responding to forces around them.

❖ In 1985, Edgar Schein of MIT put forward his perspective on the essence of organisational culture. Schein recognised that people are internally driven and identified different levels of culture which would allow us deeper diagnosis and understanding of the issue. To Schein, ritual ceremonies and artefacts are tangible components of organisational cultures but are not the heart of the matter.

While many have understood culture to be synonymous with tradition, culture in fact is a human system comprised of two

opposing forces. Tradition and innovation coexist to create necessary friction. The reinforcement of tradition enables a group
to retain its distinctive identity and provides group members
with a sense of belonging and continuity. The ongoing process
of inventiveness enables the group to generate a range of solutions to problems as the environment changes. When these two
forces exist and strive towards equilibrium, a distinctive culture
can retain its identity and survive long term. In addition, culture
is said to be essentially amoral. But within the organisational
context, morality must become part of the fabric of the culture
because only through a reputation of integrity and transparency can a corporation motivate the workforce and attract funds
and business away from the competition.

A new typology of cultures was presented that employs a
moral perspective as ethics figure to be the biggest cultural
challenge for organisations in this new era:

A culture that is healthy from a moral perspective is known
as a *culture of ethics*. It is morally sound and principle-centred
in word and spirit, encouraging the longevity of constructive
beliefs and the pruning of harmful ones. Flexibility is employed
to facilitate adaptability to a changing business environment
and to safeguard the spirit behind the law together with the
spirit of the workforce. Staff are aligned with corporate philosophy and strategy, which encompasses the needs of major
stakeholders, and they have a common sense of purpose.

A **toxic corporate culture** can take two forms: a *black-and-
white* culture or a *shades-of-grey* culture. At their most extreme,
these oppressive cultures reduce people to a common denomi-
nator — eroding all that is human in us.

❖ The *black-and-white culture* is principle-centred but flexibility has been replaced by rigidity to stifle the business. It
   demands that the letter of the law be followed, with little reflection given to the spirit intended behind the law. Independent thinking is discouraged, with creativity and innovation quashed. While the leader might be an honest individ-

ual, this in itself is not enough for the business to survive and thrive. Tradition weighs down heavily on innovation.

❖ In the *shades-of-grey culture* flexibility takes hold to over-shadow principles, becoming overly dominant. Shades-of-grey thinking can thrive where the "cult of the shareholder" prevails, as it creates possibilities and opportunities which would be inconceivable if the constraints of a fundamental sense of what is right and what is wrong were employed. To maintain control of the ranks, tradition may be overly en-forced and/or a culture of fear and intimidation will prevail.

In essence, healthy cultures are principle-centred in word and spirit and facilitate the adoption of constructive beliefs and as-sumptions while toxic cultures are perpetuated by institutional thinking on an organisational level, and by an array of human circumstances on the individual level. Therefore, being an ac-tive participant in a morally sound culture is an empowering and nurturing experience, while subscribing to a toxic corpo-rate culture is literally selling out on one's heart and soul. As staff are active participants and observers of corporate culture they are first to feel its effects. Customers are the next to ex-perience the reality of a prevailing culture, for they experience the "personality" of the organisation when they buy products and services. Remote shareholders can often be last to learn the truth when there is a gap between the espoused culture and the prevailing culture. Current affairs have taught us that it can take a whistle-blower to raise consciousness.

Corporate culture can be a high-risk issue for brand image and company performance if it is maladapted, and executive management has neither the knowledge, skills nor desire to analyse, audit and nurture it. As we move further into the twenty-first century, natural laws would appear to be correcting the path of organisations which have met their "day of reckon-ing" as a result of a toxic corporate culture. The way forward for organisations in the new millennium is to:

❖ Re-establish their commitment to all major stakeholders; and

❖ Be principle-centred in word and spirit, nurturing the spiritual core of the organisation.

The former requires a paradigm shift on the role of the organisation in the twenty-first-century global environment to embrace both economic and societal facets. The latter will involve a) centring corporate philosophy, strategy and action around a set of principles and values which are real and meaningful for the workforce and b) taking active steps to nurture a healthy culture.

Despite their differences, all cultures have in common a number of traits and learning these traits allows one a grounding on some of the basics of corporate culture analysis. Also, all types of corporate cultures produce qualitative and quantitative data that can be organised into three common levels:

❖ *Drivers* include shared needs, beliefs and assumptions;

❖ *Expressions* include shared attitudes and behaviours; and

❖ *Reflections* include artefacts, outcomes and results.

3

THE BUSINESS CASE

3.1 The Case FOR Corporate Culture Management

3.1.1 White Collar Crime

As we learnt in the previous chapter, corporate culture is a potentially productive or destructive force. Enron, Andersen, WorldCom, Parmalat . . . over and over again, the neglected corporate culture has been named as a key culprit for the disgrace, and sometimes demise, of major respected organisations. Insiders and experts talk about conspiracy and collusion, illegal practices and turning a blind eye to wrong-doing. The negative values, attitudes and behaviours of toxic cultures permeate throughout esteemed organisations, twisting policies and processes. The domino effect can only lead to downfall and disgrace.

A toxic corporate culture might trumpet ethics in annual reports but it is not principle-centred in word and spirit. Below are four recent cases which will enable us to consider the prevailing attitudes and behaviours in these profiled organisations, plus the beliefs and basic needs which drove these high-profile corporate governance scandals. In addition, the espoused cultural values of these organisations, as presented to major stakeholders in annual reports and other official communications, is highlighted. Each company was using a glossy communications campaign to misrepresent who they really were.

Case Study: Enron

The Enron collapse sent shockwaves through the financial world when it emerged that management had used off-the-books, unregulated private partnerships to absorb losses and support inflated revenues. When concerned analysts questioned where the money came from, Enron refused disclosure. Only under mounting pressure did they eventually comply, in November 2001, to communicate the overstatement of profits. This event triggered the collapse of the company and its bankruptcy filing by 2 December 2001. This resulted in the loss of more than 5,000 jobs and at least US$1 billion in retirement funds.

During investigations it emerged that Arthur Andersen, the Enron auditing firm, had supported the deceit by turning a blind eye to questionable accounting practices in order to secure lucrative consulting fees. A 217-page report by Enron's Board condemned management for inflated profit reports and failure of controls at every level. The report states the following: ". . . a culture emerged of self-dealing and self-enrichment at the expense of shareholders, as accountants and lawyers signed off on flawed and improper decisions every step of the way".

Former Enron bosses Kenneth Lay and Jeffery Skilling now face a lifetime in prison after a Texas jury found them guilty in one of the biggest corporate scandals in American history. In May 2006, Skilling was convicted of 18 charges of fraud and conspiracy, and one count of insider trading, while Enron founder Kenneth Lay was convicted of six counts of fraud and conspiracy, and four counts of bank fraud. They will receive jail sentences that could keep them behind bars for the rest of their lives.

Enron Corporation's Espoused Cultural Values:

- *Communication*
- *Respect*
- *Integrity*
- *People*

Case Study: Arthur Andersen

Arthur Andersen was founded in 1913 and in time would take its place as one of the "Big 5" accounting firms. The motto of the founder was "think straight, talk straight", and over time Andersen earned a reputation in the marketplace for his integrity. This reputation transferred across to the company brand. Unfortunately, and behind closed doors, Andersen encouraged groupthink, creating a workforce of followers, not leaders. This led to the creation of a soulless cult and by the 1990s it was all about the dollar. In *Final Accounting*[1] Barbara Ley Toffler, former partner-in-charge of Andersen's "Ethics and Responsible Business Practices" consultancy practices from 1995 to 1999, reports that, eager to rake in millions in auditing and consulting fees, Andersen executives turned a blind eye as clients such as Waste Management, Global Crossing, WorldCom and Enron cooked their books. Inward-looking executives lost sight of the customer and other key stakeholders. Staff were applauded for the amount of money they brought in, but nobody was acknowledged and rewarded for standing up to unethical conduct. Unfortunately, while there were attempts in some quarters to improve the corporate culture, these failed due to collusion, corruption and resistance to change at the top of the hierarchy. Self-interest triumphed. The culture of Andersen did not have "principles" as its central paradigm. The real paradigm was money. In her book, Toffler named the cause of Andersen's downfall succinctly:

> . . . a corporate culture emerged that put loyalty to the firm above loyalty to the client or the investing public.

This intriguing insight suggests that the organisation had come to take on a fictitious personality all of its own in the minds of employees, and that it was the duty of executive management to protect the mothership above and beyond any calling to protect the interests of the non-fictitious (shareholders, customers, the

---

[1] Barbara Ley Toffler, *Final Accounting*, Doubleday, 2002.

workforce and society). In *The Corporation*[2] professor of law and legal scholar Joel Bakan explains how this thinking took root:

> By the end of the nineteenth century, through a bizarre legal alchemy, courts had fully transformed the corporation into a "person" with its own identity, separate from the flesh-and-blood people who were its owners and managers and empowered, like a real person, to conduct business in its own name, acquire assets, employ workers, pay taxes and go to court to defend its actions. The corporate person had taken the place, at least in law, of the real people who owned the corporations.

Arthur Andersen's Espoused Cultural Values:

- *Integrity*
- *Stewardship*
- *Training*

Case Study: Parmalat

When, in mid-November 2003, the Italian dairy giant Parmalat defaulted on a US$185 million bond, concern grew amongst analysts about the corporation's failure to use the abundant cash shown in its balance sheet to repay its debts. Under pressure from regulators, the Group would eventually state that some 38 per cent of Parmalat's assets were held in a US$4.9 billion Bank of America account of a Parmalat subsidiary in the Cayman Islands. That prompted auditors and banks to scrutinise the company accounts. But on 19 December, Bank of America reported that no such account existed in the Cayman Islands. In the ensuing investigation Italian prosecutors found that, over a 15-year period, Parmalat executives simply invented assets to make up for as much as $16.2 billion in liabilities and falsified accounts. Its 2003 Earnings before Interest, Taxes and Depreciation were overstated by 530 per cent. This news forced the company into

---

[2] Joel Bakan, *The Corporation*, Constable & Robinson Ltd, 2005, p. 16.

bankruptcy on 27 December. Those under investigation included Parmalat founder and former Chief Executive Calisto Tanzi, his son Stefano and brother Giovanni. Tanzi's family controlled 51 per cent of Parmalat. On 27 December 2003, he was arrested on suspicion of fraud, embezzlement, false accounting and misleading investors. Additional charges now include regulatory obstruction and false bankruptcy. As of June 2005, Tanzi plus a number of colleagues and three financial institutions faced formal charges of market rigging, false auditing and hindering the work of regulators. While company shares have been suspended indefinitely, Eric Bondi, the new Parmalat CEO, has now formulated a turnaround for the rebranded Parmalat Finanziaria SpA and his strategy is to win billions in lawsuits against the banks who were involved in the collapse.

Parmalat's Espoused Cultural Values:

- *Quality*

- *Innovation*

- *Communication*

- *Brand*

- *People*

Case Study: WorldCom

When WorldCom, the US's number two long-distance phone company, revealed US$7.2 billion in improper accounting in July 2002, it filed for the largest bankruptcy reorganisation ever. In the ensuing investigation, the report of court-appointed monitor, Richard Thornburgh (a former US attorney general), stated:

> . . . our investigation strongly suggests that WorldCom personnel responded to changing business conditions and earnings pressures by taking extraordinary and illegal steps to mask discrepancies between the financial reality at the company and Wall Street's expectations.

In 2005, Bernie Ebbers, former chief executive of WorldCom, was declared guilty of fraud, conspiracy and filing false documents in an accounting scandal which eventually totalled US$11 billion in irregularities and made for the biggest bankruptcy scandal in history. He was sentenced to 25 years for his role in the massive accounting fraud.

Incidentally, the WorldCom top team had previously worked for Arthur Andersen!

> **WorldCom's Espoused Cultural Values:**
>
> - *Leadership*
> - *Service*
> - *Innovation*
> - *Communication*

Figure 9 shows some of the prevalent attitudes, behaviours, outcomes, artefacts and results of these corporate cultures as documented in the media. Working backwards, one can divine the basic needs and beliefs which served as the seedlings for the disastrous domino effects. These corporate cultures were not principle-centred in word and spirit.

The needs are normal and valid. It is in the central paradigms where the seedlings of malfeasance sprout, as the beliefs entertained go a long way towards influencing attitudes and the means used to achieve ends. Given that white-collar crime has proven to impact whole economies and the value of national brands, the new lack of tolerance for shady dealings means that we can expect more and more corporate governance scandals to come to light. A glance in the business section of any major newspaper, on any given day, would confirm this trend as senior executives, consultants, banks and auditors continue to be brought to task for white-collar crime.

Figure 9: A Toxic Domino Effect

Needs ?	Central Paradigm ?	Attitudes ?	Behaviours ?	Artefacts ?	Results
▪ Self-esteem needs ▪ Social and belonging needs ▪ Power	▪ Money ▪ Possessions ▪ Self-interest ▪ Pleasure ▪ Friends	▪ The ends justify the means ▪ If everyone is responsible, no one is responsible ▪ My boss is in on it, so it must be OK ▪ In the "real world" everyone is doing it ▪ Monetary results are all that matter ▪ Speak up — at your peril ▪ Conspirators are considered brilliant and their deception intellectually stimulating ▪ Those who challenge our way of doing things are trouble-makers	▪ Intimidation, harassment, conspiracy, collusion, coercion, etc. ▪ Embezzlement ▪ Misleading investors ▪ Turning a blind eye to, and rewarding, wrong-doing ▪ Signing off on flawed and improper decisions ▪ Market rigging ▪ Sweeping misdeeds under the carpet ▪ Finger pointing; e.g. "it's a US problem" or "it's an Italian problem" ▪ Directors passing the buck to accountants ▪ Nepotism, and discrimination towards minority groups ▪ Bending the rules to divert money and privileges to themselves, cronies and henchmen	▪ Falsified accounts ▪ Companies designated to the corporate governance scandal graveyard ▪ Negative media coverage ▪ New legislation (e.g. Sarbanes-Oxley Act) and compliance software ▪ Code of Ethics ▪ Court cases ▪ Books written by insiders and observers	▪ Financial ruin ▪ Loss of competitive products and services for consumer ▪ Tarnished brand and image ▪ Jail sentences and destroyed reputations for senior executives ▪ Lost jobs for the workforce and stress for their families ▪ Lost pension plans for thousands as share prices plummeted ▪ Employees are "marked" when applying for new jobs in the community ▪ Damage to the environment ▪ Bankruptcy

© O'Donovan, 2006.

The challenge in identifying a toxic culture is that it often hides behind expensive packaging, be it an organisation's glossy marketing campaign or an individual's designer suit and watch. Recent findings by International Survey Research (ISR) have confirmed that ethical (or unethical) behaviour is part of an organisational culture which develops over time. This study is based on employee surveys in 72 companies from 1999 to 2000. According to ISR, the aspects of corporate culture that are likely to put a company at risk include an environment in which:

❖ Discussion of company values is seen as a public relations ploy rather than a true commitment;

❖ Acting with integrity is seen as an obstacle to success rather than a vehicle to it;

❖ Open debate and questioning of the status quo is discouraged;

❖ Bad news is "spun" rather than confronted head-on, and there is a "shoot the messenger mentality", particularly as one goes up the chain of command;

❖ Information of all kinds is hoarded rather than shared;

❖ Behaviour of high-performing employees is not questioned and the ends are emphasised (particularly the financial ends) while the means are largely ignored;

❖ The external environment — including customers, investors, and the general public — is something to be manipulated, rather than respected;

❖ There is an exclusive focus on short-term financial results, often matched with unrealistic performance expectations.[3]

It is interesting to note that the behaviours identified by the ISR research will not surface in cultural audits through scientific-

---

[3] International Survey Research (ISR), "Ethics and Organisational Culture: How Corporate Culture Impacts Shareholder Security", September 2002.

based tools alone. Instead, they require the use of qualitative tools, including the direct observation of staff, by a neutral party, as they go about their daily business.

Organisations which demonstrate all these attitudes and behaviours in their prevailing corporate culture have a *shades-of-grey* culture and the heart of the matter is an exclusive focus on short-term financial results. Those who have closely followed the scandals will recognise that a mixture of personal arrogance and insecurity underlies many of the points above; arrogance, bred from association with a seemingly invincible corporation which has a successful track record, coupled with the insecurity of those who know in their hearts that they do not hold the authentic personal power necessary to embrace change and the courage to face new challenges. Like the fictitious "Wizard of Oz", their false power is based on position and props and they will suppress and oppress the ranks to preserve their empires. Many folded under the pressure when they were exposed.

3.1.2 Corporate Social Responsibility (CSR)

The rise of the "cult of the shareholder" in the 1990s has heightened public mistrust of corporations in recent years. This skewed mindset, which led to earnings forecasts, short-term thinking and general malfeasance, provided the environmental context which led to the growth of the corporate social responsibility movement this past decade. A recent study[4] by international opinion research company GlobeScan has found that consumer measures of CSR fall into two broad categories:

1. ***Operational responsibilities:*** treat employees fairly and with respect, provide secure employment, treat customers with respect, comply with local and international legislation, ensure safety in factories, avoid harassment and discrimination, reject the use of bribery and manufacture safe and high quality products, environmental protection.

---

[4] GlobeScan, "2005 Corporate Social Responsibility Monitor".

2. ***Citizen responsibilities:*** protect human rights, make chari-
   table donations, protect the environment and contribute to
   local healthcare and education.

Operational responsibilities are a matter of risk management
(and a matter of culture) and failure to fulfil them can seriously
damage a company's reputation, while citizen responsibilities
are not considered a part of normal business operations.
GlobeScan found that 70 per cent of consumers in 21 countries
hold companies totally accountable for operational responsibilities while less than 50 per cent hold companies fully responsible for citizen responsibilities. "Our findings show that a lack
of CSR at the operational level cannot be compensated for by
more socially orientated citizenship activities", according to
Chris Coulter, vice-president of GlobeScan.

When the "2005 Public Eye Awards" asked citizens of the
United Kingdom to vote for the most blatant case of corporate
irresponsibility, Nestlé received more than double the votes of
any other company. In relation to the promotion of breast milk
substitutes, a Colombian subsidiary of Nestlé was brought to a
government tribunal in pursuit of a claim that it had broken a
collective bargaining agreement. Commenting on the case,
Louise Richards of the *Financial Times* had this to say: "ultimately, the gap between Nestlé's marketing strategy and the
reality on the ground is one more reminder that we cannot rely
on companies to regulate themselves in a global economy."[5]

When the goal of a well-managed organisation is to further
the interests of stakeholders, face the competition in its markets
and act legally *and* honestly (what is legal is not always honest)
it has little need to justify its character. That said, it certainly
does not pay for a CEO to be humble about internal best practices as the public has come to expect organisations to have a
CSR programme in place. A successful corporate culture management programme can enable organisations to demonstrate

---

[5] Louise Richards, *Financial Times*, 25 February 2005, p. 12.

to the public in a real and meaningful way both their authenticity and character and their commitment to good internal management practices. The website of the UN Global Compact allows member organisations a forum for sharing best practices.

3.1.3 Differentiation from the Competition

A healthy corporate culture is an invisible force which can strengthen an organisation's competitive edge, enhancing customer satisfaction, staff satisfaction, the quality of life for host communities and shareholder value. Moreover, it has emerged as a key driver of sound corporate governance. As each corporate culture is unique, it is effectively the organisation's personality which customers experience. It cannot be copied, unlike products and services.

3.1.4 Mergers and Acquisitions

Research shows that cultural differences between the partners of a merger are a key reason why the majority of mergers fail. Just as a person of integrity and a self-interested person will not fare well in marriage, culturally incompatible organisations are typically doomed. The challenge in a merger or acquisition is that cultures with very different ways of doing things can be forced together to problem-solve and achieve business results. Just as history books are written by the winners, the more powerful partner in the merger will impose their culture on the weaker partner, which will result in conflict.

While compatibility studies are standard in the financial, strategic, technological and human resource areas, cultural due diligence is often ignored. Well-designed cultural due diligence will enable corporations to:

❖ Identify common ground in beliefs, attitudes and behaviours which will facilitate synergies, and also show where any gaps occur;

❖ Discern if the potential partner's culture is an asset or a risk;

❖ Discern if and how any cultural differences can be reconciled;

❖ Decide if the chemistry of the companies involved is culturally compatible or incompatible.

Successful cultural integration will determine whether profitability can be sustained and grown in the companies merged. According to research conducted by a business intelligence firm in 2002, failure to effectively integrate culture and technology is the number one cause for unsuccessful mergers and acquisitions. Companies that find the most success in their consolidation efforts are said to be those that focus on post M&A integration activities early (during strategic planning) and consistently throughout the M&A process. It is reported that top integrators (including Pfizer, Hewlett-Packard, Cisco, IBM, GE and Exxon-Mobil) use proven integration strategies which focus on cultural, technology and process integration as well as potential financial benefits.[6]

But culture clashes are not the domain of mergers and acquisitions alone. They will also be prevalent in an organisation where a new breed of executive management is groomed and positioned to drive change. A lack of leadership and support from the old guard will result in staff aligning themselves with warring factions wrestling for power, resulting in energies being directed internally rather than outwards to serve the customer.

3.1.5 Outperform the Competition

Many reputable studies have emphasised the relationship between culture and performance. Harvard Business School professors John Kotter and James Heskett studied the performance of 207 large firms over eleven years. In their findings, they wrote that corporate culture can have a significant impact on a firm's long-term economic performance. Also, the study found that organisations with cultures that emphasised all the key

---

[6] cuttingedgeinfo.com/reports/FL59_M&A.htm

managerial constituencies (customers, stockholders and employees) with leadership from managers at all levels, outperformed by a large margin organisations that did not. Over the eleven-year period, the former increased revenues by an average of 682 per cent versus 166 per cent, expanded their workforces by 282 per cent versus 36 per cent, grew their stocks by 901 per cent versus 74 per cent and improved their net incomes by 756 per cent versus 1 per cent. Other major studies on the benefits of a constructive culture include Pfeffer and O'Reilly's *Hidden Principle* (2000)[7], Katzenbach's *Peak Performance* (2000)[8] and Collins's *Good to Great* (2002).[9]

3.2 The Case AGAINST Corporate Culture Management

3.2.1 Ethical Considerations

Some researchers are against corporate culture change as they consider it unethical because through the process the individual's worldview is challenged and this can lead to stress and confusion. Challenging worldviews is in fact healthy, as through this process personal growth occurs as our minds and hearts become open to diversity. When our worldview is challenged, we are pushed out of our comfort zone into the learning zone. As our comfort zone is dynamic, it expands as we grow through these learning experiences. This enhances our ability to deal with the next set of challenges. So on an individual and organisational level we become more resilient, more confident and more inventive.

---

[7] Pfeffer, J. and O'Reilly, C.A., *Hidden Principle*, Harvard Business School Press, 2000.

[8] Katzenbach J.R., *Peak Performance*, Harvard Business School Press, 2000.

[9] Collins, J.C., *Good to Great*, Harper Collins Publisher, 2001.

Figure 10: The Dynamic Comfort Zone

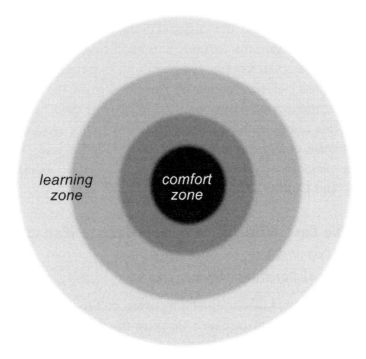

© O'Donovan, 2006

That said, a person whose worldview is challenged (whether by personal choice or through external intervention) has the right to decide for themselves which beliefs they wish to retain and which beliefs they may wish to discard.

Some culture analysts who dismiss corporate culture management on ethical grounds are concerned, quite rightly, that if the culture is not measured correctly at the outset, any intervention can cause a lot of unnecessary grief for the workforce. For this reason Appendix 2 includes a comprehensive list of tools and techniques, and practitioners should use as many as possible over a period of not less than three months so that as clear a portrait as possible is drawn. Chapter 5 addresses how to use these tools.

3.2.2 An Elusive Issue

As the social sciences of change have evolved, differing definitions of culture have been put forward. Given that academics and practitioners have been unable to agree about fundamental issues, it is not surprising that little headway has been made in terms of how to measure corporate culture. Schein was not far off the mark when he described the process of measuring culture as "difficult and hazardous" — but it can be done. Chapter 2 included a new model for corporate culture measurement which uncovers the drivers, expressions and reflections of culture. This model provides practitioners with a straightforward and practical framework for data analysis and consolation when diagnosing any culture. By using the resources provided in Chapter 5, organisations will be able to identify, for themselves:

❖ If the espoused culture and the required culture are aligned;

❖ If the prevailing culture of their organisation is an honest reflection of the espoused culture;

❖ If the prevailing culture is supportive of corporate philosophy and changing strategies;

❖ If the corporate culture is principle-centred, or otherwise;

❖ What beliefs, attitudes and behaviours are facilitating current outcomes and results, and what alternatives are needed to meet the demands of the marketplace; this in turn will point to what must change in the prevailing culture.

Chapter 13 provides detailed guidance on how to measure a culture change programme.

There is also debate amongst academics as to whether employee attitude surveys represent a viable tool for cultural assessments. Early employee attitude surveys collected data pertaining to individual opinions and so could not contribute in any significant way to cultural assessment. Over time, surveys evolved to collect data pertaining to attitudes. In the early days, culture analysts accepted these tools as valid measures of culture but over time came to dismiss them. Attitudes were not considered measures of corporate culture because staff behaviour can be influenced by situational stimuli. It can be argued, however, that both attitudes and behaviours are valid reflections of a corporate culture and a valuable source for gleaning insights into the underlying paradigm of beliefs and assumptions. One must make sure though that when conducting an employee attitude survey, every single staff member is invited to partake. If only a small portion of your workforce is included:

❖ You will not have a clear picture of group attitudes;

❖ It is unfair of those staff whose only opportunity to express their worldviews is via this mechanism;

❖ It sends out the message that management do not really value feedback from internal its customers; and

❖ It is reasonable to assume that management is either shy of staff feedback and measurement- and/or activity-centred.

Only management "gains" (by sending "happy family" results up the line), and only in the short term, when employee attitude surveys are limited to a small proportion of the workforce. Also, and when a management team considers cancelling their Employee Attitude Survey because they are fearful of negative feedback (a not altogether uncommon practice), they can expect the disgruntled workforce to vote with their feet, through absenteeism, mediocre performance and high turnover.

3.2.3 An Expensive Endeavour?

Contrary to popular opinion, a culture change programme is not an expensive endeavour in terms of financial cost. Certainly, a decent budget must be made available to get it off the ground, but once staff start to behave differently to deliver on strategies, the time and effort taken to get things done diminishes considerably and the financial outputs far exceed the inputs. That said, a culture change programme *is* very expensive in terms of the *non-financial resources* which must be directed towards its successful implementation but, apart from the dedicated core team, no one else is being asked to do much outside their normal work duties.

3.3 Chapter Summary

The case for corporate culture management greatly outweighs the case against:

❖ Recent corporate governance scandals have brought home the risks associated with a corporate culture which, when left untended, can become toxic. While the companies profiled in this chapter espoused principles and values like "respect", "integrity" and "communication" as central to their core philosophy, in reality the prevailing culture was the antithesis of those empty promises and malfeasance reigned. This led to either their disrepute or demise. Had the leadership teams of these organisations nurtured a healthy culture from the outset or implemented a culture change programme to create a culture of ethics, they could have averted these disasters. While ethics cannot be regulated, principles can be woven into the very fabric of an organisation.

❖ As no two corporate cultures are the same, it effectively is the organisation's unique personality that is a key component of corporate brand and image. Products and policies can be copied, but not corporate culture. Therefore, a healthy corporate culture can differentiate an organisation from the competition to become a competitive advantage. For deal-makers, achieving synergies from mergers and acquisitions can, more often than not, mean cutting costs by removing duplication of effort. But the real challenge is to get two different cultures working together in harmony and to create synergies so that one plus one equals three. By conducting cultural due diligence, deal-makers will obtain valuable data that will allow them to decide if the character and chemistry of two different companies is compatible and supportive of sustainable value.

❖ Many reputable studies have been done on the positive impact of ethics in the workplace. Kotter and Heskett studied the performance of 207 large firms over eleven years. In their findings, they wrote that corporate culture can have a significant impact on a firm's long-term economic performance. Also, organisations with cultures that emphasised all the key managerial constituencies (customers, shareholders and staff) outperformed, by a large margin, those that did not. Recent findings by International Survey Research confirm that ethical (or unethical) behaviour is part of organisational culture which develops over time.

❖ Corporate governance scandals have led to the blossoming of CSR over the past decade and has put the spotlight on internal management practices. Research by GlobeScan has recently found that 70 per cent of consumers in 21 countries hold companies totally accountable for "operational responsibilities" (or good internal management practices), while less than 50 per cent hold companies fully responsible for "citizen responsibilities". As the public has come to expect organisations to have a CSR programme in place, platforms like the UN Global Compact allow organisations to showcase best practices in ethical behaviour to major stakeholders. The demonstration of successful corporate culture management in the required Annual Corporate Social Responsibility Report can do much to persuade potential investors on the good character of an organisation. Certainly, it should go some way to protect the company from getting the Public Eye Award for corporate irresponsibility.

Those who do not value corporate culture change have a few main themes for their arguments:

❖ Some consider the field unethical, as it challenges a world-view and causes stress and confusion. However, this discomfort is actually part of a normal and healthy learning process which we all go through to facilitate independent thinking and safeguard our mental health. As we reflect on our experiences to gain insights and incorporate lessons learnt, our dynamic comfort zone expands. Through this process, the individual becomes more empowered and better able to cope with the next set of challenges which come along. That said, to impose a new culture on the workforce, or to instigate culture change without diagnosing the prevailing culture correctly, is destructive and to be discouraged.

❖ To date, many conflicting views have been put forth regarding the essence of corporate culture and how best to measure it. By shifting the perspective to reveal more of the phenomenon, a new model has be created which hopefully provides clarity to make culture measurement feasible for business practitioners. While corporate culture as a concept is somewhat intangible, it has a very real effect on basically everything that goes on in an organisation. Once culture is managed and key performance indicators pinpointed and tracked, outcomes and results will become measurable and investments in corporate culture management will become self-evident.

❖ Contrary to popular opinion, a culture change programme is not an expensive endeavour in terms of financial cost. Certainly, a decent budget must be made available up front, but once staff start to achieve success with the new way of doing things, the time and effort taken to get things done diminishes considerably. Typically, the financial outputs (increased revenues and cost savings) come to exceed the inputs by a wide margin.

4

Culture Myths Exploded

To wrap up Part One of this book, below are some of the more common myths that have emerged in relation to corporate culture.

4.1 Culture Myths Exploded

Myth: A strong culture is a good culture

A culture which is overly focused on tradition or innovation to the detriment of the opposite force is out of balance and is not a good culture. Still, it may be strong in that there is clarity and consistency in terms of the paradigm of beliefs that spells out the ground rules. The same can be said of a shades-of-grey culture or a black-and-white culture. This comfort-zone must be disrupted through strategic interventions to safeguard the long-term survival of the firm.

Myth: Culture is unspoken

The established order can be very vocal when inducting new recruits to their culture. Below are some little nuggets I have come across:

❖ "I've been told to decide for myself who I think will win the political struggles, align myself with them and ride on their coattails."

❖ "If a group of us got together we could push out Jack Welch."

❖ "We don't use the words 'change management' here. We use 'training' and 'communications'."

❖ "I've been told that I am a change agent, but I don't know what is expected of me."

❖ "It's 5.30. Why are you still working? We *all* leave together at 5.30."

❖ "People don't like such confidence in one so young."

❖ "Be punctual, don't miss a briefing and answer the phone on two rings (not one because you'll look like you have nothing to do, and not three because you will look plain lazy)."

Myth: People who do not fit the corporate culture should not be hired

If the prevailing culture is maladapted, it is in the interest of the company to hire those who hold the espoused principles and values of the organisation as their own. By pairing them with senior executive mentors whose behaviour is also congruent with these espoused principles and values, a critical mass of champions can be created over time. To position such recruits in an entrenched and toxic culture is a recipe for disaster as they will be neither accepted nor supported.

Myth: Innovative cultures cannot survive

Cultures which primarily promote tradition or innovation, to the detriment of the opposing force, cannot survive in the long term. To ensure lasting change in an established company, executive management needs to promote entrepreneurship and innovation. To avoid taking the path of Enron, the culture must be balanced and underpinned by principles; to avoid taking the path of Digital Equipment Company innovation must be tempered by tradition, and the business must be steered by those possessing strong business acumen.

Myth: Cultural change cannot be managed

It can be done, it has been done, and you can do it! Successes are underpinned by the belief that people prefer independence, autonomy and a chance to control their destinies; that is, they are internally directed. However, if one attempts to manage or change a culture starting with the belief that people are externally directed, responding to forces around them and preferring guidance from the environment, then "no" — corporate culture can be neither managed nor changed.

Myth: A cult-like culture is a good thing and something to aspire towards

In *Built to Last*, Collins and Porras distinguish between a movement that revolves around a charismatic leader and companies that are cult-like around their core ideologies, that is, groups that revolve around a "cult of personality" and those that revolve around a "cult of ideology". They go on to suggest that visionary companies tend to be cult-like around their ideologies and that this is something to aspire towards (they are of the view that core ideology should not change). But is this really the case? Many leading organisations were cult-like in their single-minded pursuit of the dollar and this eventually worked against them.

Also, while it is true that some of the most cult-like visionary companies have received accolades for being the best corporations for women and minorities, this is not evidence that cult-like companies are either capable of, or open to, diversity and new ways of doing things. Often accolades for diversity focus on superficial measures (gender, race, etc.) and do not take into account the fact that most organisations hire people who *think* like themselves. Different perceptions of the world, different attitudes and different ways of doing things are the true measure of diversity and there will be no space for them in cult-like organisations.

In addition, we have no reason to suppose that on day one the leadership team got it right when they settled on their core

ideology. For example, perhaps the importance of ethical principles was overlooked either because they forgot or because
this didn't reflect their way of doing business. But a core ideology that is lacking articulated moral tenets is like a ship at sea
without a compass.

Finally, it may be generally true that in the twentieth century
it was okay to have a core ideology that was not progressive so
long as staff lived it, but the world has changed. In the twenty-
first century, society at large is wealthier, more educated, more
discerning, more demanding and more informed and there is a
demand for a higher moral quality of management (or humanistic management). Any organisation that lives a core ideology
that is not enlightened or humanistic will find its days num-
bered. So if the articulated core ideology is found to be lacking
it doesn't need to be preserved, it needs to change!

Myth: You can have a cult-like culture of innovation, of competition, of change, of innovation or even of zaniness (and the implication is that this is a good thing)[1]

To draw a picture of a culture of zaniness, Collins and Porras
tell us that executives of Wal-Mart lead thousands of screaming
associates in the Wal-Mart cheer ("Give me a W!, Give me an
A!" etc.) and describe how these thousands of staff bend and
squiggle their hips in unison. Has anyone taken into consideration that this might, for some, be an affront to their human dignity? Has any staff member asserted their human right to *refuse*
to participate? If so, how were they treated?

Speaking in general terms, people who are working in low-
income jobs and those whose livelihood depends on their job
are vulnerable to the antics and pressures placed on them by
their management team. Just because an individual challenges
their manager in order to live up to their own code of conduct,
it cannot be assumed that their "lack of fit" makes their contribution to their employer organisation any less valuable. It cer-

---

[1] Collins, J.C. and Porras. J.I., *Built to Last*, Harper Collins, 2002, p. 137.

tainly does not make them "viruses" to be ejected. Moving on, and in terms of a "cult-like culture of change/innovation", the suggested cultish reinforcement mechanisms (indoctrinating people and imposing "tightness of fit") would:

a) Undermine the individual's ability to embrace change; and

b) Stifle the creativity and diversity that feed innovation.

Finally, and in terms of a "cult-like culture of competition", I suspect that the pressure to win would mean that the ends attained would come to justify the means used — bad news in these days of CSR and heightened corporate governance monitoring.[2]

4.2 Chapter Summary

As culture analysts put forward their views on the nature of culture over the years, a number of myths have emerged. Often these myths align with the definitions and models which the authors themselves put forward in the late twentieth century, and many have been left unchallenged. Based on significant industry experience and research, it can be argued that:

❖ A strong culture is *not* necessarily a healthy culture. It may not be underpinned by principles, or tradition/innovation

---

[2] In Appendix 3 of *Built to Last*, Collins and Porras share their research on evidence of cultism in major companies (Table A.6). The measures denoting "tightness of fit" and "elitism" are spot on, but those said to denote "indoctrination" are inaccurate, for most are harmless socialisation mechanisms typical of any culture, be it a firm or a family. Examples include: a) exposure to company mythology of heroic deeds by exemplary employees; b) orientation programmes that teach values, behaviours, corporate purpose and values, history and tradition; and c) internal communications that reinforce purpose and values. By reinforcing tradition in meaningful ways, the workforce can have a deep sense of belonging and be dedicated to company philosophy and purpose without being cult-like. Only when people do not have a choice to accept or reject ideas, only when they are threatened or punished for doing what they believe is right, and only when coercion or force is used on them do we move into the murky realm of indoctrination. It follows that many of the companies cited in the survey as being "high" on the indoctrination index most probably are not. So to be "cult-like" is not something to aspire towards after all.

may overwhelm its opposite force to create system imbalance. There may well be consistency in terms of attitudes and behaviors but they may be working at cross purposes with business needs.

❖ Culture is *not* unspoken. The old regime can be very vocal when inducting new recruits.

❖ People who do not fit the culture *should* be hired in some scenarios, for example if the culture is maladapted and the new recruit holds the espoused principles of the corporation as their own, pair them with executive mentors who live the core principles.

❖ Innovative cultures *can* survive. They must be principle-centred, balanced by tradition and steered by those with strong business acumen.

❖ Culture change *can* be managed. It is essential that any such initiative is underpinned by the belief that people are internally directed, preferring independence, autonomy and a chance to control their destinies.

❖ Corporate culture *is* leader-led, for the attitudes and behaviours of corporate stewards cast a huge shadow over the organisation. In a healthy culture, the leadership baton will be relayed through the ranks.

❖ Encouraging the workforce to be cult-like around core ideology is a bad idea because a) the ideology may not be balanced by ethical principles and b) the groupthink inherent in cults will undermine innovation and risk-taking.

❖ It is unhealthy to have a cult-like culture of change, innovation or zaniness because mechanisms that reinforce cultish thinking and behaviour will undermine people's ability to embrace change, to take risks and have fun. A cult-like culture of competition is a bad idea because it will encourage people to focus on the ends achieved to the detriment of the means used.

PART TWO

THEORY INTO PRACTICE

5

Back to the Drawing Board

In a perfect world an organisation's core philosophy, purpose and vision are deeply held by the workforce and guide all strategies and actions. But it is not a perfect world and most companies are not so lucky. Some have lost sight of their core purpose due to rapid expansion, mergers and acquisitions or a high staff turnover. For others, perhaps a strong vision existed only briefly at start-up stage, and was eroded as the company matured, with ownership transferred to the hands of remote shareholders. Or in some cases groupthink was encouraged to support the business model, and when individual identities were eroded in the process the company character was undermined. For organisations to ensure that their core philosophy, purpose and vision guide all strategies and actions, they must go back to basics and delve deep inside their corporate psyche. Only then can they articulate:

❖ Why they exist; what purpose they serve (core purpose)

❖ Who they are and what they stand for (core philosophy)

❖ Where they are going (vision)

❖ How they will get there (appropriate strategies).

Many companies attempt this task only to get tangled up in the process, mistaking the vision for the philosophy, the philosophy for the purpose, the strategies for the purpose and so on. But without a clear sense of identity, of where the organisation is

ɾ it will get there, any efforts to manage change
ɔlve into a list of confusing and incompatible
.d up competing for resources and diminishing
ɪat a) corporate culture flows out of corporate
.d b) corporate culture is a tool for implementing
strategies (..... l paying the bills), it is worthwhile to revisit these
key activities.

5.1 The Five Basic Questions

5.1.1 Why Are We In Business?

The *Core Purpose* of an organisation states why it is in business
and any unique contribution it makes to the market and the
community. In general terms it will hopefully translate to the responsible provision of goods and services, but for each individual organisation what this means in practice will be unique. According to Collins and Porras, core purpose is like a guiding star
on the horizon — forever pursued but never reached. It inspires
change, stimulating progress and will often be communicated as
a banner-type slogan. To reconnect with its core purpose, an organisation may need to return to the company archives to rediscover its founding concept — why it started up in the first place
and how the beginnings took shape. If an organisation was
founded in the heyday of capitalism, that core purpose may well
need to change to address the needs of a broader range of
stakeholders and the twenty-first-century business environment.

5.1.2 Who Are We and What Do We Stand For?

The *Core Philosophy* of an organisation is a system of ethics and
values that define the character of the organisation and its core
competencies. Ethical principles connect with each individual's
moral compass while company values reflect more technical
aspects of an organisation's culture. Company values can take
the form of competencies (for example, leadership) or guidelines (for example, "Thou shalt not kill a new product idea").

Ethical Principles and Values

It is generally understood that espoused principles and values of organisations are rarely lived up to and seldom do they resonate with employees. Take a look at the following examples. Only one list is authentic. Can you guess which one?

Figure 11: Company Value Statements

Example A	Example B	Example C	Example D
Communication	Customer	Integrity	Ethics
Hospitality	Commitment	Service	Environment
Actualise	Cost control	Respect	Exploration
Mentorship		Learning	Excellence
Presentation			Education
Innovation			
Optimise			
Now			

The answer is Example C. In all other cases, the company's espoused principles and values all start with the same letter or make for a snappy little acronym. Most likely, they were manufactured by an over-zealous HR team or a CEO working alone, and are not unearthed tenets which are core to the company's being. The only way to gain an accurate picture of the real core principles and values of an organisation is to conduct an in-depth assessment of the corporate culture.

Key Beliefs

When the espoused philosophy of an organisation is a true and authentic portrait, beliefs and assumptions manifest from core principles and values. While the network is vast, some key beliefs relating to specific people, places and things need to be articulated for the benefit of the current leadership team and the workforce at large. For example, what is the organisation's belief about its central purpose, or the essence of diversity, or whistle-blowing? How the corporate culture perceives key issues will have consequences because it will determine how employees respond in moments of truth.

5.1.3 Where Are We Going?

The *Vision Statement* is just that — a description of the organisation's aspirations and where it is heading. It will include a long-term goal and a description of what achieving the goal will look like. The vision will determine how technology, funds, skills and other resources are allocated.

> *I will build a motor car for the great multitude. It will be so low in price that no man making a salary will be unable to own one and enjoy with his family the blessing of hours of pleasure in God's great open spaces . . . When I am through, everyone will be able to afford one, and everyone will have one. The horse will have disappeared from our highways, the automobile will be taken for granted [and we will] give a large number of men employment at good wages. — Henry Ford, 1908*

He wasn't far off the mark!

5.1.4 How Will We Get There?

Once the organisation has reaffirmed its identity, together with its aspirations, it is time for the leadership team to organise strategic planning sessions. This will enable them to consider how they will make the vision a reality while remaining true to their core purpose and philosophy. They will obtain current information that will highlight the critical issues that the organisation faces and that its strategic plan must address.

Those influences in the external environment that hamper the organisation's competitiveness, becomes a force for change. Macroeconomic triggers include the political, economic, social, technological, environmental and regulatory. They are outside of the control of the organisation and if the leadership team does not perceive shifts before they become a reality, any response to these triggers will constitute unplanned change. Issues that could come up include a host of primary concerns such as funding issues, new product and service opportunities, changing regulations or changing consumer behaviour.

Any factor in the internal environment that affects the way the organisation carries out its activities is also a force for change. Internal forces will include inert structures like technology, policies, processes, systems and structures, and issues related to the human landscape. For example, triggers for change on the human landscape may include changes on the leadership team (particularly when a new CEO is brought in from outside and introduces a new way of doing things); high staff turnover, absenteeism, harassment, strikes, negative feedback from surveys and focus groups; poor quality standards; poor service standards; and a lack of innovative products and services. All of these issues manifest from the corporate culture and reflect on its health. In some cases the culture is toxic from a moral perspective, and in others it might be healthy on this front but from a systems perspective may be swamped by tradition. When any of these elements stop the organisation from moving forward to embrace change in the external environment, it represents a risk to be managed.

Figure 12: Internal Forces for Change

INTERNAL FORCES FOR CHANGE	
The Inert	Technology, policies, processes, systems, structures, machine productivity standards
The Human	Leadership changes, strikes and other staff issues, quality standards, service standards, capacity to generate ideas and innovations, moral standards, human productivity standards

© *O'Donovan, 2006*

As internal forces for change occur within the organisation, they are within the control of the leadership team and present a great opportunity for getting ahead of the competition. How-

ever, these issues can be so close that we may not be able to
see the wood for the trees, and that is exactly why a newcomer
or an outsider will be best positioned to notice problems on the
human landscape. If the corporate culture is unhealthy and pre-
sents itself as a risk, the organisation will need a culture change
programme; for example:

❖ Tradition or innovation overpower its opposite force, removing the healthy conflict necessary for the survival of the
  firm; a culture swamped in tradition is in danger of stagnat-
  ing and fossilising under the burden of tradition. For example, when a company has rested on its laurels based on a
  history of success; a culture which is overly aggressive in
  terms of innovation will lose touch with its roots and is likely
  to crash and burn.

❖ The culture is not principle-centred in word and spirit and
  internal shenanigans make clear that the prevailing culture
  represents a risk to brand value.

❖ Innovative strategies require of the workforce new knowledge, skills and attitudes; if the culture has been left to its
  own devices for years it may well have shifted away from
  corporate philosophy to take on a life of its own.

Also, there are two types of change in an organisation: *reactive*
change and *planned* change. Reactive change is change
brought about by a sudden or unplanned event. Planned
change is a systematic, deliberate attempt to make changes in
the way part or all of an organisation functions. Because of the
forward planning involved, it is more desirable. By conducting
a situational assessment, top management can identify the company's strengths, weaknesses, opportunities and threats and,
when plotted onto a SWOT matrix, these can form the basis of
all strategies.

Figure 13: The SWOT Matrix

	Strengths	Weaknesses
Opportunities	S/O Strategies	W/O Strategies
Threats	S/T Strategies	W/T Strategies

Once the organisation's critical issues have been identified, it is time to figure out what to do about them: the broad approaches to be taken (strategies) and the general and specific results to be sought (goals and objectives). Taking a helicopter view, one can see that:

❖ If the company's purpose, philosophy, vision and prevailing culture are all aligned but its strategies are not, the strategies will not be achievable and will need to be revisited.

❖ If the company's purpose, philosophy, vision and strategies are aligned but the prevailing culture is off-track, then a culture change programme is required to support the strategies.

If the latter case should prove true, the leadership team will need to conduct a brainstorming session around the following questions to estimate their readiness for change:

❖ Historically, has the organisation been supportive of, or hostile to, internal and external change? How does the track record stand?

❖ How are the staff currently coping with change in the environment? Has a survey been conducted on this?

❖ Which policies and processes will change as a result of new strategies?

❖ Which new roles will emerge, and which roles will become obsolete? Will any reduction in headcount result from natural wastage, redundancy or redeployment?

❖ Which beliefs must the organisation let go of, and which must it embrace? What new knowledge and skills are required to support strategies?

❖ What new attitudes and behaviours are required and how are they in conflict with the prevailing culture?

❖ How will staff respond/resist and what challenges will come up?

❖ Who is most likely to resist? What are their motives and can they be turned around? How will they react/respond to change?

❖ Has sufficient consideration been given to staff who will implement strategic change?

5.2 Conducting a Culture Assessment

As a culture assessment can take three to six months to conduct, it should start well before the strategic planning sessions so that the results are available to the leadership team when they need them. Because the prevailing culture of any organisation represents employees' worldviews, insiders will want to believe that their culture is healthy (and that they are "ok") so attempts to critique it will be met with hostility and resistance. Therefore the perception of insiders, particularly long-serving staff, is not a particularly good starting point for determining whether or not the culture should be changed. They will be unaware of their own blind spots (Arthur Andersen took executives out of retirement to conduct their culture assessment!) so to complete this part of the process an external consultant or a new hire who has the required knowledge, skills and attitude, and who will serve as an internal consultant, should be engaged.

The approach to assessing culture should be "business needs first" — in other words, starting with how the organisation can responsibly provide goods and services and working backwards from that.

5.2.1 The Process and Tools

Stage 1: Define the Required Culture

* ❖ **Methodology:** Leadership workshop facilitated by culture analyst

* ❖ **Resources:** Annual reports, induction course, company adverts, access to the internet

* ❖ **Duration:** A couple of workshops

* ❖ **Responsible Party:** The CEO and his/her direct reports

* ❖ **Output:** Profile of Required Culture plus alignment of Espoused Culture and Required Culture if necessary.

The leadership team can start the analysis by considering the outcomes and results *required* for the business (see the suggestions on pages 78–79 which can act as a guide and should be supplemented with customer feedback and data on the market situation). Then work backwards to divine what behaviours and attitudes will make the vision a reality and lead the company to future success. List the beliefs and assumptions that will drive those attitudes and behaviours needed to support the business. Having defined the required culture, now check that this is in line with the espoused culture as communicated on the company website, marketing materials and induction courses, etc. If there is a discrepancy, the management team needs to decide what they want and align the two to avoid sending staff mixed messages because if the espoused culture lacks roots it will not be reflected in the reality.

Stage 2: Analyse the Prevailing Culture

❖ **Methodology:** Varied (see "resources" below)

❖ **Resources:** see Appendix 1

❖ **Duration:** Three to six months

❖ **Responsible Party:** The culture analyst and the leadership team

❖ **Output:** Profile of Actual/Prevailing Culture.

Stage Two is labour-intensive and must be put in the capable hands of a seasoned culture analyst because it is highly complex. To support them, recruit the help of long-serving staff who will be advised what to focus on during investigations and the feedback process/mechanisms to use. The culture analyst will consider the outcomes and results *currently achieved* and work backwards to divine what behaviours, attitudes, beliefs and assumptions are being employed on a day-to-day basis. At this stage of the process, the culture analyst must use as many tools and techniques as possible to paint as accurate a portrait as possible. Corporate culture cannot be measured through the primary use of a questionnaire as no such tool can independently isolate the nuances of culture. Ensure that scientific tools (for example questionnaires) are balanced by direct observation of staff in the workplace together with focus groups and other techniques which enable direct human interaction.

If one gets stuck identifying beliefs and assumptions, it can be useful to tackle the paradigm employed in an organisation by referring to strategies and goals. As top management performance will be measured on their ability to meet these measures there will be some level of congruency between these official statements and the prevailing beliefs and assumptions. As articulated statements, they are easier to assess than their underlying drivers, and unlike official statements regarding core purpose, philosophy and values (which can often be but aspirations), strategies and goals reflect what the organisation really values. Therefore, these artefacts can act as a window into the complex network which underlies them. From this point we can progress to unearthing the inventory of operating beliefs and assumptions which guide attitudes, behaviour and results.

Once the culture analyst has prepared the first draft profile, another leadership workshop should be convened by the CEO to review data gathered and build on it. Focusing on data gathered, the team can consider the beliefs and assumptions of the prevailing culture. To help them with this, a general inventory is provided in section 5.2.2. They must try hard to overcome their own blind-spots about the culture and consider the information objectively. During this particular gathering, it is the task of the leadership team to:

❖ Scrutinise key beliefs and assumptions, together with their antithesis, identify those relevant to the challenges facing the organisation and derive consequences from each;

❖ Unearth and explore beliefs and assumptions unique to the organisation and derive consequences from each;

❖ Conduct scenario planning, making predictions which bring to life the various domino effects or outcomes of particular beliefs;

❖ Agree on those which will help the organisation move forward in a constructive manner and those which need to be discouraged;

❖ Document conclusions, and reflect findings in the core philosophy and vision statement documents.

Step 3: Culture Gap Analysis

❖ **Methodology:** Gap Analysis

❖ **Resources:** Profile of Espoused/Required Culture and Profile of Prevailing Culture

❖ **Duration:** Two to three weeks

❖ **Responsible party:** Culture analyst

❖ **Output:** Map of gap between the vision and the reality, together with strategies and tools for bridging the gap.

Having articulated the required culture, and also the prevailing culture, it is now possible to identify how reality measures up to business requirements. Is the prevailing culture in line with the required culture? If not, *where do the gaps occur* and *what needs to change?* Look at the policies, processes, strategies and structure to identify what mechanisms are reinforcing the prevailing culture and what needs to change. For example, if the organisation wants to encourage both teamwork *and* individual excellence then compensation and other reward mechanisms must reflect this. Also, find where organisational needs and goals overlap with individual needs and goals to create win-win scenarios.

Figure 14: Culture Gap Analysis

Measure Required Culture		Measure Prevailing Culture	
Reflectors	Results	*Reflectors*	Results
	Artefacts		Artefacts
Expressions	Behaviours	*Expressions*	Behaviours
	Attitudes		Attitudes
Drivers	Central Paradigm	*Drivers*	Central Paradigm
	Needs		Needs

◀Versus▶

© O'Donovan, 2006

Figure 15 is a "quick and dirty" example of what the strategic picture might look like when the required/espoused culture and prevailing culture are out of sync (the former is principle-centred in word and spirit but the latter is money-centred). By digging behind each category, a host of data can be unearthed to provide a more grass-roots viewpoint on cultural "drivers", "expressions" and "reflections" specific to the culture under review.

Figure 15: Prevailing Culture vs Espoused Culture: A Strategic View

	PREVAILING CULTURE	ESPOUSED CULTURE
Reflections **Results**	Shareholder expectations are met in the short term; brand image is at risk because of weakness in the system or the culture Customers also use competitor products and services Staff are cynical and energy is directed inwards on politicking; redundancies and high staff turnover Damage to the environment and the local community	*A network of key outcomes and results (e.g. failed strategies/poor financial performance/corporate governance related scandals/union strikes/damage to local communities/good times not shared with staff) make it clear to the discerning public that the espoused culture is a myth*
Artefacts	Documents reflecting unfulfilled strategies and goals and proposals which never got off the ground Low customer retention rates Damning Employee Attitude Survey results; low morale Media coverage condemning company for harm to local community	*A host of artefacts (e.g. negative press, staff strikes) indicate to the discerning public that the espoused culture might be just a myth*
Expressions **Behaviours**	Shareholders get the largest cut of the pie and success is not shared with staff during good times Goods and services are overpriced Failure on CSR "operational measures" but possibly good performance on CSR "citizen measures" (see pages 91–93)	*A network of key behavioural indicators (e.g. poor product and service quality) indicate to the discerning public that the espoused culture might be just a myth*

Attitudes	The shareholder is king Customers exist to serve the shareholder Staff exist to serve the share-holder Host communities exist to serve the shareholder	*A host of attitude indicators, e.g. customer complaints, indicate to the discerning public that the espoused culture might be just a myth*
Drivers **Central Paradigm**	Money-centred	Principle-centred
Needs	Power through money Power through the control of others The esteem and respect of others however fleeting and unreliable it may be	*In this case the philosophy is but window-dressing with no foundation or roots. There-fore, the espoused core principles do not carry through to cultural expres-sions and reflections*

© O'Donovan, 2006

An authentic culture that is principle-centred in word and spirit will derive from:

a) The more enduring self-respect and self-awareness of the organisation which understands what it stands for and is clear on its unique contribution to its customers and society; and

b) Authentic power through an ethical approach to challenges, the empowerment of the workforce and the betterment of local communities.

To wind up the assessment process, use the results of your cultural analysis to consider which characteristics of the prevailing culture are most likely to hinder the transition, and which are most likely to help. How much of an adjustment is required of the workforce? The results of this complete study will form the basis of any culture change programme design.

5.2.2 Compiling an Inventory of Beliefs and Assumptions

Changing attitudes and behaviours allows for an incremental shift in the internal way of doing things. Changing the prevailing beliefs and assumptions of a culture can create a quantum leap. This can only happen when we raise consciousness in our community and ask the workforce to take responsibility for the type of culture they create. The catalogue of beliefs and assumptions put forward below — outlined in Figure 16 and expanded over the following pages — will enable people to unearth some of those assumptions which have them operate on auto-pilot and provide a useful reference point for deciphering the more elusive aspects of an organisation's psyche. They can be considered in unison with those put forward by Edgar Schein (see page 176), because together this compilation touches upon the key cultural issues of the new millennium — ethics, service, learning and innovation.

Figure 16: Characteristics of a Healthy Culture

PEOPLE

The Individual's Locus of Control

Externally directed	Internally directed

The Nature of an Individual's Value

Useful to job on hand	Intrinsic to being human

The Power of Mankind

A law unto himself	Subject to universal laws

The Complexity of Human Intelligence

One-dimensional	Multi-faceted

The Nature of Corporate Culture

Dull	Intelligent

The Essence of Diversity

Differences in appearance   Differences in thinking
                                                              ✖
_____

PLACES

The Natural Environment

An externality   The centre of existence
                                                              ✖
_____

THINGS

The Organisation's Central Paradigm

Other   Principle-centred in   Principle-centred in
                            word only   word and spirit
                                                              ✖
_____

The Nature of Company Values

A meaningless statement   A public relations ploy   A true commitment
                                                              ✖
_____

Public Image

Manufactured   Authentic
                                                              ✖
_____

The Nature of the Organisation

Inert structures   The inert and the human   An Entity
                                 ✖
_____

Core Purpose

Increase shareholder value   Responsible provision of goods & services
                                                              ✖
_____

Workforce–Organisation Relationship

Human resources/tools   Members/citizens
                                                              ✖
_____

Organisation–External Stakeholder Relationship

To be manipulated   To be respected
                                                              ✖
_____

Organisation–Business Environment Relationship

Estranged	Attuned
	✗

Bad News and Whistle-blowing

A threat	A learning opportunity
✗	

Decision-making

Immoral	Amoral	Moral
		✗

Ownership for Learning and Development

Centralised	Localised
	✗

Communication

Closed	Open
	✗

How Best Results are Achieved

Self-interest	Self-interest and group interest	Altruism
	✗	

Speed of Response to Customer Demands

Low	Medium	High
		✗

The Service Provider

Front-line workers	Contracted parties	All staff
		✗

Emotional Expression

Unacceptable	To be encouraged and managed	To be encouraged
	✗	

© *O'Donovan, 2006*

The Individual's Locus of Control

"Everything we think, do and feel is generated by what happens inside us." So says William Glasser MD, author of *Control*

Theory.[1] Glasser argues that if we believe that what we do is caused by forces outside us, we are acting like dead machines, not living people. In the context of HSBC Hong Kong (see Chapter 1), for the "Together, We Win!" programme, we believed that each individual's locus of control is internally directed and people prefer to have some degree of control of their destinies. This guided our programme design. By using experiential learning materials, we demonstrated genuine value for staff's experiences and contributions. By giving teams autonomy in Phase Two — to decide locally how they would action-plan and which tools they would use — we demonstrated trust in their capabilities and insights. This approach is congruent with Douglas McGregor's "Theory Y" (1964) which states that:

❖ The expenditure of physical and mental effort in work is as natural as play or rest;

❖ Control and punishment are not the only ways to make people work, and people will direct themselves if they are committed to the aims of the organisation;

❖ The average person learns, under proper conditions, not only to accept but to seek responsibility;

❖ If the job is satisfying, the result will be commitment to the organisation;

❖ Imagination, creativity and ingenuity can be useful to solve work problems by a large number of people;

❖ Under the conditions of modern, industrial life, the intellectual potentialities of the average person are only partially realised.

The Nature of an Individual's Value

Each individual has intrinsic value by virtue of the fact that they are unique, human and precious and their value to the business goes far beyond their immediate usefulness to the job (or

---

[1] William Glasser, *Control Theory*, Harper and Row, 1984.

agenda) on hand. This has to be a fundamental core assumption of any civilised society. In *The New Alchemists*[2] management guru and writer Charles Handy states that while the world needs new ideas, new products, new kinds of associations and institutions, new initiatives, new art and new designs, seldom do these things come from established organisations — rather, they come from individuals. When an organisation considers individuals valuable only in terms of their usefulness to the job on hand, and when they are treated with derision and considered disposable, this has dire consequences for the integrity of the entire corporate community.

The Power of Mankind

Mankind is subject to universal laws which govern moral, biological and ecological matters. We cannot break these laws — we can only break ourselves against them. Having considered non-sectarian moral principles in Chapter 2, let us now consider how universal and immutable truths govern ecological and biological matters. Take, for example the case of a group of African farmers who, in their efforts to maximise profit, decided to increase the ratio of livestock per acre. For a time, all seemed well and good until one day they arrived to survey their property. Every single animal lay dead and not one showed outward signs of attack. Bewildered, they called in some foreign scientists to solve the mystery. An examination of the carcasses only added to the intrigue, but a breakthrough was made when the scientists turned their eye to the surrounding vegetation. It was found that one tree species, from which the animals fed, had mutated to develop poisonous thorns. Here lay the culprits that had quietly killed off the livestock. The scientists concluded that, in their efforts to survive and defend themselves from extinction, the trees had responded to the increased pressure of feeding more mouths by developing a set of armour. By over-riding traditional farming principles which were based on elders' learn-

---

[2] Charles Handy, *The New Alchemists*, Hutchison, 1999.

ing of the natural environment, the farmers had sabotaged their own efforts in their drive to maximise short-term returns.

On the biological front, the result of China's one-child policy is that boys now far outnumber girls and there is now the fear that by 2020 the 40 million men "left on the shelf" will become criminals and a danger to society. The government hopes to correct this imbalance by 2010 and measures include the setting up of family planning clinics in more rural areas where female babies are not valued. Chinese men have devised their own tactics to manage the problem — by marrying Russian women across the northern border. However, Russia, fearful of diluting its gene pool, is seeking to pass legislation to make illegal such marriages. Gender imbalance is also prevalent in the business world with the upper echelons still very much a male domain. Only when this imbalance is corrected will we truly be able to strive for balanced corporate cultures.

These cases serve to illustrate that we cannot break universal laws; we can only break ourselves against them.

The Complexity of Human Intelligence

Human intelligence is multi-faceted and our success individually, and collectively, is optimised when we are utilising our basic types of intelligence: spiritual (SQ), intellectual (IQ), emotional (EQ) and physical (PQ). When we are not utilising all of our natural gifts we are operating from an incomplete toolkit. This undermines our ability to take care of ourselves and limits our success in life as we try to meet challenges. Given that modern life has become increasingly unpredictable, we need to use all of our internal resources to successfully problem-solve. While our IQ and EQ can serve us well during times of stability, we need to utilise our SQ and sometimes our PQ to adapt to big life challenges.

Spiritual Intelligence (SQ)

Demonstrating spiritual intelligence was a key requirement for leaders in ancient civilisations but value for this core attribute has been eroded over time. In the corporate world, as in all facets of life, we need moral leadership. Zohar and Marshall define SQ as our unique human ability to make moral decisions and embrace deeper meanings. It is not housed in any particular church; rather, it resides inside each one of us — and it encapsulates all that is wise and good in us. As we rush around living our busy modern lives we can become cut off from this vital part of ourselves, creating a void within. For fulfilment, we tend to turn to the external environment — fine food and good living, alcohol and other mind-altering substances, shopping, overwork and constant activity to distract ourselves from ourselves.

The irony is that many resources which we need to achieve fulfilment come from *inside* each one of us. This universal truth is central to the plot of *The Alchemist*[3], a unique novel about the essential and age-old wisdom of tapping internal resources by listening to one's heart and soul. Indeed, the ancient Egyptians believed that our soul has needs and desires just like the physical body (and perhaps this is where the term "food for the soul" was coined). In the story, a boy travels from his native Spain to the pyramids of Egypt in search of his personal treasure. A fateful meeting with an alchemist takes him on a journey of learning and self-exploration, where he is taught how to trust and respect his own heart and soul, and that of the world he lives in. This is his real treasure and the path to wisdom and fulfilment and when he achieved success with this endeavour, the boy does indeed acquire worldly treasures also — and in his own hometown.

Remember, SQ is careful about the company it keeps. If we listen to it, and respect it, our SQ will become our best friend. If we ignore it, then it will simply stop talking to us until we change our attitude.

Intellectual Quotient (IQ)

A person's intellectual quotient is a reflection of their intellectual potential. It is not a measure of any wider knowledge, just as knowledge is not a measure of wisdom. Maximising our in-

[3] Paulo Coelho, *The Alchemist*, Harper Collins, 1995.

tellectual potential demands that we challenge our brains. While some would dismiss reading in favour of real-life experience, the two complement each other. Quality reading can enrich how we go about our lives while life experience can enable us to critically review new thoughts and ideologies as presented to us in books. Through reading and writing, one can grow immensely. Systematically managing family affairs and planning for the future will also require considerable cognitive activity, as will the pursuit of our careers. IQ is logical. It doesn't understand "right" or "wrong" so one who has a high IQ but is deficient in SQ is:

a) vulnerable to manipulation because they have undermined their own sense of right and wrong;

b) in danger of outsmarting themselves (the Enron top team considered their conspirators to be brilliant and their deception intellectually stimulating!)[4]; and

c) can present a potential danger to themselves, others and society.

Emotional Intelligence (EQ)

The term Emotional Intelligence refers to one's ability to manage one's own emotions, empathise with others and cope with adversity. EQ became prominent in the 1990s as a valuable tool which can be applied in the business setting to achieve high performance. While our IQ is said to be fairly firmly set by the time we reach adulthood, our EQ quotient is more malleable and can be enhanced through self-awareness as we explore our own beliefs, attitudes and behaviour, and how they impact ourselves and others. Many titles on the topic have emerged, particularly in the context of leadership, which show that in order to be able to respect and value others' emotions we can only gain credibility and trust if we are seen to value and respect our own. Learning to do so is a journey which requires daily prac-

---

[4] *The Christian Science Monitor*, 2004.

tice and reflection, and results in increased self-awareness and self-esteem. To enhance EQ, actively work on developing self-awareness, treat people with respect and kindness and be slow to judge others' behaviour.

Physical Intelligence (PQ)

Intellectually we know that, at the minimum, we can keep our bodies active and healthy with aerobic exercise, good nutrition and sufficient rest for rejuvenation. But bodies also have their own intelligence, store memories and emotions, and will communicate to us what we need to be eating and doing to enhance our well-being — that is, if we care to listen. Yoga and meditation are useful techniques which enable us to leave the world behind to listen to signals our bodies are sending us; for example, messages regarding festered illnesses may initially be communicated in the form of an increased awareness of tension or pain in certain parts of our anatomy while more urgent health problems will be communicated more visibly and dramatically and will demand that we make lifestyle changes.

By nurturing a holistic view of ourselves we can take better care of ourselves and others, and by fostering internal balance we can take strides towards filling any void within.

Figure 17: Embrace Change through Balance

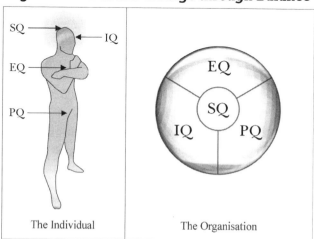

The Individual   The Organisation

© *O'Donovan, 2006*

The Nature of Corporate Culture

Culture is a living system and has different types of intelligence which parallel those held by an individual. Each culture has its own spiritual core. Corporate culture is multi-faceted. Chapter 2 included a variety of models which allow us to view the phenomenon from a number of angles to gain a better understanding. Now there is another dimension which adds to the collage. As corporate culture is a human system it is intelligent, and when we foster the intelligence inherent in our corporate culture we can gain much ground in terms of aligning each individual with the organisation's goals.

In the *organisational context*, leaders can foster the intelligence inherent in its culture by using a variety of strategies:

❖ **SQ:** Adopt the mindset that organisations are economic *and* social entities and provide goods and services in a socially responsible manner; create and nurture a corporate culture which is principle-centred in word and spirit; provide guidance and resources on ethics and personal accountability to foster good governance; apply holistic management principles to foster a concern for consequences; project an authentic image in marketing and recruitment campaigns.

❖ **IQ:** Institutionalise the process of inventiveness; allow staff to learn from mistakes; encourage a healthy mode of enquiry and dissent; provide staff with intellectually challenging roles and allow them any training they might need to fulfil their tasks.

❖ **EQ:** Create a "high trust" environment by aligning the espoused culture and the prevailing culture so that all are "walking their talk"; re-establish commitments to major stakeholders and reflect this in how end-of-year results are measured; communicate change in a timely and fair manner; avoid labelling certain emotions "positive" or "negative" (all emotions are valid); give staff tools to manage their emotions and allow them outlets for emotional expression; encourage upward communication in word and deed.

❖ **PQ:** Create a safe and healthy workplace fc
 vide all with sufficient and fair rest-time to fa
 nation; avoid over-burdening staff as this car
 ability to listen to their PQ; provide medica
 fitness and health club membership.

To explore the idea that culture has different types of intelligence, let's do a quick exercise based on the measures given
above.

Exercise

Focus on a particular organisation you know intimately. Take
out a pencil and paper, and sketch the diagram below.

Figure 18: Organisational Balance

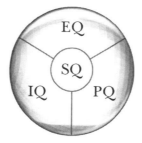

Now answer these questions by shading a part or all of the appropriate section:

❖ Does this culture demonstrate SQ?

❖ Does this culture demonstrate IQ?

❖ Does this culture demonstrate EQ?

❖ Does this culture demonstrate PQ?

Now look at your results and consider this question. How does
the culture shape up overall? What areas need nurturing? How
is the current status impacting the success of the organisation?
How does it represent a risk?

We cannot nurture what we do not acknowledge. Corporate culture is a human system and if we view it as unintelligent we cannot foster a healthy corporate culture.

The Essence of Diversity

Diversity in beliefs and perceptions stimulates new ways of behaving and is the source of nourishment for creativity and innovation. While watching a re-run of the *Star Wars* series recently, I was struck by the diversity of species co-existing on the various planets. Not only that, but the leadership groups of the warring factions had as many different species around their board tables as they did members! Yet at each table, thinking was largely aligned. We can draw a parallel with diversity as promulgated by corporations and this makes clear how crude our show of diversity is in the business world. We embrace outward differences in race, gender and disability but our recruits (be they at floor level or board level) are generally like-minded people who see the world as we see it. While it may appear to serve an organisation's interests, this practice can severely hamper progress. When new ways of thinking and behaving are systematically discouraged, tradition rules; and this undermines the organisation's ability to learn and adapt to a changing environment.

To get a more sophisticated understanding of the diversity profile of an organisation, information available on the workforce, together with psychometric tools like KAI and Myers Briggs, can create an overall snapshot in terms of personality, thinking style, geographical background and so on. If the majority population has a similar personality profile or a natural tendency towards a particular thinking style, new recruits who have a different profile may well be measured on their personality and not on their performance. It will be next to impossible to integrate such persons unless proper mechanisms are in place (for example, new job types, new performance measures, mentoring programmes, a support network) and the recruitment team reflects diversity in their own thinking and perceptions. Principles and values which will support diversity include "respect for the individual" and "open communication".

The Natural Environment

The ecological environment is not an externality; rather it is the centre of existence and the resources in our environment make the economy possible. As civilisations developed, mankind built cities and gained a sense of control over the physical environment and a level of protection from the elements and natural calamities. In our cities, we built powerful organisations which further heightened this sense of control and distance from the natural world. The illusion that we have created does not change the facts. We are the earth (every bit of energy a person uses was originally sunlight), we came from this earth and we will return to it. How many more generations of the human race get to enjoy this cycle depends on how we respect the earth during our tenure. Organisations can demonstrate respect for the natural world in a variety of ways. For example, General Electric has made a commitment to limit its own greenhouse gas emissions and many other organisations are engaging in practices like recycling, sustainable development and the responsible provision of goods and services.

The Organisation's Central Paradigm

"Principle-centred companies enjoy a greater degree of security, guidance, wisdom and power," says Stephen Covey.[5] Take a moment to visualise someone you have enduring respect for. Who is it, and why is it that you hold this person is such high esteem? Reflect for a moment. Chances are, this person knows who they are, where they are going and how to get there. They stand for something and exude integrity. This is not to say that they are infallible because they can make mistakes — sometimes big mistakes — just like the rest of us. They too have feet of clay. But their experiences with the detours and distractions

---

[5] Stephen Covey, *Principle-Centred Leadership*, Free Press, 1990, p. 24.

of life do not define who they are. Instead, their enduring character steers them back onto their path which, over time, grows into a highway to personal success. It is most probable that your hero will never have used a formal plan to articulate their personal mission statement for their life's journey. Yet some, over-burdened by the complexities of life, may well have used such a tool to help them get back to basics. Whether the details which navigate this individual are implicit or explicit, the result is the same. This is likely to be a person of substance who is worthy of your enduring respect — someone who is steered by intrinsic principles.

It is no coincidence that those companies that inspire our confidence are those that stand for something, who know where they are going and how to get there. Some may well have stumbled at some stage (as did Johnson and Johnson with the Tylenol crisis) but they have picked themselves back up to conquer higher mountains. This ability to pick themselves up and reinvent themselves in the face of adversity, this clarity of direction despite a big fall, this trust in the unknown, and this wisdom to choose an ethical course over self-interest are all characteristic of an organisation that is principle-centred in word and spirit. When facing the unknown, any organisation that does not have these capabilities is most likely to flounder like a blind man in a maze.

The Nature of Company Values

Company principles and values should reflect the authentic character of the organisation, be endorsed by the whole workforce and represent a true commitment. When company values represent the true psyche of the organisation, the leadership team has put in the work to unearth its real values and core competencies. These they have articulated in meaningful ways to demonstrate how they contribute to operations and the success of the business. Staff have been given the tools and support they need to live the values in day-to-day operations. When principles and values are a public relations ploy, there is disconnect between the promise, staff work at cross-purposes and they distrust the executive management team. When values are a meaningless statement, staff will not respect executive management, they lack direction and poor morale undermines productivity.

Public Image

A company image which is authentic reflects the real character of the organisation. This allows the general public to make an informed and sound decision as to whether or not they will work for it, invest in it, buy from it or trade with it. In simpler days, communicating an authentic public image was much easier for sole traders and local business people. Take the case of the Fitzgeralds menswear store in my Irish home town of Clonmel. I remember my mother taking me by the hand for a walk one evening in the mid-1970s. It was an autumn evening and the streets were, for the most part, deserted. Then we happened upon a sight which made my young eyes pop. Outside Fitzgeralds a group of locals were equipped with guitars, radios, flasks of tea and sleeping bags. They were clearly there for the night and were in high spirits. Mother explained to me that the store owner had marked down the price of some premium products by as much as 95 per cent to make them affordable to all, and it was a case of "first come, first served". Fitzgerald had told her that he would rather give back to his customers who had supported him for the year than spend money on an advertising campaign to promote his autumn sale. Word of mouth quickly spread and this generous act of the owner became synonymous with the Fitzgeralds brand.

In these days of the global enterprise, organisations face the complex challenge of managing their corporate image to ensure consistency across cultural and geographical boundaries. This is one of the reasons why some have come to depend on marketing campaigns which sell a corporate persona. Another reason is that they simply do not know how to manage their corporate culture and end up being led by it. So to clear up the mess, they recruit marketers to sell a package to the public.

A culture that is underpinned by moral principles will be grounded. Leaders and the workforce will know what they stand for, and this feedback will be carefully translated into marketing campaigns; that is, such outputs will be internally driven and authentic. However, when the culture has lost its footing and its connection with its authentic identity, the public image of the organisation will be manufactured by savvy marketers. The greater the inconsistency between an unmanaged corporate culture and the public image, the greater the monies that will be misdirected towards the coffers of such marketers.

The Nature of the Organisation

Organisations are made up of two types of building blocks — the inert and the human. The inert include structures, policies, technology, capital and tools while the human components include needs, beliefs, emotions and motives, attitudes and behaviours. According to Daryl Conner, former CEO of Headstrong Consulting, the inert aspects are isolated, independent features of the landscape and have no connection with each other, while the human element provides all the links and allows for the meaningful integration of components. Without this, the various inert structures would stand alone and be rendered useless. Conner argues that the human landscape is most important to the success or failure of initiatives designed to change the way an organisation functions.[6] Perhaps Henry Ford knew that when he famously exclaimed, "You can take away my factories, burn my buildings, but give me my people and I'll build them right back again!"

In Chapter 3 we learnt that at Arthur Andersen a corporate culture had emerged that put loyalty to the firm above loyalty to the client or to the investing public. Corporations are particularly susceptible to this trend of thought because the US law treats them as entities to be protected by the Fourteenth Amendment's rights to "due process of law" and "equal protection of the law"

---

[6] "Managing the Human Aspects of CRM Projects", Daryl Conner, President and CEO, Headstrong, 2000.

and this mindset has taken hold across the globe. Corporations are *not* human beings, they are not to be revered and no corporation is worth more than one single human life.

Core Purpose

In general terms, the core purpose of any organisation is to meet public demand for goods and services in a socially responsible manner. This is the fundamental basis of business for an economic and social entity. It reflects the two-way transaction between the organisation and society. Shareholder value is not an end in itself. Rather, any increase in shareholder value is seen as an indication that the organisation is delivering on its purpose by:

a) Supplying the market with goods and services that are in demand; and

b) Doing so in such a way as to gain the confidence of society.

Alternatively, when an organisation's core purpose is simply to increase the bottom line, anyone who is not a shareholder quickly loses interest.

Workforce-Organisation Relationship

"In this new world, people want to be regarded as belonging to something, not just used by it, as members not employees, citizens not human resources," in the words of Charles Handy.[7] We established earlier that the corporate community is a key component of the organisation and not something external to it, but how can we glean more insights into our own community thinking on this? Years ago a friend coached me to listen to the words people use, for they speak volumes about perceptions of people, places and things. The term "human resources" reflects a bygone era and a mindset that people are tools, because resources are things we draw upon and exploit to extract

---

[7] Charles Handy, "Democracy's New Frontier", *The Economist*, January 2005.

maximum value. As inanimate objects, we don't have to consider their well-being but we can end up treating them even better than we treat people. For example, when a machine breaks down an engineer is call in to fix it but when a person breaks down they are deemed useless and written off. We really need to reappraise our whole attitude to our workforce. Perhaps "human resources" could be repackaged as an exclusive members' club that provides an array of products and services to citizens of the organisation's community to facilitate organisational development. This would encourage a service mindset and attract recruits who wish to serve others rather than control them.

Organisation–External Stakeholder Relationship

Customers, investors, suppliers, unions and the general public are to be respected. Each group of stakeholders is critical to the success of the organisation: customers create demand for products and services; investors finance operations; raw material suppliers and other trade partners facilitate production; unions help us safeguard the rights of our corporate citizens; and the general public shares their living space with a corporation's physical structures, advertisements and other output like products and waste, etc. In Chapter 2, we explored why organisations need to re-establish their commitment to major stakeholders in the twenty-first century. To achieve success in this new world of ours and meet the rising expectations of the public, business stewards need to understand how the organisation fits into the external environment and complete the two-way "give and take" transaction with the communities with which it interacts. A company vision which does not reflect this understanding can be revised and shared, so that all can strive to meet new marketplace realities. Any organisation that does not respect its relationships with external stakeholders will give poor terms of trade to suppliers, poorly manage the business for investors, provide goods and services to customers in a way that is not socially responsible and be uncooperative with trade unions.

Organisation–Business Environment Relationship

The more attuned the organisation is to the business environment, the more capable it will be to meet public demand for goods and services, and the more able it will be to spot opportunities and threats on the horizon. To deliver on this, organisational processes, policies and people must be up-to-date with external trends. All staff must know exactly who their customers are, buy into organisational philosophy and strategies and understand how they can deliver on this in their daily practices. For creativity and innovation to flourish the internal environment needs to be dynamic. A dynamic external environment will call for more emphasis on the future, perhaps through scenario-planning. Inclusiveness towards consultants will open minds to new ways of doing things, new methodologies and market trends.

Bad News and Whistle-blowing

Bad news represents a learning opportunity, and bearers of bad news bring gifts by highlighting weakness in the system and in the culture before these become public knowledge. When bad news is seen as a learning opportunity this can safeguard the organisation's interests. Trusted mechanisms are put in place to encourage internal whistle-blowing and the formal and informal processes on how to handle such situations are the same. Bad news is confronted head-on and receivers of bad news take corrective action to improve processes, holding individuals accountable for any malpractice. Facts pertaining to a situation are documented and this file serves as a resource for scenario planning by the strategic management team. This helps to ensure that business information is managed and lessons are learnt so that incidents are not repeated. Bearers of bad news are supported, and may even be rewarded, for raising issues.

However, research conducted by Whistleblowers Australia found that people who blow the whistle on bad behaviour, mismanagement, abuse of authority or legal violations are rarely considered heroes. Rather, bad news is seen as a threat and there is a "shoot the messenger" mentality, particularly in the

upper echelons. Formal grievance procedures may just be window-dressing and most staff will learn not to go where angels
fear to tread. Whistleblowers are most often punished and even
excommunicated. With them out of the way misdeeds can be
swept under the carpet, bad news "spun" and the web of deceit
thickens as time progresses. Even arch enemies sing from the
same hymn sheet. More than 90 per cent of Australian whistleblowers lost their jobs or were demoted, 20 per cent got into difficulty with alcohol, 20 per cent saw the break-up of their long-
term relationships, 20 per cent were treated with defamation action, 6 per cent attempted suicide and 9 per cent went bankrupt.
Much of the personal trauma will have resulted from the heavy
knock to their belief system and the shattering of any illusions
they held about the integrity of their employer organisation.

Responsible Decision-making

Decision-making which is navigated by a moral perspective is the
hallmark of a culture of ethics. When ethical principles are
woven into the fabric of a community's way of being, they align
with the moral compass within each individual staff member.
This congruency fosters authenticity, creativity and trust in both
the internal environment and the external environment. Acting
with integrity is seen as a vehicle to success, and not an obstacle to it, and the means employed are given as much consideration as the ends achieved. Corporations like Citigroup understand this and are now urging staff to focus not just on making
money but on the methods used. When decision-makers give in
to short-term interest and employ dubious means to achieve
their ends, they undermine their own spiritual core and that of
their corporate culture. This has ramifications for the individual
and their corporate community.

Ownership for Learning and Development

To nurture the ongoing process of inventiveness, learning and
development should be decentralised with the organisational
community equipped for, and committed to, continuous learning

and development. When ownership for learning and development rests with the line there is a constant search amongst staff for finding a better way of doing things by applying a wide variety of tools and techniques. This fosters innovation. Insights are shared with other teams and significant learning experiences are transmitted across the organisation using a range of media. Every team leader is a trainer and facilitator responsible for developing their own team members. A lean centralised training unit acts as a support to the business and it is the key task of trainers to go out to the line to help team leaders deliver on their commitments. Team leaders support and coach each other. All members of the training team are of the highest professional calibre and their role is to help line managers understand, and action, their people development responsibilities. Organisational strategies and policies are streamlined to support the whole effort.

However, when ownership for learning and development rests with a centralised training unit, it encourages the mindset that learning only takes place in classrooms, which can severely hamper innovation in the workplace. Staff lack the power and confidence to take risks, line mangers are not equipped with facilitation skills and there are few internal best practices to share. Beware — if the latter set-up describes your organisation and if your organisation is highly political, note that the head of training may well perceive any attempt to decentralise learning and development as a threat to their power base. So before revising strategies consider how the role of training will evolve to suit the new model. To get buy-in, emphasise that the programme is temporary in nature while training is a permanent fixture. Also, the programme will result in an increased demand for training as a support for on-the-job training and as a support for those wishing to upgrade their skills. Remember, when culture change is required, it will be the responsibility of the business leaders to revise the training strategy to suit new workplace demands.

Communication

An open communication system best serves the interests of the individual, the group and the organisation. In an open system, forums are created which allow staff to present ideas, voice concerns and attack outmoded policies and processes. Such a system reflects a respect for others and the intelligent and responsible use of information. The American political drama series *West Wing* provides a frame of reference for such a system. In this series, colleagues in the White House routinely get worked up when passionately debating policy issues. But at the end of each day, "warring parties" will sit down to chat about more mundane issues and even share a few laughs. Everyone understands that the earlier conflict is not personal and while policies will be attacked, relationships seem to be only strengthened. How can we develop such a healthy approach to conflict in our workplaces? A start would be to provide training courses which focus on the development of debating skills and the transfer of such learning to the workplace. When staff gain confidence in their ability to articulate themselves and know that they will have their say, they are more likely to listen to other points of view. In a closed system, open debate and challenging established protocol is discouraged so people learn to criticise each other instead. Criticism is taken personally and people become defensive.

How Best Results are Achieved

"The maximum benefit to a group can be realised if each individual works for his own benefit and the group" (John Nash, 1950). With this in mind, I developed Interdependent Team Learning (see pages 239-252 in Chapter 9) which provides teams with a framework for achieving results through cooperation and respect. This approach to teamwork creates a win-win for all. Such a mindset can be more difficult to instil than ever before because the workforce in general has learned that they will be the first to be sacrificed when executive management is seeking to boost shareholder value. We have taught the workforce

to be self-interested and the smarter ones will either find new pastures or play the system for their own ends. When one is driven by self-interest one can lose sight of who the stake-holders are in an equation and this strategy often backfires. It pays to be considerate.

Speed of Responsiveness to Customer Demands

The organisation's speed of responsiveness to customer require-ments reflects its ability to keep pace with the external environ-ment and meet the competition head-on. We can all relate to the following poor service experiences:

❖ The customer who asks for a phone line to be put into his new flat and has to wait six months for his request to be ful-filled by the phone company;

❖ The customer who, when asking a broadband provider what special offers are available to new clients, is told that a man-ager will call him to answer the query; he never receives that follow-up call and chooses a competitor service instead;

❖ The customer who asks a freight forwarder to move 50 kg of personal effects from Europe to Australia; he is told "we only do big house moves, use the post office";

❖ A customer who is told that her new DVD player "will arrive when it arrives".

All of these tales reflect a poor responsiveness to customer re-quirements. In the examples, the providers respectively fail on speediness of service, on internal follow-up, on their attitude to smaller customers and on their lack of interest in the concerns of the customer. This happens when there is a disconnection between the workforce, organisational strategies and the ex-ternal environment. Conversely, when the organisation's de-gree of responsiveness to customer requirements is high this reflects a customer-centric culture, a strong service chain, a positive attitude to service and a strong operational network.

Organisations with this latter profile have what it takes to survive and thrive in times of rapid change.

The Service Provider

Whatever the industry, every staff member is a service provider and a member of the service chain. When this belief is ingrained in the culture of the organisation, everyone from the CEO to the most humble member of staff understands that they make a direct contribution to the service standards of the organisation. All have been introduced to the concept of the external and internal customer and all have mapped out those service chains for which they are a part. In addition, any staff member can explain what specific contribution they make to a particular service chain. They can also name those persons up and down the line who depend on them to do their part in an efficient and effective way. Everyone knows what the key products and services of the company are, and everyone knows what particular cultural beliefs promote service quality. As a result, both internal and external customers can conduct their business in a smooth way. The biggest hindrances to creating such a mindset are:

a) The industry, as those in the manufacturing industry often suppose that the only ones responsible for service delivery are middlemen who deal directly with customers; and

b) The size of the organisation, as large organisations can breed silo mentalities where the left hand doesn't know what the right hand is doing.

This causes service breakdowns and with it, relationship breakdowns.

Emotional Expression

During times of change, staff must be given the support and tools to manage any strong emotions so that they can choose constructive behaviour. All emotions are valid and should be acknowledged. When business challenges require of the workforce a new way of doing things, it is inevitable that many will find the upheaval hard-going, but well-managed communication activities will help staff keep a handle on their emotions. In the NEC Group of Birmingham, UK, it is the practice of the leadership team to share news of change with the workforce at the beginning or middle of the week and to have an open-door policy. This team understands that some will have questions and would consider it irresponsible to leave some employees with no one to talk to over the weekend. To cover evenings and weekends they also set-up a 24-hour hotline. Such a policy demonstrates a genuine caring for the workforce and a respect for people's emotions. As staff digest the implications of any news of change for themselves, some will experience strong emotions like anger, frustration and a sense of betrayal. Labelling emotions "positive" and "negative" is not helpful because if the feelings of employees are not considered or validated, this can make people very resentful. So in addition to sharing information in a responsible manner, provide staff with forums and outlets to express their emotions in a constructive way.

The Influence of National Culture

To understand a corporate culture one must understand the local context in which it is operating, and that means the national culture. Despite globalisation, national cultures vary from each other in the network of beliefs and assumptions that dominate. This fact was noted in an ISR report in 2002 which stated the following:

> Members of different societies have divergent views about relationships which should exist between colleagues, some putting a premium on individualism, others on conformity to group values and norms. Societies vary in their attitudes towards the status quo, some believing that the current state of affairs should be accepted and adapted to, others that it should be challenged and changed. Societies differ in their temporal orientation, some focusing on protecting the past, other on forging the future. Countries

vary in their modes of communication, some using implicit and tacit methods to achieve common understanding, others believing that information has to be explicitly and formally stated if it is to be transmitted successfully. Nationalities differ in their styles of decision-making, some putting an emphasis on building consensus during the decision-making process, others on achieving compliance once decisions have been made.[8]

As readers will note, this research is in fact suggesting some new categories that could be added on to Figure 16.

To understand the local culture in your own organisational context, I would solicit the input of the workforce and customers. Organise focus groups and guide the discussion using a table similar to Figure 16 but detailing the more generic issues. Have expert facilitators guide discussions and add the output to the corporate culture analysis.

To summarise, our beliefs and assumptions about people, places and things form an elaborate network and create a field of intention. By exploring our own perspectives, we can raise consciousness and, if necessary, choose more constructive beliefs. In time, these new perspectives will become unconscious assumptions and navigate our new way of doing things. Leaders can substantially increase their chances of successful corporate culture management if they engage with learned persons to challenge assumptions, bring problems to the surface and stimulate debate.

5.3 Gather Commitment in the Corridors of Power

Successful culture change is only possible with the support of a strong and united team. To gather commitment to change in the corridors of power, a number of options are available to the CEO apart from the strategic planning sessions.

---

[8] International Survey Reseach (ISR), 2002, www.isrinsight.com.

❖ **Create a "burning platform", making the status quo seem more dangerous than launching into the unknown.** If external forces have highlighted that the culture represented a risk to brand image, use artefacts (for example, newspaper reports or data relating to lawsuits) to raise consciousness. If internal forces have highlighted that the culture will not support strategies, you can use performance data (employee attitude survey feedback, etc.) to raise consciousness and spur a discussion on the issue.

❖ **Make it clear that "the way we do things around here" is no longer acceptable.** Using artefacts like those mentioned above, have the leadership team name the destructive beliefs, attitudes and behaviours which are common in the organisation, and articulate how they are contributing to harmful outcomes and results. Then ask them to identify some outmoded policies and practices. When targeting the unacceptable, make sure you ask them to focus on outmoded beliefs, behaviours and policies (not people) and let the team help decide what needs to go and what needs to stay.

❖ **Make changes to the top team** where appropriate.

❖ **Identify change agents** who will implement new strategies and position them for success by ensuring that they themselves report into other change agents.

Case Study

Citicorp

Below are some insights into how Charles Prince, CEO of Citicorp, recently set about gathering commitment in the corridors of power for a culture of ethics in the world's largest financial institution.

In September 2004, the Financial Services Agency of Japan ordered Citicorp to close its private banking business in Japan after it emerged that some staff had misled customers about investment risks, sold products that it was not permitted to sell, and failed to take proper precaution to prevent money laundering and other illegal transactions. In response to regulatory and legal pressures around the globe, Prince took great strides to reinforce the importance of ethical behaviour in Citicorp by:

❖ Taking disciplinary action against those responsible for the huge trade in European government bonds that angered European government officials;

❖ Settling a lawsuit brought by WorldCom investors (for $2.6 billion before tax) to cover legal action related to its role in other financial scandals including Enron;

❖ Hiring Eugene Ludwig, a former comptroller of the currency at the US Treasury, to conduct an internal review into the shutting down of Citicorp's private banking operation in Japan;

❖ Forcing the dismissal of three senior executives in October 2004, as a result of the above-mentioned review. All were members of the firm's management committee. Observers believe these departures stress the extent to which Mr Prince is willing to burrow deep into Citicorp's executive suite in his drive to enforce a culture of ethics and accountability at the sprawling financial institution Eleven others have left or been fired.

No doubt, the actions of the chief executive sent a strong, clear message to the management team on what beliefs, attitudes and behaviours would be expected moving forward. Citicorp has now engaged the senior management team and their 300,000 employees in discussion around the company's values and culture with a view to becoming the most respected financial services company.

5.3.1 Identify Key Stakeholders and Hidden Agendas

A stakeholder is a person or group that has a vested interest in your change programme. They may have the power to exert influence on it and for this reason alone, they need to be managed. Stakeholder management is a key discipline that people use to win support from others. It can ensure a programme succeeds where another fails and can help manage the intense politics often associated with major change initiatives. The first step is to identify key stakeholders and list them. Stakeholder groups may include staff, executive management, board directors, subsidiary companies, staff unions, the media and community groups. Then use the stakeholder mapping tool to present this information using a visual aid. Next, prioritise your stakeholders in terms of their power and interest in your programme as this will determine how much time and energy needs to be spent on each. Ask yourself how each person or group feels about your programme and what financial or other stake they might have in it. Also, it pays dividends to consider the informal network — who went through the induction process together twenty years ago, who worked together at an outpost during a time of crisis, who drink together twice a week, who has the ear of key leaders, who are members of the same exclusive club, and so on. This data will help you identify hidden agendas and plot your stakeholders' power and interest (stake) on a matrix, and this in turn will enable you to define your strategy for managing the group.

Figure 19: The Stakeholder Management Matrix

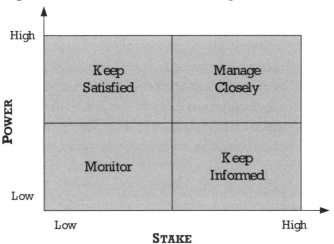

❖ **High power/high stake:** Engage them fully and keep them satisfied.

❖ **High power/low stake:** Keep them informed and share wins to subtly buy them in

❖ **Low power/high stake:** Give them ownership for helping with the details

❖ **Low power/low stake:** Keep an eye on them but don't hard sell.

When the leadership team has progressed to the programme strategy design stage, the output of the stakeholder management matrix will be used to develop high-level communications plans. This output does not need to be prepared as yet but ultimately it will help you decide how to consult with your stakeholders and how best to manage them.

5.4 Chapter Summary

For a workforce to rediscover their core purpose, core philosophy and vision, the leadership team must go back to the drawing board to determine why they exist in the first place, what unique purpose they might serve, who they are as a community and where they are going. With their identity and aspirations reaffirmed, they will be able to examine forces for change and decide on appropriate strategies to meet particular challenges.

A culture change programme does not exist as an end in itself; it exists in response to forces in the external and internal environment. External forces include the political, economic, social, technological, ecological and regulatory while internal forces in the social environment include the inert and the human. Culture change is also required where mergers and acquisitions demand internal alignment. When environmental forces make it clear that the prevailing culture is out of sync with business realities, the CEO must mobilise the top team. Having examined the environmental realities the leadership team can progress to a discussion on these issues, how they are impacting the success of the organisation and how the organisation can respond. External drivers may already be communicating, whether overtly or implicitly, that the prevailing culture represents a liability and must be changed. But first, conduct a cultural assessment so that the information is available to the leadership team. This process could take between three and six months, it must be driven by the CEO and it must be conducted by a seasoned corporate culture analyst. Hire an external consultant or a new recruit who has the required knowledge, skills and attitude.

To summarise, the characteristics of a healthy culture reflects the belief that:

❖ The individual's locus of control is internal;

❖ Each individual has value by virtue of the fact that they are human and unique;

❖ Mankind is subject to universal laws;

❖ Human intelligence is multi-faceted;

❖ Corporate culture is intelligent;

❖ Diversity in thinking and behaving is more important than superficial measures like race and gender;

❖ The natural environment is the centre of existence;

❖ The central paradigm of a healthy culture is principle-centred in word and spirit to facilitate the adoption of constructive beliefs and assumptions;

❖ Company values must reflect a true commitment;

❖ Public image must be authentic;

❖ The organisation is made up of inert structures and the human landscape;

❖ The core purpose of the organisation is to provide goods and services in a responsible manner;

❖ The workforce are members and citizens of the organisation;

❖ External stakeholders are to be respected;

❖ The more attuned the organisation is to the business environment the better able it will be to meet public demand for goods and services;

❖ Bad news represents a learning opportunity;

❖ Responsible decision-making is ethical decision-making;

❖ Ownership for learning and development should be localised to stimulate innovation and ability to embrace change;

❖ The most effective communication system is open;

❖ The best results are achieved when the individual considers their own interests and group interests in unison;

❖ A high degree of responsiveness to customer requirements helps the company survive and thrive;

❖ All staff are service providers; and finally

❖ Emotional expression is valid and to be managed.

This inventory is not definitive, and should be considered in conjunction with those suggestions put forward by Edgar Schein. The whole collection touches on service, ethics, learning and innovation. Even then there are thousands of other beliefs and assumptions that could be relevant to different organisations so the leadership team of any given organisation must put in the effort to raise collective consciousness. National cultures vary from each other in many respects and these differences need to be taken into account when striving to understand the local context of a global enterprise.

Our beliefs about people, places and things create a field of intention. By raising our beliefs and assumptions to a conscious level, we can address some of our own contradictions and choose a more constructive view of the world. When unearthing their own philosophy, a leadership team can also consider those characteristics identified by Edgar Schein, and in the process may well uncover some of their own. Get the team to discuss this proposal and sign off on the beliefs they hold about people, places and things before moving forward, as the assumptions held by this team will determine the success or failure of the programme in different parts of the business because they will drive their behaviour.

While the concept of corporate culture is intangible, culture has a very clear "cause and effect" relationship with literally everything that goes on in an organisation. Therefore, there is an abundance of internal data available. To conduct a cultural audit, first consider the features of the required culture and check if these are aligned with the espoused culture as communicated on the company website and official documents. If there is a discrepancy make corrections so that the two are aligned. Then, using a variety of tools and techniques, divine the "drivers", "expressions" and "reflections" of the prevailing culture. Compare the results with the required/espoused culture to identify any synergies and performance gaps. The output of this exercise will determine whether or not a culture change programme is required.

The CEO can gather commitment for change in the corridors of power by making it clear that the "status quo" is harmful and more unattractive than change. Organise strategic planning sessions to get the top team involved and develop a sense of ownership for creating the future. To identify key stakeholders, give careful consideration to hidden agendas as these can influence the support any new initiatives will get. List stakeholders, categorise and prioritise them according to their power and interest, tailor the stakeholder communications plan to address the profile of different parties and integrate this output into the strategic implementation plan. Stakeholders with high power and interest in your programme need to be managed closely; those with high power and low interest must be kept satisfied; those with low power but high interest need to be kept informed (as their power may increase); and those with low power and interest should be monitored from a distance.

6

FORM THE STRATEGIC MANAGEMENT TEAM

For a corporate culture to evolve with the environment it must be led by business leaders. On a good day that will mean catering to the maintenance needs of the organisation to facilitate incremental change; on a more difficult day it will mean harnessing the resources of the whole organisation to play catch-up to the external environment.

6.1 Culture Management versus Culture Change

6.1.1 Business as Usual

When it's a case of business as usual, the organisational development (OD) team will work within the normal hierarchy to *nurture the natural evolution* of the corporate culture. OD could be described as:

> The systematic and long-term application of the social sciences to improve organisational effectiveness, as measured by the ability to adapt and align organisational human and inert structures in response to change.

Social sciences include anthropology, psychology, sociology, the political sciences and the various other branches. While OD practitioners can start off in training and development and develop their repertoire of knowledge and skills in company-wide programmes and external pursuits, such knowledge and theory is not typical in traditional training or HR functions, which tend to be more operational in approach. For this reason, most often an organisation will have a separate OD function. Worker responsibilities will include working as internal consultants with the business units and liaising with support functions to facilitate alignment between strategies and culture. Often OD specialists are recruited from the ranks of external consultancies or local university research departments. Traditionally, they have tended to the maintenance needs of the organisation but their role is expanding to include change management as well.

6.1.2 Changing Tides

When culture *change* is called for, the set-up required is different as we are now moving into a different realm and need change management skills. A new team must be created to implement the strategic initiative and will be positioned *outside* the normal hierarchy. Members should be drawn from cross-functional teams — organisational development, learning and development, internal communications, marketing, operations and the front line. The greater the diversity and skill set on the team, the more capable the team will be to manage the operation through to success. In addition to being an OD professional, the head of this new team must be a change agent because not everyone is built to *drive and implement* a major change programme and take the heat which comes with it. In fact, many can find it downright uncomfortable as it is in conflict with who they are as a person. They will be more comfortable ensuring team harmony and maintaining the established order, and have an important role to play once change has been implemented. Those identified to drive strategic and large-scale change must literally be built for the job and it is this group I refer to when I talk about "change agents" in Section 6.3.

6.2 Strategic Management

The strategic management team will comprise the executive sponsor, the steering committee and the implementation champion. Where possible, all will participate in leadership meetings where the programme strategy is designed, so as to facilitate understanding, ownership and commitment.

Figure 20: The Strategic Management Team

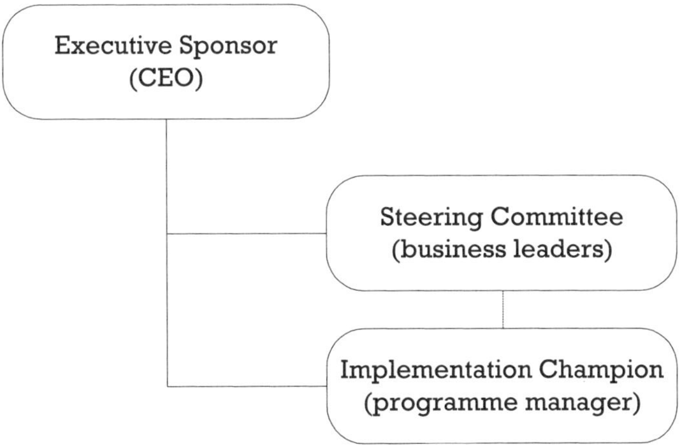

© *O'Donovan, 2006*

6.2.1 The Executive Sponsor

It is in the remit of the CEO to champion the company vision and strategy, lead the corporate culture and nurture a workforce which has the experience, ability and common objectives to execute the vision and strategy. Therefore, the CEO has a very important strategic role and has the power and influence to drive a culture change programme through to success. CEO leadership will provide the workforce with a common direction and the programme team with the support they need to deliver on their remit. As change management is a key concern for chief executives in the twenty-first century, the CEO will ideally have a successful track record in driving change. For example, at General Electric Reginald Jones chose Jack Welch as his successor, not because he fit the mould, but because Welch was a radical deviant from the prevailing culture, which revered the status quo. He was successful despite the culture, not because of it, and when Welch became chief executive he immediately set about creating a customer-centric culture. In 1989, Welch launched the culture change programme "Work-Out" to help people change their attitudes about their work and the way they approached their jobs. It helped the workforce translate strategic imperatives into their own individual actions.

As the CEO is effectively the one employee of the Board of Directors, it is those attitudes and behaviours to which the CEO is exposed at board level that will infiltrate the organisation. In "A Board Culture of Corporate Governance",[1] I put forward a practical strategy which takes corporate culture management to board level, and provides any CEO with a foundation for success leading culture change themselves. A healthy corporate culture must start in the upper echelons if it is to be taken on-board by the whole workforce.

Executive Sponsor's Role: *Champion the company vision, lead the corporate culture and nurture a workforce that has the experience, ability and common objectives to execute the vision and strategy*

Responsibilities

❖ Define and communicate the vision and objectives to the organisation.

❖ Enlist the help of executive management and key stakeholders and form the steering committee.

❖ Select the implementation champion and supply the crucial resources needed for the success of the change management project; assign core team members on a full-time basis

---

[1] Gabrielle O'Donovan, "A Board Culture of Corporate Governance", *Corporate Governance International*, October-December 2003, pp. 28–37.

to facilitate and manage the change process; position team correctly for success.

❖ Provide high profile leadership, maximising on communications media to reinforce core principles; for example, internal magazines, programme materials and so on.

❖ Meet the implementation champion on a monthly basis to provide guidance, critique designs and options honestly, making time to review the progress of the planned change.

❖ Communicate priority of the project, take personal responsibility and protect change agents from attack by opponents by meeting resistance head-on.

❖ Make it mandatory for all staff to participate and personally attend events to emphasise its importance.

❖ Solicit feedback from the organisation and seek input from all levels of management.

❖ Demonstrate congruency with the core philosophy and core values, participating in the programme actively and visibly.

If the chief executive is not a change agent, then the person nominated to chair the steering committee must have such a profile but it is the chief executive who should have the ultimate say in all decision-making and who will give the final approval for all activities. The executive sponsor may well decide to share the responsibilities with this person who will then also serve as the programme director.

6.2.2 The Steering Committee

The chair will be a business leader and a successful change agent, appointed by the executive sponsor. Key responsibilities will include stakeholder management, issues and risk management plus identifying and overcoming resistance to change. If the organisation is seeking to create a service culture or a culture of innovation, parties taking up these roles must have a successful track record. But if an organisation is seeking to create a culture of ethics, these two critical roles must be filled by modern-day Knights Templar (no less) who surround themselves with like-minded people. What will be required of them goes beyond the realm of change management as we know it because they will be seeking to rehabilitate the morally challenged.

Members of the steering committee will include the leaders of all major business areas, together with key figures from support functions, including OD, training, HR and communications. Include a mixture of both supporters and resistors in your programme committees to share responsibilities and enable those pro-change with a forum for influencing others and building buy-in. A key role of the programme manager will be to meet these members on a one-to-one basis to provide consultancy services, identify local issues and overcome resistance.

> **Steering Committee's Role:** *Guide the strategic direction of the culture change programme in a changing environment, and ensure that it is compatible with other change initiatives.*

Responsibilities

* ❖ Champion the programme and act as ambassadors of it.

* ❖ Secure commitment at all levels of the organisation, using influencing skills to overcome resistance to change.

* ❖ Act as a forum for decision-making, raising issues which will impact successful implementation in the workplace and offer solutions.

* ❖ Provide guidance to the head of the culture change team, if and when the programme runs into difficulty.

* ❖ Clarify the roles of operational managers versus the programme team, especially as the programme moves into Phase Two implementation, appointing the advisory committee and creating new roles to support the new process where appropriate.

❖ Reward behaviour and results congruent with the core principles and reward the programme team for achieving milestones.

As the CEO forms the steering committee and advisory committee, it is worth noting that members will hold their responsibilities by virtue of the positions and responsibilities they hold. This will not guarantee their support for the culture change programme. While some will champion change, others will be keen to maintain the status quo and their own power positions. The latter will be sitting on the side-lines, waiting for the programme to be derailed. They will have their own agendas and will need to be managed by the programme director and others who are pro-change, and brought onboard.

6.2.3 The Implementation Champion

This post requires huge personal energy, as does the role of the executive sponsor. No ifs and buts here — the programme manager *must* be an innovator, as changing scenarios is where they will derive energy and job satisfaction. If you are looking to create a service culture or a culture of innovation, don't think that you must choose a very senior person. However, when the creation of a culture of ethics is in order, then an older person will be more suitable. With a life experience of people behind them, more mature programme managers are more likely to have a much-needed frame of reference for what they will be exposed to.

Implementation Champion's Role: *Manage the design, development, delivery and evaluation of the culture change programme in line with the objectives and framework set with the steering committee in order to implement a successful programme that either supports staff organisation-wide to embrace change, creates a culture of ethics or creates a service culture.*

When considering the role of the programme manager, you may also wish to identify the main challenge of the post in your organisation so that all are clear on what is expected of the programme manager. For example, the main challenge of my TWW! post at HSBC was "to act as a change agent in a largely conservative culture". To achieve this I would need to:

❖ "Demonstrate creativity and the ability to challenge/ question existing paradigms, policies and procedures but with sensitivity to cultural differences, operational requirements and varying priorities;

❖ Produce a high quality and innovative product that would support people in a rapidly changing work environment, promoting the programme key principles and values; and

❖ Organise, manage and control the operational delivery of the programme."

When detailing this remit, the Executive Sponsor should ensure that it is communicated with key players as it will provide the programme manager with a necessary platform for forging new frontiers.

Responsibilities

❖ Programme needs analysis, design, delivery and evaluation.

❖ Project portfolio design and management.

❖ Education and development of team up and down the line.

❖ Stakeholder management.

❖ Issues and risk management.

❖ Identify and overcome resistance.

❖ Communications management.

❖ Maintain programme momentum.

❖ Oversee the emotional and behavioural issues.

❖ Quality and cost control.

The programme manager cannot be looking to win any popularity contests and must be able to stand up in the face of adversity to do the right thing. Avoid those candidates who wholly subscribe to the shareholder-value mantra as they will not really care about the workforce and how they cope with, and adapt to, change.

6.3 Identify Change Agents

The Chinese say that where there is crisis, there is opportunity. Change agents thrive on change, have highly creative minds and will naturally have great tenacity and resilience. The Kirton Adaption-Innovation Inventory (KAI)[2] tool measures thinking style and is used internationally for major change projects. The underlying theory states that people differ in the cognitive styles in which they are creative, solve problems and make decisions. These style differences, which KAI measures, lie on a normally distributed continuum and range from "high adaptive" to "high innovative". They are stable and no life experience will change them, so we must learn to use them well. The more adaptive are said to prefer to solve problems by using the rules, and the more innovative solve them *despite* the rules. As we can see in the diagram below, which illustrates different thinking styles along this continuum, the "Adaptors" on the left tend to perceive a problem within one major paradigm (the box), whereas the "Innovators" on the left are said to find problems and juggle out puzzles that lie across more than one paradigm (the shapes).

Figure 21: Diversity in Thinking and Creativity

Adaptors 32 48 64 *96* 112 128 144 160 Innovators

Population
Norm

---

[2] Kirton M.J., Kirton Adaption-Innovation Inventory booklet, 1985.

Adaptors are said to be essential for ongoing functions, since they are the vanguard of an organisation's rule and order, while innovators are critical in time of change because of their willingness to venture into the world of the unknown. Instead of being enemies, the adaptors and innovators can achieve excellent synergies. Yet when the two meet, each has difficulty understanding and coping with the others' thinking style and behaviour. Adaptors may see innovators as abrasive, risk-taking, impractical, creating confusion or even "changing for the sake of change", disrupting adaptors' comfort zone. Likewise, innovators may see adaptors as dogmatic, compliant, close-minded and timid, hindering innovators' efforts to move forward. This is where conflict arises.

In the early days of TWW! at HSBC Hong Kong, an incident made it clear to me that my new team was having communication problems. Having studied a number of team-building tools and activities, I chose KAI for its relevance to change management programmes and asked a colleague from Human Resources to administer KAI to my team. Sarah had our full attention when she plotted our individual marks on a graph to create a team profile. My team members' profiles fell between 87 and 107. My individual profile of 134 explained my orientation to change management from the outset. We were told by the KAI administrator that a gap of more than 15 points creates communication problems which can cause conflict. The smallest gap I had with any of my team members was 27. The manager went on to explain the strengths of each individual team member, and how we each could contribute to enhance our teamwork and communications. I sensed a light had been switched on amongst us and any personal judgements we held about each others' style or approach to things quickly dissipated. With our new awareness of this diversity in the team, and using our KAI profile and follow-up exercises, we were able to understand how each individual could contribute to the team. For example, at the extreme ends of *our* continuum, one colleague would be particularly strong at institutionalising new approaches. I was best suited to carving out new frontiers — which was fortunate, given my remit. We did not have a "bridger" in our team (someone whose score fell midway between both ends of our team continuum and who could recognise both points of view) but with our new awareness and resulting efforts, this did not become an issue. As a conscientious team, we simply used the input to identify how we should adapt our behaviour to capitalise on our diversity. For example, I realised immediately that I had to adjust my fast-paced style when talking with one team member and she automatically sped up her pace somewhat so that we met at some point in the middle. This joint effort eliminated the frustrations we had been experiencing when communicating one-to-one. Our team was committed to the job on hand, and we would do all that was required to deliver.

Incidentally, these discussions created a new sense of openness in my team and it wasn't long before another obstacle to our communication was brought to my attention. It emerged that it was considered unacceptable for team members to speak directly to their manager without first going through the chain-of-command. I never would have worked this one out by myself (given that they were not talking to me in an open manner). Apart from making the ramifications of such an approach very clear to the team, I turned the manager's office into a meeting room and took up residence right in the middle of them. Our open plan seating had been designed so that we four faced each other, though we did have partitions which allowed some privacy. They got comfy managers' chairs just like mine, because they would be working just as hard and their backs would tire just as easily, and we all had the same size workspace — regardless of our differing positions in the hierarchy.

While my team were impressed with the armchairs, they were initially appalled with the idea of communicating directly with me but, given how extremely busy we were, they quickly learnt to appreciate this more informal approach to getting things done. We had a lot of fun in the process and started to gel as a team. As they got used to my leadership style, grew into

their roles and increased in confidence, they became less concerned about making mistakes or losing face. While my assistant
manager initially felt that she was losing some power, she
quickly learnt that our new approach to teamwork took a burden
off her shoulders. In 2001, discussions were already underway to
flatten the HSBC Group hierarchy from a whopping 22 levels to
eight. In 2005, this structural change was implemented and
should do much to loosen up perceptions of positional power.

Returning to KAI for a moment, whether one is an "Adaptor"
or an "Innovator" is relative both to the population norm and to
the profile of the team or group in question. There are no abso-
lute boxes into which people can be slotted. Let's take a look at
how our team profile would have changed had a colleague,
Matt, joined our team. His KAI profile is 156. With Matt on the
team, I would have become the "bridger" between those on
either end of our continuum — and, with 22 points between us,
to Matt I would have been an Adaptor. In another scenario, if I
had moved on to another post to be replaced by someone with
a KAI profile closer to the population norm, the change team
would have been more homogeneous in terms of creativity,
problem-solving and decision-making and less capable of carving new frontiers. Also, some business leaders might be worried about the sound of "Innovators". Here's a little insight.
Using another psychometric tool called "Life Orientations"
(LIFO) which approaches the individual from another perspective, I have learnt that while I am daring in everyday situations I
am conservative in a crisis, preferring to limit any damage. This
might well reflect the profile of other "Innovators".

6.4 Chapter Summary

When it is a case of business as usual, corporate culture management will be driven by the organisational development
function and it will be the responsibility of this team to nurture
the maintenance needs of the organisation. Members of this
team will work as internal consultants to support the business

units, and work alongside the support function to ensure that policies and process align strategy and culture. However, when culture change is required, a different set-up is in order. The new team must operate outside the normal hierarchy to ensure that they are not subject to prevailing norms and protocols (in direct conflict with their remit to change the way of doing things). The head of the team must be an OD specialist *and* a change agent because strategic change should be driven by individuals who are literally built for the job. Heaven to them would be hell for another. Team members will be drawn from cross-functional teams to harness knowledge and skills.

The strategic management team will consist of the executive sponsor, the steering committee and the implementation champion, and this core team will remain intact for the duration of the programme. The CEO is responsible for nurturing a corporate culture which delivers on strategies, ensuring that the right staff are recruited, motivated and retained so they are the obvious choice for the role of executive sponsor. When top management demonstrates authentic leadership through congruency with the espoused principles and values of the organisation, the right messages are cascaded through the ranks and the right behaviours are rewarded. The steering committee will comprise the leaders of major business areas, plus key support partners, for example, OD, training, human resources and corporate communications. The implementation champion must be an OD practitioner and have it in their DNA to drive change.

The Kirton Adaptation-Innovation Inventory is a tool which is used internationally for major change projects. It helps identify those who will thrive on the challenges of change ("Innovators"), and those who will be more comfortable maintaining the established order ("Adaptors"). By including a mixture of Adaptors and Innovators on the programme team, the CEO can maximise on problem-solving abilities in the face of challenges. Create a career path for change agents so that their creative energies can be utilised to drive other transformation initiatives at the end of the programme.

7

CREATE PROGRAMME VISION AND DEFINE STRATEGY

As we established in Chapter 5, a culture change programme does not exist as an end in itself. Instead, it exists in response to forces in the internal and external environment. For example, a corporate governance scandal may demand the creation of a culture of ethics, eroded market share may demand the creation of a culture of innovation, or an inward-looking mindset could demand the creation of a customer-centric culture.

7.1 Strategic Vision and Planning

Once the results of a culture assessment indicate that a culture change programme is in order, the CEO will next request of the culture analyst a programme proposal. This document will outline the strategic vision and plan for the programme, and will include the following:

❖ Terms of reference

❖ Company philosophy and related strategies

❖ Vision statement and programme philosophy

❖ Core principles and values

❖ Strategic goals and objectives

❖ Blueprint of the transformed organisation

❖ Scope and timeframe

❖ Key players

❖ Stakeholder map

❖ Methodology

❖ Programme portfolio of projects and activities

❖ Budget.

Below is a description of each of these key areas and advice on how to tackle some of the trickier ones.

7.1.1 Terms of Reference

This refers to key words and phrases that define the programme and will be used repeatedly throughout the lifespan of the culture change initiative. Examples include background, goal, purpose, scope, timeframe, cost, quality, blueprint, principles and values, stakeholders and so on.

7.1.2 Company Philosophy and Related Strategies

During the strategic planning sessions, and as part of the culture audit, the leadership team will have defined or reaffirmed their philosophy about people, places and things (see Chapter 5). They will also have decided on appropriate strategies to meet business challenges. Include in the programme proposal a summary of any such information that relevant to the culture change programme so that the linkage is clear to all.

7.1.3 Core Purpose and Programme Philosophy

The *programme core purpose* will be a broad, long-term goal; for example: "To deliver service straight from the heart". It will remain true and valid over many lifecycles of the culture evolution. The *programme philosophy* will flow out of the corporate philosophy and will describe each of the beliefs that are key to the success of the programme; for example: "Company values are a true commitment", "The individual's locus of control is internal", "All staff are service providers", "The core purpose of the organisation is the responsible provision of goods and services", "Bad news is a learning opportunity". The philosophy will act as a compass for programme methodology, content and results, because we reap what we sow. This must be congruent with the new attitudes and behaviours required of the workforce. Best results will be achieved when the set of beliefs agreed upon reinforces some of the old and introduces some of the new. This will make culture change less of a shock for the workforce. Do not progress any further until agreement has been reached on the programme philosophy, as the beliefs held by leaders and functional heads will greatly impact the success or failure of your programme in the different parts of the business.

The beliefs detailed in the programme philosophy will serve as important building blocks of programme strategies. For TWW!, we sought to institutionalise continuous learning and continuous improvement so that we could fulfil our primary objective. Schein put forward a theory on which assumptions should prevail to create a learning culture and in Figure 22 we see how much of his thesis underpinned aspects of the "Together, We Win!" (TWW!) programme at HSBC (see Figure 3 in Chapter 1), as outlined below.

Organisation–Environment Relationship

"The more turbulent the environment, the more important it will be for leaders to argue for and show that some level of control over the environment is desirable and possible" (Schein, 1992). My own view is that the relationship between the organisation and the environment can at best be symbiotic. Organisations (and individuals) interact with and influence their environment. Larger companies can exert some degree of influence, and will get involved in dealings with regulators to ensure new legislation

Figure 22: Characteristics of a Learning Culture

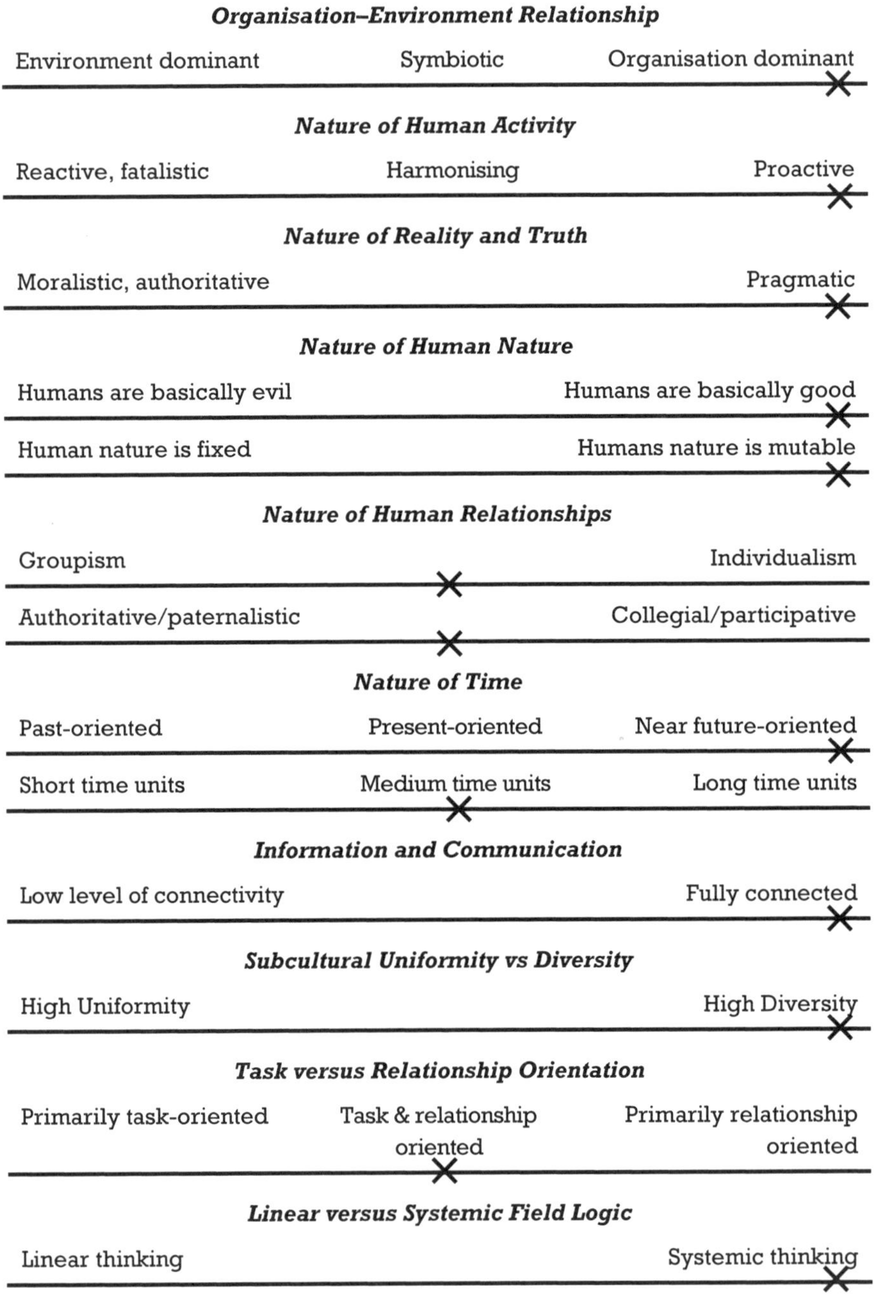

Organisation–Environment Relationship

Environment dominant	Symbiotic	Organisation dominant
		X

Nature of Human Activity

Reactive, fatalistic	Harmonising	Proactive
		X

Nature of Reality and Truth

Moralistic, authoritative		Pragmatic
		X

Nature of Human Nature

Humans are basically evil	Humans are basically good
	X

Human nature is fixed	Humans nature is mutable
	X

Nature of Human Relationships

Groupism		Individualism
	X	

Authoritative/paternalistic		Collegial/participative
	X	

Nature of Time

Past-oriented	Present-oriented	Near future-oriented
		X

Short time units	Medium time units	Long time units
	X	

Information and Communication

Low level of connectivity		Fully connected
		X

Subcultural Uniformity vs Diversity

High Uniformity		High Diversity
		X

Task versus Relationship Orientation

Primarily task-oriented	Task & relationship oriented	Primarily relationship oriented
	X	

Linear versus Systemic Field Logic

Linear thinking		Systemic thinking
		X

does not adversely impact their business, but this is generally small-scale stuff compared with the major economic and political changes that are really making the world economic environment so turbulent. TWW! came from a recognition that the environment for HSBC Hong Kong was changing, and becoming more turbulent. We were conscious that many external environmental factors (regulatory, technological and customer behaviour) were changing; not only that, they were becoming more unpredictable. Our response, however, was not to try to control these changes, but to position HSBC to deal with the changes, see them as opportunities and leverage them for our continuing success. In essence, it is more important to position the business to steer through choppy waters than to try to control the waters. I would be very concerned about any management team who suppose that they can control the external environment as it could a) involve a great deal of wheeling and dealing with politicians and b) lead to a "God complex".

Nature of Human Activity

"A learning culture must contain a core shared assumption that the appropriate way for humans to behave is to be proactive problem solvers and learners" (Schein, 1992). Three of our programme values in TWW! were "Continuous learning", "Continuous improvement" and "Take personal responsibility". For the latter, materials used included an in-house designed video entitled *A Problem Owned is a Problem Solved* and, moving away from the "get it right first time" mentality adopted in the 1980s, learning through trial and error was now encouraged. Instilling the belief that continuous learning was possible in the work environment was initially a challenge, as our Hong Kong workforce believed that learning takes place primarily in classrooms. The design of the programme did much to open minds to learning opportunities in the workplace.

Nature of Reality and Truth

"What must be avoided in the learning culture is the automatic assumption that wisdom and truth reside in any one source or method" (Schein, 1992). The variety of resources provided would encourage the exploration of different truths and deeper meanings. For Phase Two of TWW! we changed tactics, moving from experiential learning activities in a centralised environment to action-planning in the workplace. Learning materials varied greatly in nature and staff were encouraged to use their own tactics, and explore deeper meaning through books.

Nature of Human Nature

"Learning leaders must have faith in people and must believe that ultimately human nature is basically good and in any case mutable" (Schein, 1992). The book *Lord of the Flies* reflects the view that people are essentially evil, whereas the central theme of *The Celestine Prophesy* is that people are essentially good. I can't say that we ever had a discussion on this issue at the bank, but we did design materials working from a philosophy which was respectful and supportive of people. For more on this, turn to Chapter 5.

Nature of Human Relationships

"Learning organisations have a complex blend of individualism and groupism, and therein lies the key. Neither extreme on this dimension is inherently favourable to learning" (Schein, 1992). In HSBC teamwork is a core value, which we reinforced with the TWW! programme. However, given the inherent dangers in "groupthink" and the importance of individualism for creativity, innovation and growth, our focus when designing programme materials was on how the individuals within the team have specific value and how they can contribute to the sum of the whole. This approach instils a sense of ownership and pride for each individual to create stronger bonds and relations within the team. Programme reward and recognition mechanisms catered for both the individual and the team.

Nature of Time

"The optimal time orientation for learning app *where between far future and near future"* (Sc strategic goal of the TWW! programme — "To embrace change and allow HSBC continuing twenty-first century" — will continue to be relev.... ior the span of the century. Given that we had no benchmark to refer to, the two-and-a-half-year lifespan of TWW! was considered an appropriate time unit for measuring whether or not our approach was working. Each Phase 2 module was, on average, three months in duration, allowing staff shorter time units to measure their success as they applied their learning in the workplace.

Information and Communication

"Anyone must be able to communicate with anyone else and everyone assumes that telling the truth as best one can is positive and desirable" (Schein, 1992). TWW! mechanisms which enhanced communication and transparency amongst staff bank-wide included the following:

Phase One	Top management members hosted a live "Q&A" session with 120 staff each day and did much to answer questions to the best of their ability.
	Event participants were arranged in cross-functional teams to facilitate relationship building and the flow of information.
Phase Two	The electronic forum "Ask Top Management" on our programme intranet allowed every staff member to post questions and receive an answer within seven days. The steering committee, who governed this communication vehicle, did their utmost to ensure that answers were as honest and transparent as possible, and that commitments to the workforce were kept.
	Our "Teamwork" module focused on the service chain to include team members up and down the line, and all other modules reflected this extended view of "our team".
	Team action-planning results were posted on the programme website, facilitating the dissemination of best practices across the organisation.

₂ural Uniformity versus Diversity

₂he learning leader should stimulate diversity and promulgate* *the assumption that diversity is desirable at the individual and sub-* *group levels"* (Schein, 1992). As mentioned earlier, when we think of diversity we tend to be referring to the more tangible differences, for example, race and gender. As our programme was about embracing change, we focused specifically on thought diversity — that is, how individuals approach problem-solving and decision-making in the face of change. To support teams, we recommended the KAI tool to those in need, during our leadership workshops. As outlined in Chapter 4, the more diverse a team is in terms of individual team members' approaches to problem-solving, the stronger will be the team's ability to generate a broad range of solutions in response to environmental challenges.

Task versus Relationship Orientation

"In a turbulent environment, one needs to value relationships in order to achieve the level of trust and communication that will make joint problem-solving and solution implementation possible" (Schein, 1992). The extraordinary TWW! event and attractive programme materials did much to communicate to staff that they were valued by top management, and again the cross-functional mix for event teams facilitated relationship-building. For Phase Two, we were careful to include a fun introductory activity which would provide staff with a safe forum for exploring themes and issues before they implemented their action plans. Line feedback collected towards the end of the programme reflected that TWW! gave staff a legitimate platform for raising issues with their teams and driving change locally. Trust is a two-way street and the workforce repaid the compliment by utilising communication forums and TWW! materials to produce significant outcomes and results in respect of the programme goals and objectives. To this day, our event facilitators still meet up on an annual basis to celebrate the event and the friendships they forged.

Linear versus Systemic Field Logic

"As the world becomes more complex and interdependent the ability to think systemically, to analyse fields of forces and understand their joint and causal effects on each other, and to abandon simple, linear causal logic in favour of complex mental models will become more critical to learning" (Senge, 1990).[1] The programme philosophy was centred around holistic management principles. The Phase One event raised awareness to change as top management shared with the workforce the change issues they face, and how they were embracing them. This input, supported by line speeches and presentations, provided staff with the strategic view of the world the bank was operating in. This would help them process information and generate appropriate solutions to problems they faced in the workplace. During Phase Two, the tools we provided (for example, force field analysis) did much to encourage the use of different approaches to problem-solving.

Finally, when the underlying assumptions of individual leaders differ in any dimension, this will result in conflict and resistance to the culture change programme. For example, if the executive sponsor drives the programme based on the assumption that people are intrinsically proactive and positive, but a functional head operates from the "Theory X" assumption that people are lazy and to be controlled and threatened, then the implementation of the culture change programme in this part of the business could be seriously undermined, as the local subculture will be geared to reinforce the negative prophesy. We create our own realities. Note that the part of the programme most likely to challenge the sensibilities of "Theory X" managers is the team action plan, as it empowers staff to decide for themselves which goals they will focus on and which team processes they will improve.

---

[1] Senge, P.M., *The Fifth Discipline*, Bantam Dell Publishing Group, 1990.

7.1.4 Core Principles and Values

Of the thousands of beliefs and assumptions that make up any corporate culture network, just a handful tie it all together in a nutshell and define the unique character of the organisation. These are the core principles and values. In Chapter 2 we touched upon the differing nature of principles and values (we cannot break principles, we can only break ourselves against them; whereas values lack constancy and can be eroded over time). Because corporate values typically reflect *competencies*, every corporate vision statement should include at least two principles which will act as a compass for good values and keep them on course long term. It goes without saying that bad values must be outlawed.

*Figure 23: **Examples of Core Principles and Values***

Principles	Good Values	Bad Values
Authenticity	Teamwork	Collusion
Wisdom	Quality	Deception
Integrity	Excellence	Dishonesty
Honesty	Personal responsibility	Disrespect
Justice	Continuous learning	Injustice
Trust	Continuous improvement	Nepotism
Respect	Win-Win	Discrimination
Service	Learn from mistakes	Win-Lose
Change/flexibility	Ethical decision making	Closed communication
Human dignity	Open communication	Self-interest
Co-operation	Positive reinforcement	Covetousness
Sharing		Rigidity
Compassion		Negative reinforcement

© *O'Donovan, 2006*

Increasingly, it is common to see "integrity" on company vision statements but "wisdom" has yet to be recognised generally as a valid and necessary consideration. I think its day has come. Wisdom is a prerequisite for ethical decision-making and only through a history of such behaviour can we build our personal integrity. Integrity and ethics flow out of wisdom.

If they are not underpinned by such principles, good values can become corroded over time to hamper productivity. For example, when Lou Gerstner of IBM found that the value "respect for the individual" had devolved into a system of pervasive non-action he changed the core values of the organisation by removing "respect for the individual" and replacing it with "teamwork". But the value of teamwork can also devolve over time to hamper productivity and put a company at risk. In most instances, corporate governance scandals came about due to the toxic teamwork of a cast of characters who worked in tandem to satisfy their own selfish ends.

Toxic teamwork on the operational level can look like this:

❖ There is little movement in and out of a team in order to safeguard the status quo;

❖ Team members collude to reject those who rock the boat by giving the company their full commitment and raising the benchmark in terms of performance standards;

❖ Presiding line managers rest on their laurels, sabotage team members and pass off their colleagues' efforts as their own contribution to the company;

❖ Some have a toxic reporting line; malfeasance can be traced up through the hierarchy;

❖ Team members collude to work minimum hours and reap company benefits, maximising on time out of the normal working day with visits to the doctor.

The key word here is *collusion*, and this feature is a measure of teamwork at its most toxic. Collusion can occur in an immediate team, a cross-functional team, through a reporting line or in the informal network. The fact is, neither "teamwork" nor "respect for the individual" is superior to the other. Rather, the strategic management team needs to identify during the cultural analysis which value is integral to the organisation's identity and which will support strategies. A combination of the two approaches would seem to reap the best benefits — interdependent team-work which respects the individual and encourages co-operation. Besides, to encourage passion, creativity, loyalty and integrity, we need to nurture the individual; and to complete ambitious tasks, serve customers and manage large corpora-tions, we need excellent teamwork.

If a corporate culture analysis finds an organisation to be lacking in ethics, then principles like "integrity" and "wisdom" will need to be made explicit and woven into programme mate-rials so that the spiritual compass of the culture is nurtured. This will facilitate enduring value and help ensure that good values do not become corrupted over time. While ethical principles are applicable in all scenarios, specific cultural challenges will demand focus and attention on specific values; for example:

Figure 24: Matching Values to Business Needs

Challenge	Good Values/Competencies	
Service Culture	Customer service	Independent teamwork
	Quality	Personal responsibility
Culture of Innovation/ Learning Culture	Continuous learning	Lateral thinking
	Learn from mistakes	Interdependent teamwork
Culture of Ethics	Personal responsibility	Interdependent teamwork
	Communication	Ethical decision making

These cultural challenges are not mutually exclusive but exist to address specific organisational needs because the culture is lacking in certain areas.

Finally, when securing agreement on core principles and values, keep in mind that different business environments may well require different focus. The local religion, educational sys-tem and national culture have produced a workforce which is strong in its congruency with certain principles and values but weaker with others. Use staff feedback, the results of your cor-porate culture assessment and data on marketplace demands to determine which core principles and values need reinforcement locally.

7.1.5 Strategic Goals and Objectives

To align staff across the organisation with core ideology and envisioned future, choose programme goals and objectives which complement the corporate vision and the programme vision. The *strategic goals* should cover all major stakeholders. Goals should be refined further into *objectives* to reflect how success will be measured in each area.

7.1.6 The Blueprint

The Blueprint provides a model of the transformed organisation outlining the policies, processes, practices and technology that will enable the organisation to deliver on the capabilities described in the programme vision statement. It will put forward the business case for the change initiative and allow the leadership team to visualise the desired state. Using the template below, leadership teams can first consider their vision, goals and objectives and then consider the specific changes which must be made in different parts of the business to deliver on the vision.

Figure 25: Blueprint Design Template

Vision, Goals and Objectives (insert here)							
	Sales	*Mktg*	*Finance*	*HR*	*IT*	*other*	*other*
Human Structures • Culture							
Inert Structures • Policies • Processes • Technology							

© *O'Donovan, 2006.*

7.1.7 Scope and Timeframe

Scope

As we saw in Chapter 1, the HSBC programme encompassed the whole of HSBC Holdings Hong Kong plus five subsidiaries. This approach is a major undertaking but promises the best results, as in their daily work all will be aligned with the common vision. Many CEOs under pressure may seek to instigate a programme for a particular segment of staff — for example, front-line staff or the research and development team. If you do take this path, it is imperative that the top team are actively involved every step of the way. Apart from providing good role-modelling, this serves to communicate to the whole organisation the value and importance placed on corporate culture as a competitive advantage. However, as front-line staff are dependent on their colleagues up and down the service chain, this selective approach will be limited in its successes unless it is cascaded throughout the organisation. The same can be said for the creation of a culture of innovation as innovation is not the domain of R&D staff alone. We are all equally capable of being creative.

Timeframe

The duration of each phase of your programme will depend on the number of core principles and values, the size of your workforce, how long it takes to get everyone through the event, and the time given over during Phase Two to each module. The shorter the gap between Phase One and Phase Two the better. Evolving environmental demands (for example, a large-scale product launch or some unforeseen event) may demand that a break is taken before the roll-out of Phase Two. If this happens, a competition will keep momentum up and bridge the gap.

7.1.8 Key Players

CEO Led

Some, like the CEO of General Motors, will drive the programme as executive sponsor, working in partnership with the Director of Change Management who was responsible for the design and implementation of the GM culture change programme "Go Fast", which has been implemented internationally. Others chief executives will also take the reins but create a new and dedicated programme team responsible for corporate culture management specifically. Others still will appoint a Chief Change Officer who works hand-in-hand with the CEO to direct all change management programmes. The set-up in each corporation will differ but no matter who is given responsibility for the implementation of a culture change programme, it simply *must* be led by the CEO. The CEO will command the respect of the business leaders, be closer to the customer, have the power and the influence to speak on behalf of the leadership team, and be able to cross functional boundaries to deal with resistance. To delegate this role is to abdicate on broader responsibilities.

Steered by a Powerful Guiding Coalition

The steering committee will be chaired by a person appointed by the CEO. This successful change agent will be a powerful business leader and committee members will share responsibility for ensuring the programme is aligned with an evolving environment and positioned for success.

Implemented by a Dedicated Core Team

Saying that, the executive sponsor cannot spend all of their time driving a culture change programme; nor can the programme director. A dedicated core team will be able to focus single-mindedly on driving the culture change programme to success. In HSBC, we learned that with strong backing from the executive sponsor, a small team can be a major catalyst for change when they have the right make-up and skill set.

Benefits of being a team member include the following:

❖ Recognition: being asked to be part of the change team is an endorsement by the top team of members' track record and potential;

❖ When positioned correctly and backed consistently, the dedicated core team is protected from interference;

❖ Regular progress reporting and feedback, together with regular line wins, is hugely motivational;

❖ Team members get much greater opportunities for multi-skilling than do staff in typical project management and line management roles.

However, it is not all a bed of roses. Below are some of the thornier aspects one has to contend with:

❖ The elevated status of the team conferred by their role and responsibilities can be hard to swallow for those who made their way up the hierarchy, based on their years of tenure and the old way of doing things, as it challenges their view of themselves and their own accomplishments;

❖ The team will take much of the heat in the face of resistance to change as aspects of the programme will be, by its very nature, counter-cultural.

Saying that, success always attracts flak and these thornier aspects will not act as a deterrent to bona-fide change agents. The leadership team needs to consider what is being asked of the programme team and how they will be supported and protected.

7.1.9 Managing the Political Environment

Stakeholder management is a highly complex discipline but it is key to winning support from others. It can ensure a programme succeeds where another fails and can help manage the intense politics often associated with major initiatives. Stakeholders have a vested interest in the outcome of your change pro-gramme. They may have the power to exert influence on it and, for this reason alone, they need to be managed because they represent a risk. Every programme exists within a political envi-ronment whereby different stakeholder groups are seeking to have their own interests met with regards to the outcome of the programme. In the private sector stakeholder groups will in-clude board directors, business leaders, functional/department heads, general staff, subsidiary companies, staff unions, the media, employment agencies and community groups. In the public sector stakeholder groups can run into the hundreds.

For example, when the Hong Kong Airport Authority moved airport operations from the old Kai Tak airport to the new Chek Lap Kok terminal, stakeholder groups for this major construction programme included the following:

❖ **Internal stakeholders:** The "multi-headed" client (the Hong Kong government, the Chinese government and the British government); the head of the airport authority (who acted as the interface party between the client and others); airport authority rank-and-file employees; trade unions; construction workers, consultants, etc.

❖ **External stakeholder groups:** The airlines together with airline alliances and handling agents, aircraft maintenance, aircraft fuellers, passengers, airport banks and other retail outlets, car hire companies, hotels, airport security, regulatory authorities, people living close to both airports, local chambers of commerce, recruitment agencies, the press and media, business groups, the public, etc.

The stakeholder map names all key players and describes their particular interest in the programme. It will have been designed alongside the strategic planning sessions and a summary of it will be incorporated into the programme proposal together with the stakeholder management matrix. This groundwork will enable us to determine how to effectively consult with different stakeholders so as to minimise any risk.

For example, the output of the stakeholder analysis matrix can clarify for us why we need to closely consult with certain stakeholder groups more than others. To give structure and meaning to this output, develop a stakeholder communications plan for each group starting with those with high power/high stake and finishing with the low power/low stake group. Figure 26 is a cut from a high-level stakeholder communications plan.

Figure 26: High Level Cut of Stakeholder Communications Plan

Group I.D.	Stakeholder Group	Why Consult?	Profile	Consultation Channels	Line Owner	Facilitator
RA11	Regulatory Authority	They have the influence to restrict company activities	High Power/ High Stake	Meetings comprised of presentations, discussions and Q&A sessions Correspondence to highlight more specific issues and requests	Manager - Regulation	Programme Stakeholder Management Consultant
WF21	Airport Staff	They are creators of the new way of doing things	Medium Power/ Medium Stake	Internal magazine articles FAQs booklets Intranet articles Roadshows & exhibitions Focus groups & Workshops	Corporate Communications	Programme Stakeholder Management Consultant
RA31	Recruitment Agencies	They source employee for the organisation	Low Power/ Low Stake	Press releases Newspaper articles Job advertisements	Human Resources and Public Relations	Programme Stakeholder Management Consultant

© *O'Donovan, 2006*

The Executive Sponsor has ultimate responsibility for the success or failure of the whole programme, but this will be shared with the strategic management team. Line owners are responsible for implementing the plan. The level of power and interest a stakeholder group has in the programme will determine the involvement of the senior executive group with them, for example:

❖ In the first case (regulatory authorities) the Executive Sponsor and Programme Steering Committee will own the relationship and, because this is a "high power/high stake group", they will manage any interventions by direct involvement in meetings with government regulators. Also, a single point of contact will be appointed to deal with any related correspondence.

❖ In the second case (airport authority staff) the strategic management team will ultimately own responsibility for the effective management of the stakeholder group, but as this is a "medium power and medium stake group" they will only oversee the process. To support them, line owners will be identified to facilitate the process; e.g. corporate communications will work alongside the party responsible for programme stakeholder management to develop an appropriate plan and utilise communication channels for the best result. To manage the process a "comms steering group" can be established comprising personnel from corporate communications and stakeholder management. The strategic management team will establish terms of reference for this body and any responsibilities/sign-off authority they may have in terms of materials content, quality and development. This will allow the strategic management team to focus on other priorities. To track overall performance, establish a metric for output generated (e.g. number of intranet articles, internal magazine articles per month), monitor any shifts in employee perceptions and issues and monitor how often (if ever) the quality of such materials is questioned by the comms steering group.

❖ In the third case, the group has a "low power and low stake" profile. However, they need to be monitored and kept advised of ongoing progress. In this instance human resources will interface with public relations to agree upon and implement suitable communication activities. Given the profile of the group and the lower level of output to be generated, there is no need to set up a steering group to oversee the process.

Implementation

Once the high-level stakeholder communication plans have been established the party responsible for programme stakeholder management will:

a) Interface with all stakeholder groups and project managers to kick start the consultation process; more operational level communications plans will be designed to identify key messages and suitable communication channels;

b) Feedback activity and results to the strategic management team on a regular basis; and

c) Revise plans to suit the evolving business and evolving stakeholder profiles;

d) Reinforce that the line owns the stakeholder relationships and is responsible for outcomes and results

7.1.10 Strategy and Methodology

Culture change strategies should be learning and development centred and recommended methodologies include self-directed learning and interdependent team learning. The process is overseen by a strategic management team headed by a key business leader. Inert structures like people systems, technology, policies and processes can help make the core principles and values part of the fabric of the organisation. They can reinforce tradition, or be crafted to institutionalise new approaches (some of which will become tradition in time). Chapter 9 is devoted entirely to the finer details of the programme methodology.

7.1.11 Portfolio of Projects and Activities

This portfolio will include a list of all of the projects and activities that will allow for delivery of the capabilities described in the blueprint. The sample portfolio on page 11 can be used as a frame of reference.

7.1.12 The Budget

The operating plan is a derivative of the strategic plan. When the majority of the budget is drawn from the operating plan, it is clear that this initiative is driven by business needs and business leaders. Human Resources can be asked to make a contribution as the programme will do much to assist HR in delivering on its responsibilities. For example, 75 per cent of my TWW! budget came from the operating plan and 25 per cent came from Human Resources.

For Phase Two of a programme designed to create a culture of ethics or a culture of innovation, ask the workforce to focus on implementing change which does not incur extra costs. People often assume that to find a better way of doing things, extra resources are required. While sometimes this will be the case, it is good practice to get the workforce to focus on maximising resources that are already in place. Pressure stimulates creativity. Of course, common sense is required. Manning a busy retail branch with just three tellers instead of the usual six will not cut it, so have managers refer to company standards when in doubt. However, if the programme is designed to create a culture of innovation, then a handsome budget must be made available for research and development purposes.

Ultimately, the programme proposal will be used by the leadership team to determine whether or not to formally commit to any culture change programme. When examining the proposal, the leadership team must carefully consider their motives before endorsing the initiative because if, at the bottom of their hearts, they are really seeking a "rah-rah motivational programme" which looks good and distracts staff from bad news, they will lack the courage and commitment to support the programme when resistance to change shows its head. They will fail in "moments of truth". But if their intentions are honourable and they themselves are dedicated to the future success of the organisation they will have the drive and courage to embrace change themselves.

7.2 Winning Strategies

Below are some of the key features of a successful corporate culture management programme.

7.2.1 Vision and Strategy Aligned

When an organisation nurtures its spiritual core by being principle-centred in word and spirit, it enables the organisation to tap into a well of latent potential. And when staff are working towards programme goals and objectives which are aligned with corporate vision and strategies, the prevailing culture and the espoused culture are in-sync. This alleviates any conflict in the workplace which can come about when staff are receiving mixed messages on what is expected of them. It removes bottle-necks and encourages the flow of positive and constructive energy. As corporate vision serves as the central paradigm of the whole organisational community, underlying principles and values will always filter down through the ranks, regardless of whether or not they are constructive and explicit, so ensure they are both!

7.2.2 Strives to Balance both Tradition and Innovation

Any CEO of a major corporation will immediately recognise where their own company is generally, in terms of how tradition and innovation weigh in as a whole. Leaders can reflect on the indicators below to gain further insights:

❖ **External perception:** What does the public and the competition have to say on how innovative or traditional the company is?

❖ **Track record:** What is the company record for product and service innovation?

❖ **Energy level:** What does it feel like inside; is it notably dynamic or lethargic? The former suggests innovation has the upper hand while the latter suggests that tradition rules.

❖ **Risk tolerance:** To what extent are staff encouraged to take risks and learn from mistakes? Fear of making mistakes is typical of cultures weighed down by tradition.

❖ **Change agents:** Are identified change agents supported for the good of the company, or sabotaged/forced out? The former suggests a change-friendly organisation, while the latter suggests hostility to change.

❖ **Creativity and ideas:** What mechanisms are in place for generating, collating *and actioning* ideas across the organisation and how much credibility do these mechanisms have? For inventiveness to flourish, creativity and ideas must have convincing and respected forums of expression which staff utilise.

❖ **Tradition and identity:** What programmes and mechanisms are in place to reinforce company history and corporate vision?

By considering their corporate culture using each of these indicators, any leadership team will be able to get a good feel for how their own organisation is doing in terms of nurturing the dual forces.

7.2.3 Results Driven

Schaffer and Thomson (1998) advise us that too often corporate improvement programmes have a negligible impact on operational and financial performance because management focuses on activities, not results. While both activity-centred and results-driven programmes aim to strengthen fundamental corporate competitiveness, the approaches differ dramatically. Activity-centred organisations will be shy of measurement as it exposes poor performance. Such organisations will breed a management team and workforce that lose sight of the consequences of their actions. For TWW! we referred to Schaffer and Thompson's model[2] to direct our programme design, adapting it slightly for a culture change programme specifically (see below).

Results-Driven Programme

The improvement effort is defined in long-term, global terms. *Also, there are measurable short-term "team behavioural outcomes" so that staff can track their progress and create momentum.*

The strategic goals and objectives, together with the core principles and values, will determine up front what measures will need to be used to gauge the eventual success or failure of the programme. These need to be identified early on and can include historic measures managed by the line, or external interventions implemented by external parties. In Appendix 2, I share a selection of measures and indicators. As each corporate culture is unique, the measures chosen used will vary from company to company. More guidance on how to choose instruments and approaches is provided in Chapter 13.

7.2.4 Top-Down, Bottom Up

A "top-down" approach will provide great controls and ensure that staff go through the motions. But there is no guarantee of staff commitment to the change initiative. A "bottom-up" approach alone will gain participation and encourage interest but

---

[2] Schaffer, R.H. and Thomson, H.A., "Successful Change Efforts Begin With Results", *Harvard Business Review*, January–February 1998.

those in the lower ranks do not have the power to sustain the momentum of a culture change programme. At HSBC, we decided on a combination of the two approaches which would allow us to get the best of both worlds and create synergies. Top management were responsible for guiding the programme strategically, advising on the suitability of toolkits for the line and championing the programme in their own business areas. At grass-roots level, line pilot teams had the first say in terms of materials suitability for the business. Action planning activities for Phase Two were open-ended, allowing line staff to decide for themselves what local issues needed to be addressed and which tools they needed to use. In fact, all Team Leaders were told during their workshops that if they preferred to use their own tools and techniques for action planning then that was fantastic! They had our full support.

7.2.5 Designed to Engage Hearts and Minds

To implement the programme strategy, we used experiential learning, as it engages staff emotionally, and in activities which are seemingly unrelated to work life (see Figure 27). This introduces an element of fun and we all know we learn more when we are having a good time. Our extended team wanted to move the workforce beyond mere intellectual awareness to influence and capture peoples' hearts. By using the "pull" influencing style (see Figure 30), we built enthusiasm, commitment and ownership. Only then could we engage the workforce in action planning and the application of learning on the line.

The experiential learning cycle has four stages — Do, Reflect, Connect and Apply — and it is based on Kolb's Experiential Learning Model (Figure 28). Kolb recognised the need to address individual differences in learners. He believed that in order to be effective, instruction must be modified to accommodate a variety of learning and learning styles. He defined a four-step learning process and went on to describe the four learning styles (preferences) used within this process. The learning cycle is a series of experiences, and each stage of the cycle caters for a distinct learning style. While we each have our own learning preference which enhances our effectiveness, we use the other learning styles on a daily basis.

Fig 27: Experiential Learning vs Traditional Learning

Experiential Learning	Traditional Learning
The source of learning and information is ***primarily internal***:	The source of learning and information is ***primarily external***:
• Facilitator as coach	• Trainer as teacher
• Facilitator empowers others to tap their own knowledge and experiences	• Trainer is expert filling delegates who act as "empty vessels"
• Delegates speaking 90 per cent of the time	• Trainer speaking 90 per cent of the time
• Focus on insights, encouraging exploration and experience sharing	• Focus on "right" answers and encourages compliance
• Delegate-centred, encouraging ownership	• Trainer-centred, encouraging compliance
• Caters for individual learning preferences	• Geared for only some learning preferences (e.g. cognitive)
• Adult → Adult interaction	• Parent → Child interaction

© O'Donovan, 2006

Figure 28: Kolb's Experiential Learning Cycle

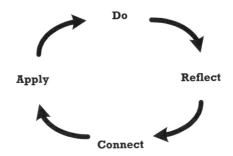

7.2.6 Transfers Learning to the Workplace

Prepare the workforce for culture change by raising awareness of business realities, and providing a centralised forum and common language for discussing change issues. In your centralised event environment, your staff will cover the first three steps of the experiential learning cycle. Then provide staff with relevant tools and techniques to behave in a new way. In the workplace they will cover the final and crucial step of the experiential learning cycle with the guidance and support of programme materials and line champions.

Figure 29: Raise Awareness — Apply Learning

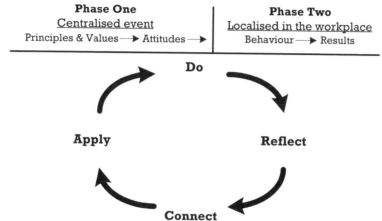

© O'Donovan, 2006

❖ Attempting to have staff apply learning without going through Phase One, which engages them emotionally, provides a common language and shifts attitudes, is a value-destroyer.

❖ Equally, having a Phase One type initiative alone will simply raise expectations and shift attitudes without providing staff with the tools and techniques to act in new ways. This will lead to frustration and again destroy value. Unfortunately, it is a common approach.

❖ A piecemeal approach to Phase Two (where only certain pockets of staff are engaged) will do little to align staff collectively with corporate vision to implement strategies. Instead, the intervention will create a minority group (or subculture) whose modus operandi is different to that of the larger population. This will not facilitate productivity up and down the line.

❖ When rolling out the programme in new parts of the business, don't separate learning materials from the overall philosophy and framework or hand them to training staff for delivery, as this will water down the culture change programme into a training product.

7.2.7 Balances Commitment and Compliance

Everyone in the organisation must have a formal role in the programme; activities will be "part and parcel" of staffs' everyday work. For TWW! we used a mixture of approaches to influencing people so as to balance commitment and compliance. While participation in the programme had to be mandatory, everything else about the programme (philosophy, methodology, policies, processes and systems) was geared to facilitate rational and emotional associations plus line ownership.

Figure 30: Approaches to Influencing People[3]

PUSH ◄			►PULL
Press	*Reason*	*Connect*	*Engage*
▼	▼	▼	▼
Compliance	Rational association	Emotional association	Ownership
(strong push)	(weak push)	(weak pull)	(strong pull)

---

[3] Author unknown.

While all staff must participate in the programme, allow them to decide for themselves whether or not they wish to share their team action planning results at the end of each module. While the scientist in me was initially very frustrated when the programme director decided not to insist that every team shared their results, I learnt to understand the value of this approach. As he explained, we did not want staff to feel that we were burdening them with additional pressures and breathing down their necks to measure their output. If we were to empower staff, demonstrate trust and encourage a culture of fun and creativity in the workplace, we had to give staff ownership and allow them to decide for themselves what remained amongst the team and what was shared with external parties. Besides, the advisory committee was against compulsory measurement as it would create an administrative burden on the line. The proof was in the pudding when, over time, many teams across the bank chose to share their action-planning wins for my team to advertise on our programme's intranet website.

7.2.8 Complements Other Change Initiatives

Major change initiatives should be driven strategically, and not through local piecemeal programmes which will conflict. In "Managing Change"[4], Jeanie Duck recounts how the COO of a large corporation told her of his frustration with managing change. "It's like the company is undergoing five medical procedures at the same time," he told her. "Each operation is successful but the patient dies of shock." Duck's advice to him was that the key to the change effort is not attending to each piece in isolation, but connecting and balancing all the pieces and recognising how changing one element changes the rest. Often, your culture change programme will not be an isolated event. Other major change management initiatives can include a CRM programme, projects to streamline processes and restructuring activities. In the context of the HSBC programme,

---

[4] Jeanie Duck, "Managing Change", *Harvard Business Review*, November 1993.

the head of the retail bank worked in tandem with the head of corporate and institutional banking to ensure that all initiatives are aligned.

When planning a range of change programmes, allow the different initiatives to retain their own identity and autonomy. If one is derailed through resistance to change, you don't want the whole stack of cards to fall.

7.2.9 Ownership Rests With the Line

Giving the line ownership for the success or failure of the second phase of the initiative creates some major benefits:

❖ It builds buy-in;

❖ It makes line management accountable for implementation and results; and

❖ It frees up the programme team to focus on materials design and consultancy services.

We had nearly 100 per cent attendance for the TWW! event, which is no small feat given that, over the seven-month period, some 15,000+ staff left their busy workplace to join us for the day. When Phase Two brought culture change out into the workplace, we initially had varying degrees of success ensuring participation across the different functional areas. As momentum built and short-term wins materialised, more and more came onboard to create the critical mass necessary to make possible the results eventually achieved for the industry service award.

7.2.10 Cascades the Baton of Leadership

At HSBC, the Executive Sponsor realised that to enhance customer service, it was essential to empower those on the front line to make decisions and use their initiative. Through the TWW! programme, he cascaded the baton of leadership throughout the organisation, providing annual leadership workshops for 1,400 line managers from both front and back office staff. In these workshops, we shared again with staff the unacceptable "managerial" behaviours prevalent in the prevailing culture. Also, we shared the leadership behaviours required and how they would help us compete in the twenty-first-century environment.

7.2.11 Manages the Trade Union Relationship

As an organisation seeks to modify the general way of doing things in its community, many of the established employment rules will be renegotiated. For example, rules regarding employee evaluation, reward and recognition may be shifted from a practice based on years served to one of employee performance and contribution to the company. Or the notion of lifetime employment may be done away with as the workforce starts to realise that their jobs are no longer guaranteed. Perhaps responsibility for employee development is passing from a centralised training function to line managers. All of these changes in the culture are a potential source of conflict between top management and general staff and can act as a force for labour union activities. To manage the process as smoothly as possible, the leadership team and trade union representatives should cooperate from the outset and address any changes to the rules of engagement.

In the rapidly changing environment, there has been an increased tendency since the 1990s for US employers, trade unions and workers to come together to create non-traditional structures aimed at meeting their various interests at work.[5] Approaches include collective bargaining, new methods of communication and conflict resolution and joint decision-making.

---

[5] The Role of Industrial Relations in the Structural Change of Organizations, *European Industrial Relations Observatory* online, David Thaler, 2002

7.3 Chapter Summary

The programme proposal will include terms of reference, company philosophy and related strategies, the vision statement and programme philosophy, core principles and values, strategic goals and objectives, a blueprint of the transformed organisation including proposed measures and indicators, the programme scope and timeframe, manpower, the stakeholder map, methodology, portfolio of projects and activities and the budget. The leadership team will use this document to determine whether or not to commit to the culture change programme.

A winning culture change programme has a number of distinctive features: it is aligned with vision and strategies, strives to balance both tradition and innovation, is results-driven, uses a top-down/bottom-up approach, is designed to engage hearts and minds, transfers learning to the workplace, balances commitment and compliance, complements other change initiatives, ensures ownership rests with the line, cascades the baton of leadership throughout the organisation and the leadership team cooperates with trade unions with regard to any changes in the rules of engagement.

8

ORGANISE THE WORKFORCE

In *Built to Last*, Collins and Porras advise us that building a visionary company requires 1 per cent vision and 99 per cent alignment.[1] The same rings true for creating a healthy corporate culture, and in this chapter we learn how to organise the workforce to support that alignment. Giving every staff member clear roles and responsibilities will facilitate their sense of ownership and provide them with focus for working towards the company vision. And by harnessing resources to create synergies, great feats can be achieved in the face of adversity. While the make-up of the strategic management team will remain the same for each phase of the programme (Executive Sponsor, Steering Committee and Implementation Champion) other roles will evolve and dissolve as the programme changes form.

8.1 Key Roles: Phase One

8.1.1 Change Team Members

A small team can be a major catalyst for change if it has the right makeup. I would recommend six to eight core members. When the team has a good mixture of Adaptors and Innovators this will maximise problem-solving potential. Also, when each individual has their own recognised contribution to team results, this will allow for a sense of personal responsibility and

---

[1] Collins, J.C. and Porras, J.I., *Built to Last*, Harper Business Essentials, 2002.

pride in the sum of the whole. Team members must have a strong commitment to the company. Look beyond current job descriptions to review candidate profiles. The role and responsibilities of individual team members will depend on the size of the team and how the responsibilities of the programme manager are divided up.

In the early days of TWW! I sat with my core team and asked them what they had done prior to HSBC and prior to their new job posting. Below is an overview of some of the hidden talents and skills which emerged:

❖ Sam: Manager of a publishing house (and very well versed in print-based materials production, with many local contacts to draw upon). Also, he had a Chinese language degree and so would be the obvious choice for translating learning materials and communication articles into Chinese on behalf of our team.

❖ Gwen: Fifteen years' experience as supervisor in the retail banking sector made Gwen well versed on line staff mentality and their issues. Also, she would have a huge network of contacts for collating informal feedback on the programme content and operations over the next few years. In addition, her commitment and attention to detail was second to none, making her ideal for overseeing major logistical issues.

❖ Angel: With many years in training and development, Angel would be able to support us with facilitator training and Phase Two materials design. Angel expressed a strong interest and talent for designing processes, and we had quite a few to develop from scratch.

Clearly, there was more to this bunch than met the eye! Besides their hidden talents, the team members had strong preferences for the type of work they would rather do and this was taken into consideration when deciding on roles and responsibilities. Given how tight our team was, individuals could be matched to tasks according to their strengths in the early days. Only when the programme matured with responsibility passed to the line, was I able to cater for personal preferences and allocate work differently. Also, accepting new talent and enabling team members to grow is essential for healthy team work. The programme director told me that my team would have to role-model best practices to colleagues who were looking to us for cues. They all understood from Day One that they would have to work very hard indeed, demonstrating passion and commitment, stretching themselves in ways they had never been stretched before. This is what the programme director expected, and this mammoth task could only succeed as a team effort. In return for their efforts, I promised to reward them — if, and only if, they delivered. It was very personally satisfying to watch them stretch and grow over the duration of the programme, and to be able to reward them for their dedication. By the time we had reached mid-way through Phase Two, I had a very good idea of who was ready to move onwards and upwards to share their new knowledge, skills, etc. I promoted my Assistant Manager out into a new role in Training, and promoted a general staff team member up to executive level. Towards the end of Phase Two, I was able to reward and promote our remaining core team member into an exciting role in the retail bank.

8.1.2 Top Management Speakers: Event Live Q&A Session

The top management speakers will be nominated by the executive sponsor, and drawn from the ranks of executive management.

Top Management Speaker's Role: *Demonstrate congruency with the core principles and values as a top-management speaker for the phase one event live Q&A session.*

Responsibilities

❖ Give a ten-minute presentation to event participants on how the core principles and values are being actioned in the speaker's business area.

❖ Follow up with a twenty-minute live Q&A session, answering staffs' questions with knowledge, transparency and integrity.

❖ Liaise with the programme manager pre-event on "hot questions", "common questions" and suggested answers provided by the various "line owners" of more technical issues, and engage in on-location debriefing with the programme manager post Q&A session.

Prior to the event, arrange a briefing session for all speakers. Event representatives can share the background and logistics of the programme, the event layout and the role of the senior management speaker. Speakers can share the generic materials provided and amend these to suit their own style. It would be beneficial, where possible, for speakers to participate in the event prior to their attending as a speaker. All of our speakers did so. In this way, they had the same experience as the audience and were completely familiar with the event. This process enables top managers to build relationships with the workforce, and to broaden their understanding of current issues in other business areas.

8.1.3 The Pilot Teams

The collective make-up of the pilot teams will reflect all areas of the business and all levels of the hierarchy.

> **Pilot Team's Role:** *Test suitability and effectiveness of prototype experiential learning materials*

Responsibilities

❖ Participate in event pilot runs, testing suitability and effectiveness of activities and processes.

❖ Provide constructive feedback to programme team.

Ask your pilot team members to "wear two hats" when engaging in activities: that of participant and that of critic.

8.1.4 Event Facilitators from the Line

Event facilitators should be recruited from the line. Ideally, they will represent a cross-section of high performers from varying levels of the hierarchy, so as to cater for different customer needs. How many are recruited by the programme team will be determined by how large the workforce is, how many staff attend the event each day and the size of the team groupings. A couple of extra facilitators should be on hand to cover for sick leave, etc. Also, take into consideration how long you expect a team of facilitators to be attached to the event, when determining final numbers. Event facilitators should formally report into the programme manager for the duration of their attachment, and be accountable for how they perform their duties. Low performers must be held accountable while high performers can be rewarded with a Certificate of Merit to bring back to their line manager.

Event Facilitator's Role: *Facilitate event experiential learning activities under the supervision of the programme team, contribute to the continuous improvement of the whole event and champion the core principles and values on return to the workplace*

Responsibilities

❖ Act as ambassadors of the programme, welcoming each event participant as an honoured customer.

❖ Facilitate experiential learning activities for teams which will include top executives and staff from the most junior levels.

❖ Assist in the logistical running of the event as required, facilitating smooth traffic flow on a daily basis by keeping to schedule with team activities.

❖ Wear specially designed event attire so as to be easily recognisable to guests and the programme team.

❖ Attend debriefing sessions led by the programme team at the end of each day.

❖ Champion the core principles on return to the workplace.

8.1.5 Line Coordinators

> **Line Coordinator's Role:** *Liaise with the programme team to arrange for local staff to attend the event while ensuring that attendees' work is covered in the business*

Responsibilities

❖ Liaise with the programme team to identify dates where places at the event are available.

❖ Consider line needs and arrange roster for staff to attend event so that all line roles and responsibilities are covered.

❖ Advise programme team on final roster and any last minute changes, maximising free places by arranging for others to attend e.g. when the original attendee rostered is ill, etc.

❖ Distribute formal invitation cards sent by programme team, and ensure all staff in their area attend the event before it closes.

8.2 Other New Roles: Phase Two

8.2.1 The Advisory Committee

The Steering Committee will establish an Advisory Committee for Phase Two to ensure senior management ownership and direction locally, and to provide strong line support to the programme team. This committee will comprise members of senior management who represent major staff areas of the corporation. It will provide much needed input and direction on the suitability of activities for each business area, and the impact these activities will have on line operations as the programme moves forward. The Advisory Committee is critical to the success of Phase Two and should remain in place until completion of the programme.

> **Advisory Committee's Role:** *Ensure that the programme is practical and suitable for diverse areas of the business and advise the Steering Committee on local implementation issues*

Responsibilities

❖ Review prototype learning materials and provide feedback to the programme manager on their suitability for differing business areas.

❖ Give advice on how the Steering Committee can respond to line issues which impact programme strategy.

❖ Support the strategic management team in facilitating the success of the programme.

8.2.2 Module Sponsors

The level of ownership and commitment demonstrated by the line will determine the success or failure of the programme. To alleviate the time commitment of the executive sponsor in overseeing materials and to encourage a sense of ownership amongst senior management, department heads can be encouraged to volunteer for the role of module sponsor. Module sponsors may well be members of the Steering Committee and Advisory Committee.

Module Sponsor's Role: *Take ownership for championing a programme module, facilitating its success all across the business*

Responsibilities

❖ Provide input on module materials design to the programme manager and check prototype materials before they go to the Advisory Committee for consideration.

❖ Encourage own department staff to come up with innovative ways to ensure success of module on the line.

❖ Sign off on all elements of module materials design.

❖ Sign off final draft of internal articles related to specific module.

❖ Communicate with other senior managers to get their support.

❖ Consider what organisational support is appropriate for the module and come up with suggestions for the programme team to implement.

❖ Prepare module launch e-note for the programme team to disseminate organisation-wide with other launch communications.

8.2.3 Department Heads

As department heads for the smaller business areas may not be on either of the committees, it is important to keep them in the loop and provide them with official responsibilities for driving culture change in their area of the business.

> **Department Head's Role:** *Fully support the whole pro-gramme, ensuring its successful implementation in own business area, facilitating the transfer of core principles and values to the workplace*

Responsibilities

❖ Attend programme briefings by programme manager to gain a full understanding of the programme.

❖ Cascade market realities and key messages with local line staff.

❖ Nominate direct reports Local Line Champions who will assist the Department Head in their role.

❖ Encourage department staff to participate in programme activities, including Customer Feedback Surveys and competitions, leadership workshops, etc.

If the Department Head is Team Leader for their own direct reports, they should run the programme activities for each module and attend the leadership workshops. Each Department Head should have final discretion on the make-up of their own teams and monitor progress in the department, providing feedback and coaching where necessary.

8.2.4 Senior Line Champions

In the larger areas, the department heads may well decide that they need help implementing the programme in their own area. These Champions will be their direct reports and this group of people will have a key role in monitoring the implementation of the programme in their workplace, supporting staff where necessary.

> **Senior Line Champion's Role:** *Assist department head in ensuring the smooth and successful implementation of the programme in their own functional area, to facilitate the transfer of core principles and values to the workplace*

Responsibilities

❖ Nominate Team Leaders as per criteria set by Steering Committee and communicated by the programme team.

❖ Ensure Team Leaders attend leadership workshops.

❖ Identify practical distribution points for programme materials, feedback details to programme team, oversee distribution and update the Department Head on progress.

❖ Identify local Phase One facilitators who can help Phase Two Team Leaders in need of assistance with group facilitation.

❖ Oversee all department teams, providing support and coaching where necessary.

❖ Run activities with own team if nominated as a Team Leader.

❖ Perform any programme-related work as requested by Department Head.

❖ Review modules results forwarded by local teams, and share wins with department head and programme team who will share best practices across the organisation.

8.2.5 Team Leaders

Research by international experts says that, in addition to action-planning, one of the most powerful interventions in terms of the transfer of learning to the workplace is to engage line managers and supervisors as coaches and role models of new behaviours in the workplace. A key behavioural change for line managers in changing times can be to shift from their traditional role as managers to the more progressive role of leaders. Facilitators coach and motivate their teams, empowering them rather than simply dictating to them what to do.

> **Team Leader's Role:** *Ensure the smooth and successful implementation of the programme with one's own team, by transferring the core principles and values to one's own workplace*

Responsibilities

❖ Participate in leadership workshops run by the programme team.

❖ Inform own team of team meeting dates and rundown, etc.

❖ Do required preparation work to run team meetings and activities.

❖ Run activities and facilitate team to develop their own Action Plan.

❖ Enforce and monitor the Action Plan, providing support and coaching where necessary.

❖ Encourage Team Members to revise plans if their learning suggests this course of action.

❖ Organise meetings to reflect on progress and plan future action.

❖ Ensure that new Team Members are briefed.

❖ Track behavioural shifts, measure results and, if the team agrees, share results with Line Champions and programme team.

❖ Fill in Module Evaluation Form and return it to the programme team

8.2.6 Team Members

Team Members will more commonly be the direct reports of the Team Leader nominated to guide their activities.

Team Member's Role: *Work with own team to action core principles and values in the workplace in line with programme strategy and goals*

Responsibilities

❖ Participate in team meetings related to the programme.

❖ Design Team Action Plan.

❖ Implement Action Plan, logging personal and team experiences.

❖ Revise plans where necessary to reflect learning.

❖ Meet to reflect on progress and plan future action.

❖ At module end, compare team progress to "Team Behavioural Outcomes" provided in programme materials to measure behavioural improvements.

8.2.7 Pilot Teams

Again, the collective profile of the pilot teams will reflect the diversity of the workforce, with representative teams chosen from every business area. When Department Heads are deciding on teams, it's worth considering any planned movement amongst staff or downsizing and how it may impact pilot teams. You don't want to lose half your pilot teams over the course of the programme.

Pilot Team's Role: *Test prototype materials and provide feedback to the programme manager on their suitability for line use, piloting each module before it is officially launched*

Responsibilities

❖ Conduct activities and measure team results.

❖ Provide detailed feedback to the programme team.

❖ Keep prototype materials "under wraps" from other staff.

❖ Pilot each module before it is officially launched in a timely manner, to facilitate the overall module development and distribution.

8.2.8 Line Materials Distributors

Often, large organisations have already in place a list of key personnel who receive, and distribute to line staff, materials relating to internal campaigns. This resource can be shared with the programme team and utilised for the dissemination of programme materials. Also, it makes sense to draw on the pool of staff who acted as Line Co-ordinators for Phase One of the programme. The relationships with the programme team are established and the workforce will readily identify these staff as points of contact on the line.

Line Materials Distributor's Role: *Ensure that the distribution of programme materials is smooth, timely and accurate in one's own business area*

Responsibilities

❖ Receive programme materials.

❖ Advise local Team Leaders when materials have arrived, by sending email (template can be prepared by the programme team).

❖ Store, distribute and keep stock of the materials.

❖ Advise programme team of any changes to the quantity of materials required for area.

❖ Advise programme team if the person responsible for the materials distribution changes.

❖ Monitor collection and follow-up with Team Leaders who are late collecting materials.

Once all the roles and responsibilities have been mapped out, the programme team will build databases to store the contact information of Line Coordinators, Team Leaders, Department Heads and Line Champions. They will also determine what communication channels are used to communicate differing roles and responsibilities (e.g. Team Leader Guides, FAQs booklets for all and/or the programme website). The outputs of this whole process will put the scaffolding in place for work-force alignment.

8.3 Strategic Partners to the Change Effort

It is the job of all strategic partners to the change effort to cre-ate the right conditions to support the smooth implementation of the culture change programme.

It will be essential, now more than ever, that the most suit-able person is chosen to lead *Training*. This person must de-velop a strategic view of their professional craft and practise continuous development. The head of training will partner with line managers and executives in accomplishing organisational objectives with their goal to contribute to corporate strategy, facilitate organisational change, enhance productivity and in-crease the quality of work life — outcomes that are important to all. The biggest contribution Training can make during a cul-ture change programme is to send trainers out to the workplace to support line managers in their efforts (once the programme is completed and dissolved, this practice should continue). In addition, courses offered by Training will need to be aligned with business strategy and needs and the principles and values of the programme must be reflected in all materials. Pro-gramme logistics will require support in the form of suitably qualified and seasoned facilitators and training rooms for any support workshops.

Human Resources also has a key role in assisting the CEO with the implementation of a culture change programme, ensur-ing that HR policy and processes align the workforce with cor-porate strategy via recruitment, job descriptions, core compe-tencies and behaviours and compensation arrangements, etc. HR should also encourage the inclusion of change agents in the organisation by a) creating career paths for identified change agents and b) organising succession planning to build on past successes to ensure that any future initiatives are also driven by bona-fide change agents. Too often, HR is the biggest obstacle to the change process.

If *Organisational Development* is a separate entity to HR, then I would transfer a couple to the programme team to develop their change management skills and utilise their knowledge of the business. Any remaining staff can continue on with their normal job responsibilities and serve as advisors to the programme team. As *Communication* activities are integral to the success of the programme, the head of communications can help by a) sharing internal communication vehicles with the programme team and b) ensuring that the integrity of core values and messages of the programme is upheld.

8.4 Chapter Summary

Building a healthy corporate culture requires 1 per cent vision and 99 per cent alignment. Once strategic management have outlined their strategy, they can then progress to aligning staff across the organisation to work towards the common vision. To put the scaffolding in place, create a Roles and Responsibilities Map and build databases of Department Heads, Line Champions, Team Leaders, and Materials Coordinators. As the programme evolves, other roles will be created and pruned as required.

Partners to the change effort include Training, Human Resources, Organisational Development and Communications. Training can help by aligning their offerings with corporate strategy and sending trainers out to the workplace to support Team Leaders with their new people development responsibilities. On the logistics side, they can also provide facilitators for leadership workshops and provide rooms and other resources if necessary. Human Resources can facilitate the integration of change agents, align their offerings with corporate strategy and give the maximum support via culture embedding mechanisms that fall into their remit (e.g. recruitment, talent management, staff profiling, etc.) Members of the OD team can come aboard the change programme team to share their skills and knowledge while any remaining team members will continue on with their normal jobs and serve as advisors and interface contacts. Corporate Communications can help ensure that the integrity of the core values and messages of the programme is upheld and share communication vehicles to avoid the duplication of efforts.

9

DESIGN CORE PROGRAMME AND EMBEDDING MECHANISMS

Just as the seasons are cyclical and renewable, so are the stages of culture change. Building on this analogy together with my learning and development-centred approach to corporate culture management, I have created a model that reflects the culture change cycle (see Figure 31), incorporating Kurt Lewin's classic model for changing organisations (unfreezing, changing and refreezing); Hickman and Silva's model for building a strong, successful culture;[1] and Edgar Schein's culture embedding mechanisms.

Each phase of the change cycle represents a season; each season serves a specific purpose; and once the cycle is completed it must begin afresh to sustain life and evolution. The first two structured phases of the cycle are learning and development-centred and supported by cultural embedding mechanisms. Upon completion, these two phases will be followed by a period of consolidation before the cycle repeats itself in response to new business challenges.

---

[1] Hickman, C.R. and Silva, M.A., *Creating Excellence*, Allen and Unwin Ltd, 1985, p. 70.

Figure 31: The Culture Change Cycle

UNFREEZING ▶	CHANGING ▶	REFREEZING
Phase One *Centralised Event*	*Phase Two* *Localised*	*(Phase Three)* *Consolidation and* *Readjustment Period*
Instil *commitment* to a shared philosophy and purpose, recognising that employee commitment to a corporate philosophy must concur with both individual and group interests Unfreeze cognitive maps using experiential learning activities	Develop and reward *competence* in key principles and values, keeping in mind that one will foster greater competence by focusing on one principle or value at a time rather than by addressing a host of them in unison	*Consolidate* learning, reinforce alignment with common philosophy and purpose *Consider* new environmental demands and the culture's synchronicity with these before starting the cycle afresh
Use "culture embedding mechanisms" to anchor the new way of doing things into everyday practices and to perpetuate *consistency*		

© O'Donovan, 2006

❖ Phase One of the programme is designed to appeal to the minds and hearts of the workforce and build commitment to the way forward. By engaging staff in experiential activities we can unfreeze old mindsets and open people to new possibilities.

❖ Phase Two enables teams to change how they work together and the results they achieve, creating tens of thousands of opportunities for staff to manage change in their own workplace.[2] Competence in actioning key principles and values is developed via action-planning and rewarded via competitions and line reinforcement.

---

[2] For TWW!, 1,400 teams actioned three Team Behavioural Outcomes (TBOs) for each of the six values. Each action plan consisted of, on average, twelve specific activities relating to the core value in focus. This equates to 100,800 examples of line teams using programme materials to manage change in the workplace (1,400 x 6 x 12) over an eighteen-month period.

❖ Phase Three is a period of consolidation and readjustment. For the workforce there are no structured culture change programme activities and deadlines but, as workforce learning is consolidated, behavioural norms and the inert structures of the organisation are aligned to perpetuate consistency. The culture refreezes in its new form.

❖ Cultural embedding mechanisms (see Section 9.2.2 below) support all three stages of the change cycle, so the more the merrier.

At some point, feedback will start to indicate that the prevailing culture is at odds with the external environment and to keep abreast with external demands, the cycle will need to be repeated. For the second culture change cycle, each phase may take on a new form to evolve with the evolving business. Lewin believed that the new state needs to be a more fluid one that does not require the degree of effort that the original paradigm for developmental change required. To help achieve this, I suggest that you keep the scaffolding of Phase Two in place, so that the programme Team Leaders continue to manage the learning of their teams in the workplace, with help from support functions and top management. The assortment of template tools and techniques provided during the first run of the programme can be reused to address new issues as they arise, and training can utilise the programme databases to contact Team Leaders for further developmental opportunities. In this way, staff understand that the primary learning environment continues to be the decentralised workplace, with the training function supporting line managers in their efforts to develop their teams. Learning and innovation become institutionalised.

General Electric is an organisation that is totally committed to managing its culture long term and addressing new cultural challenges as they present themselves. Since the launch of the first programme in 1989 (to eliminate bureaucracy and free up people's time) the leadership team has rolled out five culture programmes focusing on productivity and then process improvement, followed by the change acceleration process, making customers winners and six sigma quality.

9.1 The Core Programme

The methodology and tools recommended in this section reflect the philosophy of a healthy culture. The broad philosophy, principles and values outlined in the programme proposal can become tangible through the use of experiential learning and workplace action planning which help staff understand and apply abstract concepts.

9.1.1 Phase One: Methodology, Content and Processes

Having explored the nature of experiential learning in an earlier chapter, I would just like to reiterate that in Phase One of the culture change programme, staff will go through the first three stages of the experiential learning cycle (Do, Reflect and Connect) and in Phase Two they will complete the last step (Apply). Let us now explore what such activities look like, first in the centralised environment and then in the localised environment, and consider who should facilitate them.

Indoor Activities

To participants and observers alike these activities are colourful, challenging and fun, and in the first instance seem completely unrelated to the workplace; this opens minds to new possibilities. Below, I suggest some ideas for the three most common challenges facing organisations — teamwork, service and ethics — as they will require different approaches.

Teamwork

One of my favourite activities is "The Maze", as it allows one powerful insights into how individuals operate on a number of levels in the team context.

For TWW! we had each of the break-out rooms in the event hall designed for specific activities, and in this room the carpet reflected the design of the maze: a grid, six squares by nine squares; each square was one foot in diameter; the pattern was like that of a chess board. When a team entered this particular room in the event hall, their facilitator would welcome them and then proceed to brief them on the objective of the activity: "to get the whole team from one end of the maze to the other in 20 minutes". As the team would have no idea which squares on the maze were "go" and "no go" zones, they would have to learn through trial and error. They would get a (fictitious) budget up front, be told the rules of the activity (e.g. they had to take turns on the maze and they could not touch a person who was on the maze). They would be advised that penalties would be applied for rules broken. They would then be given five minutes of preparation time to work out how they would meet the objective. Once the preparation time was up, no one was allowed to speak until the objective had been met or the twenty minutes was up. Then, the facilitator would check in with participants to learn how they were feeling and what emotions had come up (these could range from warm feelings to annoyance and frustration).

Having acknowledged the participants' emotions, the facilitator would then elicit input on what had happened during the process (feedback could reflect a range of issues which are relevant to teamwork in the workplace e.g. leadership, communication, use of resources, sharing of information, willingness to take risks, ability to learn from each other and from mistakes, following instructions, etc.). As each issue came up, the facilitator would list the key points on a flipchart. Then, the team would be asked if these issues came up in the workplace. At this point an "Aha!" light bulb would come on and the group would proceed to link their learning points to workplace issues and have a focused discussion around these. Learning points would be consolidated in the final review.

For TWW! all of our six activities followed this same process. However, as the focus was different with each core value, the activities varied, as did the learning points. Every team approached the activities differently and drew from them their own insights, but some patterns emerged in terms of the attitudes and behaviours across the board. As my team moved from room to room, coaching the twelve event facilitators through 72 activities a day and over a seven-month period, we gleaned more rich insights into the organisation's culture. This input helped us to design Phase Two materials.

Service Recovery

It costs ten times more to advertise for new customers than it does to retain existing customers. Therefore, it makes sense to utilise whatever opportunities we have to retain those whom we are already doing business with, particularly those customers who are loyal to us. "Service Recovery" is about taking care of a customer especially well when things go wrong during product or service transactions. If a difficult situation is handled well, the customer's loyalty can increase to a point higher than before the mishap. So if customer retention is a key challenge for an organisation, I would run two activities related to service, one experiential learning activity focusing on customer service and a second focusing on service recovery. The latter can take the form of a simulation exercise which will include role-play activities. Simulation exercises require a larger space and can take anywhere from two to six hours to process. In 1998, I delivered such workshops for Cathay Pacific Airways in many locations globally and below I share what the exercise looked like for airport operational staff, who were set the task of handling a delayed outgoing flight, and an army of unhappy customers.

Service Recovery Activity

Presentation

To set the scene, I shared with the group a story about a man whose loyalty to his bank increased after he experienced service failure. This outcome was due to the excellent service recovery skills of the bank staff. As I told the story, I depicted on a graph how his loyalty first increased incrementally with each transaction, took a large nose-dive when he was double-billed on his credit card, but quickly climbed back to a loyalty level higher than before the incident. This was made possible by the team of bank staff who worked speedily and in concert to regain his trust.

Simulation Exercise

Having learnt how to work together to recover a situation, the group set about a simulation exercise which would allow them to apply their knowledge and skills in a high-pressure but controlled environment. The participants were general and supervisory staff whose job it was to handle a work situation (the inevitable flight delay) and carry out tasks as if the situation was really happening; they would discuss options and make decisions based on the challenges and resources available to them. The Resource Centre Manager was a managerial level staff member who provided information to participants as and when required. This person gave feedback in the debriefing as to the consequences of certain decisions and explicit strategies. Roleplay Actors were staff from other departments and/or course participants. Their role was to read the task cards given to them, listen to their briefing, approach the relevant section, take part in the role-play and give feedback during the debriefing on how their complaint was handled. Facilitators were Airport Managers, facilitators from head office and the local port trainers. Some ports ran the simulation activities themselves by using the comprehensive package of materials provided.

The simulation workshop:

❖ *Started off as a "short delay", became a "creeping delay" and then a "long delay";*

❖ *Was based on "real time" and reflected the pressure of a fast-paced work environment;*

❖ *Had general and supervisory staff deal with impromptu customer complaints on-the-spot;*

❖ *Had general and supervisory staff swap roles and responsibilities to allow them insights into the reality and pressures of each others' jobs;*

❖ *Took over six hours to process.*

Again, each team will approach the activity challenges differently and draw from them their own insights. They may well start off the day with their own biases towards each other and their work environment. An astute facilitator can use these insights to determine who does what during the simulation exercise. For example, while running the exercise at the airport in Anchorage, Alaska, we noticed that one member of the operations team was somewhat dismissive up front of the role and responsibilities of the Airport Services Manager and was convinced that he could do the job just as well. So we assigned him with this post for the simulation exercise. As the activity got more and more intense and the pressure rose, he got visibly stressed out. When the practical exercise ended, his relief was tangible, as was his new-found appreciation for the role of the Airport Services Manager. In the debriefing, he was at pains to let the rest of the team understand his "traumatic" experience, as he was called upon from all directions to make decisions. He even drew on the real Airport Services Manager to validate his experiences and the Airport Services Manager was only too happy to oblige. Our strategy worked a treat!

To support staff in applying their learning in the workplace, Cathay Pacific Airways enhanced their service recovery policies and processes, changed operational roles and responsibilities and raised the authority levels of operational staff. Airport communication vehicles were enhanced, and a team of Managers on Duty was created to oversee the big picture and provide personal service to airport customers. The company added to their array of food and drink vouchers for staff to distribute to customers in the case of a flight delay. By creating a supportive work environment for staff, Cathay Pacific Airways positioned staff to utilise their learning and increase customer retention figures.

Ethics

It is a sign of our times that personality tests have gained precedence over tests of integrity. Every HR department I have heard of uses personality tests like Myers Briggs for recruitment and talent management activities. However, one can have a "winning personality" but no personal integrity. On issues of character we cannot use the same type of development interventions which we employ to explore competencies and skills. While there is no great social stigma attached to being identified as in need of some skills development (e.g. leadership, customer service or teamwork), once a person's character and reputation is brought into question the damage is done. But before we consider how to raise consciousness on the issue of ethics, Figure 32 outlines how experiential learning activities, simulation exercises and role plays compare on the ethics front.

Figure 32: Comparing Methodologies on the Ethics Front[3]

Experiential Learning Activities	Simulation Exercises	Role Plays
Participants engage in problem-solving activity which draws out workplace attitudes and behaviours	Participants engage in work-related activity; they are assigned work roles and are required to complete work-related tasks	Participants act out prescribed roles
Emotions are spontaneous but may be kept in check as participants will be conscious of workplace hierarchy and power others wield in the workplace	Emotions are influenced by corporate culture as participant acting is based on a workplace scenario and draws on their knowledge of workplace and internal ways of doing things	Emotions, motives and personalities are provided by the role play cards
No real world ethics are involved except the spirit of "fair play"	Real world ethics apply insofar as examining how ethical the corporate culture is and/or how ethical the individual is	Real world ethics apply insofar as examining how ethical the corporate culture is and/or how ethical the individual is

---

[3] Adapted from "Games, Simulations and Roleplays", Guila Muir and Associates, 2003.

Simulation exercises and role plays can be designed so that participants can deal with ethical issues as they are raised. However, I am not convinced that this approach has any enduring value, as participants will be very aware that observers are watching their every move, and this will influence their behaviour. Also, I do not believe that knowledge-based ethics workshops go the distance in terms of creating a culture of ethics. Every person joins their employer organisation with an innate sense of "right" and "wrong", "justice" and "injustice", etc. To create a culture of ethics, what is required is more symbolic action (behaviour) on the part of leaders at all levels and not more knowledge. That said, a centralised environment allows us a forum for tackling some thorny issues central to the creation of a culture of ethics.

With Phase One activities we are looking to open hearts and minds to new possibilities so I have devised the following activity which aims to encourage each individual to explore their own inner dialogues as they make decisions, because when our internal moral compass and our immediate self-interest are at odds with each other we have conversations in our heads and internal dialogues begin. The culture of our organisation will influence and can even determine how dubious these dialogues become and whether our moral compass or immediate self-interest will win out. For example:

❖ In *a culture of ethics*, a mode of enquiry is encouraged. People think for themselves by engaging in reflective internal dialogues, make up their own minds and are navigated by their internal compass to make ethical decisions. The individual's spiritual core/moral compass is nurtured and complemented by a principle-centred culture which respects the spirit intended behind the law and the spirit of the workforce. Colleagues appreciate, and encourage, good conduct and the management team articulates how a culture of ethics makes good business sense.

❖ In a *black-and-white culture*, a mode of enquiry is discouraged. There is little inner reflection or personal understanding of the belief system which dictates decision-making. Peter Singer warns us that a belief system which is based on no inner reflection, and which fails to consider human motives, is as dubious a course as is the immoral path. It can be a vice and not a virtue. Diversity training and education can go some way towards opening minds to new ideas but should be supported with real experiences of travel and exposure to other cultures.

❖ In a *shades-of-grey culture*, the spiritual core of the community has been undermined such that the moral compass of each individual is eroded. Dubious inner dialogues have a field day and the individual ends up confused and unable to think for themselves. Decision-making may be delayed, so that the individuals can weave a web of grand myths to deceive themselves and their peers that the easy course is the righteous course. Their sense of judgment is impaired as groupthink takes hold. When short-term self interest and/or pressure to conform wins out, it chips away as the individual's heart and soul as they take another step away from their authentic self. Internal misgivings are suppressed. Below is an activity which I have designed to raise consciousness of this very important issue.

Activity: Shady Inner Dialogues

Write "When Good People Do Bad Things" on the board to set the scene.

Step One: Group Brainstorming

Ask participants to quickly brainstorm on how everyday situations can impede one's ability to live a moral life. They can write bullet points on a whiteboard or use "Post-Its" and stick them to a wall. Leave their input on the wall for later reference.

Step Two: Facilitator Storytelling

The facilitator tells a personal story which relates to a day-to-day experience and outlines their own personal struggle to forego personal self-interest and do the right thing. For example:

> *These days, I rarely walk past a beggar without giving them some money and a few friendly words. It's relatively new behaviour which I adopted having examined my own thoughts and motives about helping those in need. When I was younger, my head was filled with well-meaning social dictates about why I should not be giving to them (e.g. "Be careful, you might be followed", "They'd probably spend it on drugs", "Don't draw attention to yourself as a young woman") and my own internal dialogue ("I'll help the next person, I'm in a hurry now", "I only have large notes with me", "Hmm, he does look a bit dangerous", etc.). So I did what I was told to do and hurried along, but the conflict went on in my head as my conscience continued to nag at me. It was only when I stepped out of the corporate world to write this book that I found the time to examine my behaviour and thought processes. I came to realise that my behaviour had been dictated by a cynical attitude which I had first learnt and then nurtured because it was convenient. I chose to stop these shady inner dialogues and choose new behaviour.*

Most participants will be able to personally relate to the story and this type of sharing will get their attention and foster an environment of trust and openness. Refer to the output of the brainstorming activity to cluster examples which come under the heading "Shady Inner Dialogues/Self-Deception" and write this up under the first one to name the behaviour.

Step Three: Individuals Reflect and Share in Pairs

Now give each participant a copy of the handout in Appendix 5 and ask them to spend five minutes reflecting on a similar struggle they experienced. Put them in pairs and ask them to share their experience with their partner.

Step Four: Group Sharing

Ask a handful of participants to volunteer to share their stories. Make sure they stay on track and that the group is respectful and non-judgemental as they listen. Avoid an overly pious tone and let them have their fun as they relate their "misdemeanours".

By the end of the sharing session it should be clear that such inner conflicts are common everyday occurrences. Emphasise that our conscience has an uphill battle because its directives can clash with what seems to be in our immediate self-interest. Highlight that by choosing the easy path, we maximise on short-term pleasure but undermine our own moral compass. When we give in to environmental demands and "groupthink", we sell out on our heart and soul and undermine ourselves. By choosing the ethical path we take another step towards building our own personal character, learn to know our own minds and become a person of substance who can make a meaningful contribution to our community.

Elicit the principles of ethical decision making, fill in the gaps in knowledge and then give each participant a copy of the handout in Appendix 5 to use as a workplace tool.

Transfer to the Workplace

Ask the group to brainstorm on how they can support a culture of ethics in their own workplace. Teams share their findings.

Wrap Up

Facilitator summaries key learning points and wraps up the activity.

Creating a culture of ethics is not going to come about by drumming core principles into the workforce and attempting to teach grown adults the difference between right and wrong. Most certainly it is not dependent on the creation of a company guide to ethics (though there is great value in sharing such a document with the workforce). To create a culture of ethics, leaders need to demonstrate to the workforce through their behaviour that integrity is valued and will be rewarded. Staff watch management behaviour very closely and will quickly recognise when there is any disconnect between espoused values and prevailing values. Also, if a firm is seeking to create a culture of ethics, it must align recruitment processes with the espoused culture to provide new recruits with a consistent message. The firm ABN Amro encourages potential recruits to assess their cultural fit with the organisation right at the outset. One can participate in six "Dilemma Challenges" on the company website. These case studies call upon the individual to exercise integrity *and* good judgment to solve a set of practical problems. They give one a good feel for the culture and what is expected of staff.

The Facilitators

Having considered the nature of the indoor activities, let us now consider who should facilitate them. Initially, I had expected that our TWW! indoor activities would be run by experiential learning experts, but the programme director was firm in his view that they should be facilitated by line staff who would become champions of the core principles and values on return to the workplace. Although I understood the rationale I just couldn't see how it would work. Becoming a good facilitator takes years of practice — it does not happen overnight. As my protests were falling on deaf ears I complied with the request, and my team proceeded to interview hundreds of staff nominated by the line. In the process, I was delighted to learn that many had developed good facilitation skills over the course of their careers so we had very good raw material to work with. The sixty we hired we put through a train-the-trainer programme on experiential learning philosophy and skills. They put in a great amount of effort each day to give it their best, and we met with them at the end of each day for a debriefing so that they could hone their skills. These line facilitators had a lot of credibility with the workforce and could talk in specifics about workplace issues, so I learnt a lot from this approach. It would work equally well for service recovery simulation exercises and activities which focus specifically on ethics. For the latter, and if the culture is strong and homogenous, an outsider's perspective will be required for discussions on workplace issues. Long-serving staff particularly will not recognise their own blind spots as they will identify with the culture and be protective of it. If your company does not have trained experts available internally for *experiential materials design*, don't hesitate to hire outside consultants for this task because these materials *must* be designed by trained professionals — or else the whole programme will fall flat. Free sample activities can be downloaded from the internet.

Outdoor Activities

I am a great advocate of outdoor experiential learning activities. They are very powerful, do much to facilitate teamwork, trust and confidence, are similar to outward-bound type activities and often take the form of ropes courses and climbing walls. If the programme budget and organisational needs allow, follow the one-day event with a half-day of outdoor experiential learning activities to get the best effect. Two experiences have impressed on me the value of such activities for both the team and for the individual.

In 1996, I was involved in the implementation of the Cathay Pacific culture change programme for service staff. Both indoor and outdoors experiential activities were being run at the Gold Coast Resort in Hong Kong. As we briefed a new team one day I noticed that one young man was standing apart from his team. He looked surly and unapproachable. When I introduced myself to him, Ivor's manner was rude and confrontational so I quickly let him be, switching my focus instead to the task ahead of us. Each team member, fitted with a safety harness, was expected to climb up a high pole and walk across a tightrope to reach a second pole. Some looked forward to the activity while a few were terrified at the prospect. When one young woman became distressed halfway through her turn and wobbled precariously on the tightrope, guess who stepped up to the task of motivating her? Ivor. He came out of the shadows shouting encouragement, reassured her that he would personally hold the safety rope to support her steps, insisted that she could do it when she said she couldn't, and talked her through each step of the process. And when she and others came down, he was on hand to applaud their successes and give comforting hugs where needed. It was just inspirational to observe the metamorphosis and see the team accept Ivor in his new role as coach and motivator. He probably never had such an opportunity to show his strengths in his junior operational role at Kai Tak Airport but now he had discovered his personal contribution to his team.[4]

The other story is my own. As part of our preparation for facilitating such activities, each trainer had to experience each one of the challenges for themselves. In this particular instance, our task was to climb a 40-foot pole and, harnessed with a safety rope, jump off a platform at the very top. The individual would swing across a line before landing on a waiting platform. It all looked straightforward enough, so GI Jane (me) decided to get the ball rolling and volunteered to go first. It was all well and good until I got half way up the pole and remembered that I do not have a good head for heights. I froze for a few minutes but with the encouragement of my team I edged myself slowly to the top, trying ever so hard not to look down. The consultant waiting at the top was going to have to work for his money to get me to jump. The world from the "diving board" looked tiny and suddenly it all seemed very, very dangerous. Having checked out the size of the tiny platform my feet were glued to, my eye carefully examined the line I was supposed to swing across for any flaws. For a good ten minutes, I tried to summon up the courage to jump but kept losing my nerve. As I struggled with myself to overcome my fear I went through a very powerful process as I discovered a newfound love for every little part of my anatomy. It was probably the first time in years I

---

[4] It is very important that facilitators keep a note of such stories and work with line management to follow through so that valuable information can be utilised to develop individuals and teams.

was focusing on me and me alone. The "jump" itself was easy once I eventually closed my eyes tightly and stepped off the platform, but I got the most value from those ten minutes I spent wrestling with myself. I will never forget it. A big learning point from that activity for me was that, firstly, it is normal and healthy to feel fear in a scary situation and, secondly, I don't have to be held hostage by my fearful feelings but can accept the emotions while forging ahead anyway. I have no doubt that it had a positive impact on my attitude towards challenges moving forward. Also, I was better able to empathise with the emotions of others as I helped them through the course activities.

The Facilitators

For health and safety reasons, such activities must be led by *licensed facilitators* who have gone through safety training. Local service providers can be found through an internet search or by contacting the local chamber of commerce, as they often allow registered consultants to use this platform to advertise their wares.

9.1.2 Phase Two: Methodology, Content and Processes

The overall design of Phase Two incorporates a number of important learning transfer strategies:

- ❖ The psychological support of transfer by top management who communicate support;

- ❖ The provision of opportunities to transfer learning to the workplace;

- ❖ Having team members participate in decision-making, end-of-module debriefings encourages positive reinforcement;

- ❖ Role-modelling by leaders at all levels;

- ❖ The setting of mutual expectations for improvement;

- ❖ The provision and support of learning tools and techniques;

❖ The support of team revisions to action plans as they take into account their workplace learning;

❖ The reward and recognition of successes.

It also incorporates the four conditions for empowerment:

❖ Allow for self-supervision;

❖ Create a win-win agreement;

❖ Provide a helpful structure and systems;

❖ Make accountability a requirement.

For Phase Two we are seeking to develop and reward competence in core principles and values. While in a perfect world staff would be demonstrating excellence in all areas at any one time, this is rarely the reality. Therefore, we need to concentrate on perfecting competence in one core principle or value within a fixed timeframe via action-planning.

Figure 33: One Step at a Time

THREE MONTHS	THREE MONTHS	THREE MONTHS	THREE MONTHS	THREE MONTHS
Integrity	Leadership	Embrace Change	Service	Learning

At the end of each module, teams across the organisation will be advised to wrap up their activities in preparation for the new module. That said, and subject to their completing their responsibilities in terms of any particular module, a team that wishes to carry over work on a particular principle/value as they start with a new one should be encouraged to do so. A blend of methodologies will achieve the best results.

Self-Directed Learning

Self-directed learning encourages empowerment and ownership. When it is organised on a company-wide scale, it facilitates the creation of a critical mass of individuals who are committed to, and have the ability to manage, their own development. For TWW!, all 15,000 staff received individual study materials and resources for personal and professional development, prior to the launch of each programme module. These included a resource list detailing internal and external structured learning opportunities; an introductory pamphlet highlighting key concepts; a theme-related self-awareness questionnaire; a book to explore deeper meanings behind specific core values; short-term behavioural measures; a personal learning plan; and a small gift (for example, a mousepad with core values printed on it). Two weeks prior to the official launch of each TWW! module, every Team Member received module inserts for their programme package. Some materials came in hard-copy form while others were downloaded from the programme website to save paper.

Interdependent Team Learning

I devised Interdependent Team Learning (ITL) to support individuals in the team context (see Figure 34). It targets teams' needs, beliefs, attitudes, behaviour and results. ITL is relevant in a change context, and is also appropriate when dealing with the maintenance needs of the organisation. The notion was inspired by governing dynamics theory which revealed to us that the best results are achieved when everyone is doing what is best for themselves *and* the group. The process is underpinned by experiential learning principles.

ITL zeros in on enhancing interdependent, interpersonal relationships. It provides teams with a platform for continuously improving work processes as they take control of their own performance and decisions to get the best results. It can be used by local teams and cross-functional teams alike. ITL respects and empowers the individual in the team context. As teamwork can mean many different things to many different people, we worked with the following definition which resonated with us:

A team is a group of interdependent individuals who have complementary skills and are committed to a shared, meaningful purpose and specific goals. They have a common, collaborative approach, clear roles and responsibilities, and hold themselves mutually accountable for the team's performance. Effective teams display confidence, enthusiasm, and seek continuously to improve their performance. (Source unknown)

Figure 34: Interdependent Team Learning: Design and Work Process

Step	Activity	Method	Target
1	Revision and Preparation Work	Individuals study Team Member package materials for the module to: a) focus on core principle in question ; b) explore deeper meanings in resources provided; c) complete questionnaire to enhance self-awareness; and d) design own personal development plan to direct their own learning. They don't have to share their results with others.	Individual Needs, Awareness and Attitude
2	Team Meeting 1 1. Introductory Activity	Teams gather to engage in Introductory Activity facilitated by their line manager and Team Leader to: a) focus as a team on core principle in question; b) share their insights and reflections on the topic; and c) come to a common understanding on what the core principle means to them in the workplace.	Individual and Team Needs and Attitude

3	2. Team Self-Assessment	Teams review Team Behavioural Outcomes (TBOs) and use scoring mechanism to create a self-assessment of how the team currently performs in relation to the TBOs. Teams now chose 3 TBOs to focus on over the duration of the module (e.g. those areas where they scored their performance as the weakest).	Individual and Team Attitude
4	Revision and Preparation	Team members review work processes and tools provided to prepare for Team Meeting 2	Individual and Team Behaviour
5	Team Meeting 2 Team Action Planning	The team create an action-plan of tasks to perform over the duration of the module (e.g. 3 months); tasks will centre around chosen TBOs and will be open to revision as teams learn through trial and error.	Individual and Team Needs, Attitude, Behaviour
6	Line Implementation of Action Plans	At this stage, the team goes back to the workplace and individuals, pairs and team as a whole perform a variety of work-related tasks as per their team compact (action-plan); team leader monitors, coaches and motivates.	Individual and Team Attitude, Behaviour and Results
7	Team Meeting 3 4. Team Results Assessment	The team gathers at the end of the module to share their successes and failures with action planning, and use the scoring mechanism to measure their performance and progress in the workplace. The team can choose to share wins with their line management and with the change team. To facilitate the dissemination of sharing and learning the change team can post action plans and results on the programme intranet.	Individual and Team Attitude, Behaviour and Results

© *O'Donovan, 2006*

To maximise on ITL, Team Leaders need to have a good understanding of their own leadership style and capabilities (hence the need for leadership workshops). They also need to understand their own team, e.g. who works well together, where some relationship-building is in order, what contribution each Team Member makes and how this could be enhanced, who needs to better understand what their colleagues do, who might be ready to move on and share their skills and where fresh blood might enhance effectiveness. This data the Team Leader can use to capitalise on opportunities which present themselves in the Team Action Plan. It can be used to identify who will complete solo tasks and who will work together in pairs. At least one Team Action Plan activity should require the input and effort of the whole team working in unison.

To support the process, packages of materials will be distributed to staff in the workplace. A flexible and buildable format allows for the inclusion of a large range of media.

Revision and Preparation Work

When the programme team sends module materials to the line circa two weeks prior to the official launch of Phase Two, Team Leaders will collect module materials from their local Line Co-ordinators and distribute Team Member Packages to their own direct reports. The Team Leaders will review the Team Leader Guide and module materials and set the date, time, and venue for the first team meeting. They each will also receive their own Team Member Package. All Team Members will review the resources provided in their individual packages to prepare themselves for the first team meeting, and create their own personal development plan. The books distributed by the Team Leaders allow staff to explore the deeper meanings behind each core principle; for example:

❖ *Who Moved My Cheese?*[5] — for a module on "Embrace Change";

❖ *Jonathan Livingston Seagull*[6] — for a module on "Continuous Learning".

---

[5] Dr Spencer Johnson, *Who Moved My Cheese?*, Vermilion, 1998.
[6] Richard Bach, *Jonathan Livingston Seagull*, Turnstone Press Ltd, 1972.

Choose books which present complex concepts in a straight-forward manner so that they can be appreciated by all.

Team Behavioural Outcomes (TBOs) provided staff with a short-term measure for principles in action, translating the abstract to the tangible. Each module Resource List provided individual staff members with direction on how they would go about designing their own personal development plan.

Figure 35: Module Resource List

RESOURCE LIST

Module Core Principle "Interdependent Teamwork":

- Module Team Behavioural Outcomes

- Books (available in-house/in local shops/on the internet)

- Related web-links

- Related in-house training courses

- Related Professional Development Programmes (universities/on-line etc)

- · Self-Awareness Questionnaire

- Booklets

The Team Meetings

An informal Meeting One encourages freedom of expression, emotional security and the avoidance of pressure. Subject to company insurance policy terms, allow the teams to decide for themselves where they will hold their meetings. Some of our teams chose the local park or the company gardens, while others arranged for the meeting to be held at a team member's home over dinner and a few beers. This we encouraged so that company meeting rooms would not be blocked solid for the duration of the programme. While we advised Team Leaders of this policy during the Leadership Workshops we decided not to put our policy on this issue in black and white, to avoid a mass exodus.

Team Meeting One

Activity 1: Introductory Activity

The purpose of Team Meeting One is to set the scene, create a focus point (the core principle), facilitate the development of trust and create a positive learning environment. The Team Leader explains the programme philosophy, policies and processes to the team and kicks off the introductory activity. This may take the form of a short experiential learning activity, learning maps or something else. Whatever the form, the activity must be carefully designed around the core principle/value so that it sets the groundwork for all other activities — and it must be fun. We chose "learning maps" given the different ability levels of Team Leaders, the different levels of staff and the different resources available across the functional areas.

Activity 2: Team Self-Assessment

The Team Leader progresses to facilitating the generation of a Team Self Assessment which will identify which areas the team needs to work on over the next three months. To do this, Team Members will first consider each of the TBOs and rate the team's current performance.

Team Behavioural Outcomes

In *Spiritual Capital*,[7] Zohar and Marshall provide us with some excellent examples of behavioural outcomes which support a culture of ethics (see examples below). TBOs are focused on grass-roots behaviour, guide staff on principles and values (which can mean many things to many people) and provide them with short-term behavioural measures. While the sample below shows the TBOs for just one value (truth) related to the core principle "integrity" to share the concept with readers, you can give staff more options when considering their performance in relation to a particular core value. This will allow them more choice when assessing their performance. When designing

---

[7] Zohar, D. and Marshall, I., *Spiritual Capital*, Bloomsbury Publishing, 2004.

TBOs (and all other materials), get the pilot teams and the Advisory Committee involved as this facilitates line ownership and ensures that materials are practical and relevant for line use across diverse areas of the business.

Figure 36: Team Behavioural Outcomes

TEAM BEHAVIOURAL OUTCOMES
Module Core Principle "Integrity"
1. Truth
• We can believe the information that senior management gives us
• We are encouraged to give managers honest and timely feedback on any matter affecting current performance, or the reputation or future of the organisation
• When changes are planned in this organisation, the likely impact is fully discussed with those who will be affected by them
• There are few hidden agendas in this organisation
• The public documents published by this organisation give stakeholders a true and complete account of its performance, character and intentions
• We are encouraged to tell the truth

Having considered the TBOs as a group, each Team Member will proceed to assess their team performance and give themselves a score. To provide emotional security, allow Team Members the option of using a secret ballot when submitting their ratings. The Team Leader will collate these, find the average score and post it on a large A0-size poster which reflects the team perception. If teams have nine TBOs, they can rate each from "1" to "9", with "1" being the strongest and "9" being the weakest.

Figure 37: Team Self-Assessment

TEAM SELF-ASSESSMENT
Module 3 "Respect the Individual"
Team Rating

Principle-Centred in Word and Spirit	☐
Empowerment	☐
Fairness	☐
Truth	☐
Respect for Diversity	☐
Field Independence	☐
Holistic	☐
A Mode of Enquiry	☐
Unique Contribution	☐

This assessment will provide the team with a snapshot on how they perceive their performance in specific areas related to the core principle under review. The Team Leader will facilitate a discussion on the results and get consensus from Team Members on which three areas they will focus on for their action-planning.

After Meeting One, the team will return to the workplace to

a) Identify which work activities and processes need their attention; and

b) Review the Tools and Techniques templates provided together with their own local processes and tools.

Tools and Techniques: The Nuts and Bolts

Continuous Quality Improvement (CQI) — a systematic, organisation-wide approach for continually improving all processes that deliver quality products and services — is the strategy many organisations are adopting to meet today's challenges and to prepare for those down the road. It is an approach one can utilise to create a service culture. The CQI Process is underpinned by four principles:[8]

* ❖ Develop a strong customer focus;

* ❖ Continually improve all processes (using quality control and management planning tools);

* ❖ Involve teams;

* ❖ Mobilise both data and team knowledge to improve decision making.

The tools used by line staff represent the nuts and bolts of the programme. They must not be used in isolation but in response to line issues. Common tools and techniques which focus on quality control and management planning include:

* ❖ Force-field Analysis

* ❖ Network Analysis

* ❖ Histogram

* ❖ Service Chain Mapping

* ❖ Stakeholder Mapping

* ❖ The Change Curve

* ❖ Affinity Diagram

* ❖ Pareto Chart

* ❖ Mind Map

---

[8] Brassard, M. and Ritter, D., *Memory Jogger*, GOAL/QPC, 1994.

- ❖ Scatter Diagram
- ❖ Porters Model
- ❖ Flowchart
- ❖ Fishbone Diagram
- ❖ Gantt Chart
- ❖ Team Meetings Process
- ❖ Lateral Thinking Activities
- ❖ TRIZ Problem Solving Process
- ❖ ASIT Methodology
- ❖ SCAMPER Process.

These tools will suit different core values/modules. For example, the Lateral Thinking Activities, TRIZ and ASIT, would be best suited for the core value "Innovation" while "the Change Curve" and "Force Field Analysis" would suit the core value "Embrace Change".

If an organisation is seeking to create a culture of ethics, the programme team may need to design new materials in-house, as the tools on the marketplace most often lack a moral perspective. Turn to Appendix 6 to see a tool which I have designed to help teams through the decision-making process navigated by an ethical perspective. Many of our tools followed this same format. On the whole, the tools are mostly interchangeable between modules and can be reused by teams as new challenges come up. To help staff, the set of tools provided for each module can be coded for easy reference.

To support the workforce in delivering on their responsibilities, provide them with a wide range of options. Then allow them to decide for themselves which tools and techniques they wish to use. In a large corporation, there will be great diversity in terms of what prior knowledge staff have of such applications. Do not assume that more senior staff know more and are better able, as such tools may not have been part of their formal education. (To get an insight into how approaches change, try to help a ten-year-old with their homework!) Also, if continuous learning does not prevail in the upper echelons, where one's position is seen as an indicator of one's heightened level of knowledge, such tools may well be perceived as rocket science.

Team Meeting Two

When a team attends Team Meeting Two soon after Team Meeting One, they can share their ideas to generate a Team Action Plan, based on what they think they need to action and how they will go about it.

Activity 3: Action Planning

Action planning under the guidance of line managers is recognised internationally as one of the most powerful interventions to transfer learning to the workplace. It builds a capacity for doing things in a new way. An action plan's content is focused around the answers to five key questions:

❖ **What?** What issues do we need to focus on?

❖ **Why?** Perhaps we scored ourselves low in the Team Self Assessment or maybe there was a specific incident which highlighted our weakness in this area.

❖ **How?** What specific and measurable actions shall we take? Which tools will we use?

❖ **Who?** Which individuals and pairs should take up specific tasks? Which tasks should be taken up by the whole team?

❖ **When?** When should specific activities be actioned? (Include specific dates and deadlines!)

After a brainstorming session, the team can consolidate their findings and come to an agreement as to how they will proceed. Give every team an A1-sized template Action Plan poster to fill in. They can post the completed action plans in their workplaces right across the organisation.

Figure 38: Team Action Plan

TEAM ACTION PLAN Module 3 "Respect The Individual"				
WHAT?	**WHY?**	**HOW?**	**WHEN?**	**WHO?**
Empowerment				
Fairness				
Truth				

The Team Leader will be responsible for monitoring progress and supporting Team Members in their efforts. Allow for revisions to the Team Action Plan as staff learn and revise their plans in the workplace.

Team Meeting Three

Activity 4: Team Results Assessment

At the end of a module, the Team Leader will gather their Team Members to debrief on the action-planning process and generate a Team Results Assessment. To kick off the process, they can post up the original "Team Self Assessment" and ask the team to consider how far they have come. The team will review their experiences and discuss what worked and what didn't. This will enhance their understanding of themselves (as individuals and as a team) and of their environment. Then they will give themselves a new rating for each of the three TBOs they focused on during the course of their action-planning. As mentioned earlier, they are under no obligation to share their results beyond their team. But if they wish to receive recognition for their successes, they can send their results to the programme team who can post them on the programme intranet. Of course, teams can share their results with their Line Champions who may organise local reward and recognition schemes. In IBM, and under Gerstner's leadership, all staff made three Personal Business Commitments (PBCs) and listed the actions they would take to deliver. Performance against these commitments was a key determinant of merit pay and variable pay.

The job of the Team Leader represents a developmental opportunity for line managers. Also, when leadership workshops are organised to train them on how to lead and develop their teams in line with the required culture, they will be best positioned to get the most out of their team members. Therefore, I would not recommend that Team Members be allowed to take up the role of leading programme activities. The division of action-planning activities will allow them ample opportunity to develop their leadership skills.

Finally, keep in mind that introductory activities may need to vary to maintain staff interest, so consider different options (e.g. learning maps, videos, simulation games) if the staff survey feedback suggests that a change is in order. I wouldn't make a habit of changing the type of activities, though, as it will be next to impossible to bring every line manager back for training each time a change is made to the methodology.

Packaging

Budget aside, how materials are packaged will be determined by the objectives of the programme, the local culture, and the make-up of the target audience.

For TWW!, we were looking to introduce fun into the workplace, which was comprised of more than 90 per cent Cantonese staff, the majority of whom were non-executives. Having lived with a local Chinese family for my first few years in Hong Kong, I had valuable insights into the local culture and what might appeal. One aspect of it is that the local adults enjoy cartoons and gimmick products. To sell this idea to the programme director in the early days, I told him that Hong Kong is the birthplace of "Hello Kitty" and I could recall fights breaking out at the local McDonalds in the early 1990s as scores of adults queued for promotional giveaways during their lunch breaks. Looking around, we could see plenty of examples where the local government and businesses used cartoon images to sell everything from new legislation to mobile phones. So we went with this approach and designed module posters, intranet notes and materials packaging which centred around six fun images e.g. a beaver working on a dam represented "continuous improvement", a group of ants carrying off a chocolate represented "teamwork" and a beautiful butterfly emerging from its pupa represented the core value "embrace change". The posters displayed around the bank brought a smile to most faces and helped us to bring fun into an overly serious workplace.

I found that top management bought into the thinking behind the packaging very quickly and the locals loved it, but some middle management expatriates did not find the packaging and posters to their liking. One expatriate told me so as I had a drink at the company bar one evening. When I explained the rationale behind our choice to him, and why it was prudent to go with the majority audience, he was able to look beyond the cover and was more accepting.

9.2 Support Activities and Embedding Mechanisms

A programme of any nature is a portfolio of projects which is managed as a whole. Programme management allows organisations a structured framework for defining and implementing change, and has the potential to deliver benefits that are of strategic importance. While some projects represent core activities (learning materials development and facilitator training) others will support programme implementation (workforce alignment, distribution activities and communications activities). The remainder will act as longer-term embedding mechanisms for the new culture (what leaders pay attention to, measure and control, leadership workshops, performance management, reward and recognition, etc).

9.2.1 Support Activities

The purpose of support activities is to facilitate the implementation of the programme. Such activities are temporary in nature and will terminate when they have fulfilled their purpose or when the programme has come to an end. For example, with the close of the phase one event, it will no longer be necessary for the programme team to work with line managers to organise attendance. Catering activities will halt, as will other activities designed to facilitate event logistics.

9.2.2 Cultural Embedding Mechanisms

Cultural embedding mechanisms anchor the new way of doing things into the company culture. Projects which come under this heading are more permanent in nature and can endure long after the programme ends. As each core principle is taken into consideration for materials development, the strategic management team will be considering ideas put forward in the programme proposal which will embed the new culture. Top management and functional heads will work in concert to implement ideas and institutionalise new approaches. Schein has identified *primary embedding mechanisms* and *secondary rein-forcement and articulation mechanisms* (see below) used by founders and leaders to embed and transmit culture and below I share some of my thoughts on each of these.

Primary Embedding Mechanisms

❖ **What leaders regularly pay attention to, measure and control** reinforces to the community the key beliefs and values held in the upper echelons. This is why the very design of the strategic implementation plan in this book allows leaders with a concrete mechanism to pay attention to, measure and control the evolution of their corporate culture.

❖ **How leaders react** to critical incidents and organisational crises serve as "moments of truth" because the decisions they make and how they make them will either reinforce the old rules of the game or set new standards. During culture change, this is probably the single most important measure because leaders' approach to decision-making will be tested again and again. Just one mishandled incident can undermine a Trojan effort on the part of the workforce at large and when executive management slip up repeatedly, this undermines the whole change effort.

❖ **The observed criteria for resource allocating** will show if leaders put their money where their mouth is. The criteria will also reflect the central paradigm of the organisation and any hidden assumptions. From this staff will be able to answer some questions for themselves; for example, is the focus on bottom-line cost containment or top-line growth?

❖ **Deliberate role-modelling, teaching and coaching** on the part of leaders might well be the hardest part for some because it means walking the talk and being congruent in word and action. But it helps considerably when the CEO cascades the baton of leadership and all line managers are given leadership training in the desired beliefs, attitudes and behaviours. When leaders across the board give peer reinforcement and encouragement this builds trust and creates a positive shift in the climate. Training can provide support with coaching and other skills development courses.

❖ **Observed criteria for allocation of rewards and status** include a) the formal organisational processes and b) any informal processes used by cliques to divert privileges to their cronies. Make no mistake, if there are two sets of rules, the workforce will be well aware of this. During times of culture change, informal and unethical practices must be done away with if the leadership team is to build trust. Also, the new attitudes and behaviours must be rewarded, with status given to those who demonstrate them.

❖ **Observed criteria for recruitment, selection, promotion, retirement and excommunication** are among the best measures of a corporate culture at any one time because they reflect what is rewarded and what is punished in each of these different areas. Ideally, all people systems should be aligned with the core principles and values.

Secondary Articulation and Reinforcement Mechanisms

❖ **Organisation design and structure** reflect founders' and leaders' ideas about how to share power and organise themselves. A tall hierarchy encourages central control whereas a matrix structure facilitates line decentralised decision-making but can cause great confusion.

❖ **Organisational systems and procedures** encourage consistency and the development of a strong culture. They must be aligned with the vision and strategies (which in turn must be constructive and well thought out) because a strong culture is not necessarily conducive to productivity and results.

❖ **Formal rites and rituals** can include ceremonies and documented *procedures* for dealing with a range of situations. Because corporate cultures are, for the most part, unmanaged, formal corporate ceremonies often lack the depth and meaning typical of religious and national ceremonies. However, **informal rites and rituals** have a more powerful effect because they are part of the regular way of doing things and constitute the unwritten rules of the game.

❖ **The design of physical space, façades and buildings** can tell us a great deal about a company. Buildings might be glamorous and sexy or plain and staid and this will affect how people feel about working in them and how they feel about themselves and their employer organisation. Grand symbols like statues, fountains and state-of-the-art buildings can often be more than decorative as they can serve to influence how the world perceives the organisation and how the workforce perceives themselves.

❖ When preserved, **stories about important people and events** are a very powerful way of reinforcing the corporate identity, e.g. Henry Ford's vision and the story behind the launch of the Model T automobile. It is extremely rare for such stories to carry more than a grain of truth because storytellers are just as susceptible as anyone else to being "right-sized" or "down-sized".

❖ **Formal statements of organisational philosophy, creeds and charters** usually reflect the *espoused culture*, or maybe even the required culture, but most probably not the prevailing culture. As such, they are often no guide to the actual beliefs and assumptions that direct the workforce. That said, during the implementation of a culture change programme such formal statements can serve to guide the workforce when the leadership team recommits to them and follows up on this by providing tools that help transfer abstract values to real situations.

Overall, the levers you choose for your programme will depend on the challenges your organisation faces, how much support you are getting in different parts of the business, which aspect of the existing culture you wish to retain and how much change the prevailing culture can absorb. The greater the organisation's ability to embrace and absorb change, and the greater the support in different parts of the business, the greater will be the range of mechanisms implemented. Figure 2 on page 11 demonstrates how one can map the differing nature of activities and projects for a culture change programme. I would encourage programme managers to do the same for their own initiatives. In Appendix 1, a selection of the TWW! support activities and cultural embedding mechanisms can be reviewed.

9.3 The Setting

9.3.1 Phase One: Centralised

A centralised environment creates a captive audience and allows management a lot of control over the internal customer experience, the quality of facilitation, the purity of information regarding vision, philosophy and principles and attendance/ participation levels.

You don't have to pull out all of the stops and have a purpose-built event hall as we did, but if floor space is available, and the workforce runs into the thousands, then it is cost-effective to do so. Also, the event hall does not have to be elaborate unless you are looking to communicate a significant change in the culture. When one contractor could not accept that each payment took a few days to process and threatened to stop work so that I would have to cancel the official opening, I told him in no uncertain terms that all I needed was four walls and a roof, and the show would go ahead with or without his help. As soon the words were out of my mouth, I realised the truth in the statement; the materials are the heart of the programme and once you get those right and have trained facilitators in place, then you can improvise in other areas if necessary. Keep in mind that as the programme is running, in-house training courses may well continue to run and Training may well require the use of their own facilities. If you do decide to use a training facility or hired hotel rooms, then bright posters with meaningful messages will jazz up the learning environment. If an organisation is looking to break down silo mentalities and/or enhance the flow of information across the organisation, arrange event logistics so that participants are grouped in cross-functional teams.

If you decide to go with outdoor activities also, you may want to take a leaf out the Cathay Pacific Airways book. For their programme, they hired hotel rooms at a local resort which has an outdoor "ropes course". It only took us five minutes to walk from one setting to the other. Also, as all service staff went through the programme, the company was able to secure great deals for the use of the premises and facilities.

9.3.2 Phase Two: Localised

In a busy workplace, the idea of rolling out a major programme can seem daunting and unappealing, as it may seem to some that an extra burden is being added to the line. However, if the cultural needs analysis and/or other feedback indicates that the prevailing culture is harmful to the company, then there is no easy way out. The learning of core principles and values must be transferred to the day-to-day workplace so that staff find better ways of doing things. Having already reviewed the roles and responsibilities map together with the programme philosophy and methodology, it should be patently clear by now that the workforce is not being asked to do anything which would not be part of their job anyway. As the workforce goes through the learning curve, the new way of doing things will become second nature and require less effort.

When the programme moves to the workplace, the line has responsibility for its success or failure. For the first couple of modules, the programme team may find that the line is trying to pass responsibility back to them. This must be discouraged. The programme manager can certainly listen to feedback and work with the top team to smooth the way for line staff but ownership now rests squarely with the line. I would strongly recommend that the first time this programme is run, staff are organised to work in their own teams, inviting colleagues up and down the service chain when appropriate. Teams must embrace the new way of doing things with their immediate team, and in their immediate environment, before they can aspire towards good cross-functional teamwork (extra modules can be run for newcomers). Only if cross-functional colleagues make up a staff member's immediate team, does this principle not apply.

9.4 The Implementation Plans

A core task of the programme manager is to manage the portfolio of projects and activities, managing the interdependencies and spreading risk. The programme implementation plans can be designed using Gantt Charts and/or Critical Path Analysis. Each has its own strengths and weaknesses. I would use both, and in this order.

9.4.1 Gantt Charts

Gantt charts are a project planning tool originally designed for the construction industry. Computer software has taken away much of the hard work, making them a very user-friendly option for project managers. The steps required to track a project are simple: make a list of tasks and sub-tasks, assign each a "start" and "finish" date and assign the person responsible for each by marking in their initials. Insert milestones (interim goals and important checkpoints) because these can be used to highlight scheduling problems early. For a complex *programme*, manageability can be an issue when using this tool, so to keep everything under control create a Gantt chart for each *project* and keep tasks and subtasks to less than twenty. This will help ensure that each of your Gantt charts (or project sheets) fits onto a page and is easy to read. When all of the project sheets are completed, use the data to create a basic programme overview that outlines tasks only and fits onto one page. This will become your masterplan or overall snapshot of projects and activities. Be flexible and on top of things; as the different projects evolve update the relevant project sheet and also the programme masterplan.

9.4.2 Critical Path Analysis

Once a Gantt Chart has been prepared for each project, the programme manager can adapt traditional Critical Path Analysis to suit programme management. Simply account for *projects* in the network, rather than *project tasks* to track the big picture. Critical Path Analysis is good at distinguishing between critical and non-critical projects. Critical projects are those projects that, if not completed on time, will cause the whole programme to be delayed unless additional resources can be invested to recover the slippage. Non-critical ones are those that can be delayed without necessarily impacting the overall programme deadline. The distinction between critical and non-critical projects helps the programme manager when deciding on priorities, both at the beginning of the programme and during it, and facilitates the decision-making process.

If implementation plans are to have any chance of being an accurate guide to the future, they must be "live" — that is, working documents which are revised and rewritten by the programme manager, who takes into account circumstances as they unfold. They should be fluid and not be a series of predictions "carved in stone".

9.5 Chapter Summary

The culture change cycle has three phases. Phase One un-freezes mindsets via experiential learning and instils commitment for a shared philosophy and purpose; Phase Two gives staff the tools to change their way of doing things and fosters competence in key principles and values. A period of readjustment follows (Phase Three), where the workforce consolidates learning while the leadership team reinforces alignment. For all three stages of the change cycle, culture embedding mechanisms anchor the new way of doing things into everyday practices to perpetuate consistency.

The programme methodology will reflect the programme philosophy defined by the leadership team. Through a combination of experiential activities, Self-Directed Learning and Interdependent Team Learning, the workforce will weave principles and values into their everyday work, translating the abstract to the tangible. Tools and techniques will support the process and represent the nuts and bolts of the programme. They can focus on competencies like "service" and "innovation" and should be underpinned by moral principles like "integrity" to allow for enduring value. Tools should not be used in isolation but in response to line needs. While many resources are available on the internet, much of the materials may need to be designed in-house to suit organisational needs. This will certainly be the case if an organisation is seeking to create a culture of ethics, as tools in the marketplace often lack a moral perspective. Materials packaging will reflect the local culture and must appeal to the majority audience.

As the core materials are being designed, a host of supporting activities will get underway. Some of these projects will support programme implementation while others will act as long-term cultural embedding mechanisms. The strategic management team will refer to the original programme proposal to reach consensus on how new approaches will be institutionalised. For each core principle, specific initiatives will be identified which will embed the new culture and support workforce efforts as they implement their action plans. While the top team and functional heads will have responsibility for implementing any proposals, the programme manager can follow up on work-in-progress and advise the Steering Committee on this.

A centralised environment for Phase One allows top management a lot of control over the internal customer experience, the quality of facilitation, the purity of information regarding vi-

sion, philosophy and values, and attendance levels. It also provides a captive audience. If the workforce runs into the tens of
thousands it may be more economical to make use of internal
floorspace to create a purpose-built event hall. For a smaller
workforce another option is to hire local hotel rooms and deco-
rate them with theme-related posters. A localised setting for
Phase Two gives top management little control over the quality
and level of participation. It is now up to the Department and
functional heads to drive the programme in their own area of the
business. High-quality programme materials and the smooth
implementation of programme logistics will inspire confidence
and generate momentum in the workplace. For best results,
have staff apply the ITL process with their immediate colleagues
before aspiring towards excellent cross-functional teamwork
(which will require the full support of the business heads).

To design programme implementation plans a number of
tools are available. Gantt Charts and Critical Path Analysis have
different strengths and weaknesses and can be used in unison.
Create a Gantt Chart for each project and, when all the details
have been nailed down, develop a Critical Path Analysis which
highlights the critical path of *projects* in the overall programme.
This will help the programme manager to manage the portfolio
of projects, manage interdependencies, and spread risk.
Whichever tool you decide on, don't get too hung up on the first
draft, as environmental changes will demand a degree of fluid-
ity and responsiveness to change.

10

COMMUNICATE VISION
AND PROGRAMME ROLL-OUT

Having completed the strategic planning and design stage, it is now time to implement that culture change strategy. To prime the workforce for this it is necessary to:

❖ Communicate the vision before the implementation of Phase One and reinforce why the change is happening;

❖ Share more detailed information on the mechanics before any rollout.

How these tasks are actioned can make or break the programme.

10.1 Communication Channel Analysis

Different communication mechanisms serve different purposes. We have interactive channels that are consultative in nature and one-way channels that simply impart ideas and messages. Some mechanisms are suitable for internal or external use only, while others are transferable to both environments. These differences we need to take into careful consideration when choosing the most effective means to consult with our stakeholders and convey key messages because to secure buy-in we need to be clear on the difference between the consultative and the one-way, and for governance and audit purposes we need to be able to demonstrate a practical understanding of the difference between the different options available to us (e.g. a focus group and a workshop). If these subtleties are not understood then it will spawn an activity-centred communication plan that does not secure buy-in or stand up to third party scrutiny.

Figure 39 illustrates how a variety of approaches measure up against one another in key areas.

Figure 39: Communication Channel Analysis: Usage

	Consultative	One-way	Internal Stake-holders	External Stake-holders
Articles	☒	☑	☑	☑
Booklets	☒	☑	☑	☑
Briefings	☒	☑	☑	☑
DVDs/VCDs	☒	☑	☑	☑
Emails/Memos/Letters	☑	☒	☑	☑
Events	☑	☒	☑	☑
Exhibitions	☒	☑	☑	☑
Focus Groups	☑	☒	☑	☑
Interviews	☑	☒	☑	☑
Intranet	☒	☑	☑	☒
Internet	☒	☑	☒	☑
Meetings	☑	☒	☑	☑
Newsletters	☒	☑	☑	☒
Posters	☒	☑	☑	☒
Practical Tools	☑	☒	☑	☒
Presentations	☒	☑	☑	☑
Press Releases	☒	☑	☒	☑
Progress Reports	☒	☑	☑	☒
Q&A Session	☑	☒	☑	☑
Roadshows	☑	☒	☑	☒
Speeches	☒	☑	☑	☑
Surveys	☑	☒	☑	☑
TV & Radio	☒	☑	☒	☑
Workshops	☑	☒	☑	☒

Below, we take a closer look at each of these options.

❖ **Articles** are stories and news features that focus on specific topics. They can be posted in the internal magazine to share programme successes together with news of any milestones reached. If the local newspaper gets wind of your programme there may be a request to share programme details in newspaper articles. Hold back until some significant wins come through and there is something to celebrate.

❖ **Booklets** can come in varying formats and can be used for a number of purposes; e.g. to share vision/mission/values statements together with strategic imperatives; to share core principles and values and how your culture change programme can help staff action them on a day-to-day basis; or to answer those questions that are central to staff concerns.

❖ **Briefings** are often used internally by line managers to update operational staff about any day-to-day changes. Briefings are one-way and mostly suitable for internal use.

❖ **DVDs/VCDs** can be visually appealing and fun; such media can add a bit of jazz to your change programme and help win hearts and minds.

❖ **Emails/Memos/Letters** are often used to follow up and seek clarification after meetings. The very nature of correspondence is such that it elicits a response of some sort, be it compliance or otherwise.

❖ **Events** require a considerable amount of time, money and organisation, provide the opportunity to demonstrate top management commitment to the stakeholder engagement process and raise the profile of a change programme. Events generally include a mixed bag of communication activities; e.g. presentations, videos and DVDs, question-and-answer sessions, workshop activities and focus groups.

❖ **Exhibitions** are one-way channels that publicly display information. They can be used internally or opened up to the public.

❖ **Focus Groups** are the most commonly used method of social research. A facilitator leads a group through a structured discussion to gain feedback on the specific issue or issues under review. Handouts with bullet points can help keep the discussion focused. The facilitator is seeking input for a specific purpose and nothing other is expected from participants apart from their candid views.

❖ **Interviews**; can be held with one or more individuals. During the strategic planning and design stage they are most useful for identifying local issues and securing the buy-in of senior executives.

❖ **Intranet**; internal websites can act as a portal to all programme communication activities that have already been put in the "public domain"; e.g. presentations, booklets, brochures, newsletters, speeches by the chief executive, articles, maps, survey results, any programme competition related information and team action-planning results. When considering this option, check what percentage of the workforce is computer-literate and how many have intranet access because this will have a direct impact on the value of this approach.

❖ **Internet**; all major organisations have a webpage that shares some basic company information (e.g. history, objectives and annual reports). These days *blogs* (or digital diaries) have become very common and are used by individuals to shared their personal interests and issues of concern to them. To keep internal issues off the internet, ensure that staff have internal communication channels that they trust.

❖ **Meetings and Discussions**; *bi-lateral meetings* are those meetings that are held on a one-to-one basis. They are most suitable when individuals and issues require confidentiality.

Sometimes less powerful stakeholders might have genuine concerns that are not in line with the thinking of bigger stakeholders. Bilateral meetings allow them the opportunity to be heard without any negative repercussions. *Group meetings* are suitable when discussion and consensus is required. This channel is most effective when all are given a chance to be heard and when the environment is conducive to teamwork. Round tables work best because the politics of "who sits next to whom" are removed. Also, it's a good idea to arrange seating so that parties from different groups or organisations are next to each other. This helps remove any sense of "them" and "us".

❖ A well-written **newsletter** will provide a high level snapshot of activities and projects within the programme. Different departments within the organisation might decide to print their own newsletters. Encourage this ownership because custom-made tools that celebrate local wins and share progress reports can only be a good thing. Email newsletters and e-zines are very popular these days

❖ **Posters** can have a dramatic effect and fun images can help improve the social environment in the workplace.

❖ **Practical Tools** are interactive in that they facilitate learning and the application of learning, encouraging users to measure their own progress and adapt their approach where necessary; such tools are mostly suitable for internal use where guidance on their use is readily available.

❖ **Presentations** are another one-way communication channel often used to sell an idea or a product. They comprise of visuals (e.g. slides) supplemented by a narrative from the presenter. Presentations are suitable for internal use and also lend themselves to use with business groups, local chambers of commerce and government agencies.

❖ **Press Releases** should be prepared by the Public Relations department. It helps if writers are experienced journalists who understand their external audience very well. Press releases are often used to share milestone events, programme successes and to respond to inaccurate and negative press.

❖ **Progress Reports** are regular updates used to help overseers keep abreast of development. For example, where Department Heads ask Line Champions to produce a one-page summary report once a month to outline local programme activity, points covered might include:

- Percentage of teams who received their materials in a timely and effective manner;

- Percentage of teams who have rolled out a particular module (local activity);

- Any team issues and concerns;

- Team challenges and learning;

- Best practices, outcomes and results.

❖ **Q&A Sessions**; during times of change a lots of questions are going to be raised and it is best if the workforce hears the answers directly from the leadership team. Organise regular question-and-answer sessions on a local level. Also, and if the situation demands it, put in place a process to protect the identity of those who raise questions.

❖ **Roadshows** can be a cross between exhibitions and events; ideally a team of champions would organise a show focused on a particular theme (e.g. vision/mission/values) and this show moves from one location to another to facilitate work groups. A poor roadshow is one-way, while a good one is informative, interactive and consultative.

❖ **Speeches** impart opinions, knowledge and ideas and, depending on the oratory skills of the speaker, can be very motivating or very dull.

❖ **TV and Radio**; once results come through and the culture change is confirmed this can be celebrated in company advertisements on television.

❖ **Workshops** equip participants with knowledge or skills and can encourage a change in attitude; a trainer or facilitator leads a group through a structured activity, participants explore new ways of doing things and practise their newly acquired skills (or test new insights) in a controlled environment.

Apart from these formal and structured communication mechanisms we also have informal channels like sporting activities and social functions. It is a well-known fact that most major business decisions are made on the golf course. And it is common practice for business people to take key clients and stakeholders out for sumptuous meals. These options are examples of informal communication channels and they are best suited for managing those powerful stakeholders who need extra special care and attention.

During the strategic planning and design stages the leadership team will use a lot of consultative communication channels to get the input of key stakeholders to inform programme design. At programme roll-out stage, the communication channels will be mostly information-sharing in nature (key dates, key values and messages, answers to "what's in it for me?", etc), and when line teams start to gather for their first module and action-planning activities the local process will again become more consultative from the grass-roots up.

10.2 Communicate the Vision

Having considered the theory, we can now move on to a more practical perspective. For the workforce to understand the significance of the strategic programme and why they should embrace it, it is essential for the Executive Sponsor to set the stage. This will include communicating the vision and getting

across to the workforce the fact that, in the face of business realities, changing the culture is a safer option than sticking to the
established way of doing things. The Executive Sponsor will be
the face of the programme and be responsible for spearhead-
ing all communication activities, with the leadership team taking up the baton to cascade messages.

To communicate the vision in a convincing manner, a sense
of urgency must be established. This is easier to achieve when
costs are under pressure, revenues are being squeezed or market share is being eroded. When the workforce has become
complacent because of past successes, a bigger communication effort with stronger messages is required of the leadership
team. In *Who Said Elephants Can't Dance?*[1] Lou Gerstner shared
a story which captures so very well many of the key issues that
CEOs face when attempting to establish a sense of urgency in a
large and complacent workforce.

In the spring of 1995 Gerstner, then CEO of IBM, convened
his senior management team at a hotel in New York. Over 400
people from around the world were present, representing
every part of the company. Gerstner kicked off the convention
by drawing attention to two charts: one for market share and
one for customer satisfaction. IBM had lost more than half its
market share since 1985 in an industry that was expanding rapidly, ranking eleventh overall. The customer satisfaction chart
was equally dismal. He shared photos of CEOs of some of their
top competitors and read quotes where they belittled IBM publicly. Making deliberate use of passion, anger and directness,
Gerstner made personal what competitors were doing to the
company in the marketplace: "They're coming into our house
and taking our children's and our grandchildren's college
money. That's what they're doing"; and "They took that market
share away and caused this pain [125,000 IBM employees lost
their jobs] in this company." Gerstner expressed frustration

[1] Lou Gerstner, *Who Said Elephants Can't Dance?*, Harpers Business, 2002.

and bewilderment about the recurring failure of the workforce to execute strategy and the company's endless tolerance of it:

> We don't demand implementation and follow-up. We don't set deadlines. Or when they're missed, we don't raise some questions. But we do create task forces; and then they create task forces. We don't execute, because, again, we don't have the perspective that what counts outside [the company] is more important than what counts inside. Too many IBMers fight change if it's not in their personal interest.

The CEO shared his feelings about the company's opportunities and prospects. He considered the people in the room to be the finest collection of talent assembled in any institution in any industry, and he was convinced that the company had unlimited potential — but only if the workforce was willing to make the behavioural changes in the corporate culture. After this convention, Gerstner knew he needed to provide risk-takers with a symbol and a structure to validate their new way of doing thing, so he created the Senior Leadership Group, inviting "living, breathing role models" to join. Members would be asked to focus on topics of leadership and change.

At HSBC Hong Kong, Executive Sponsor Raymond Or launched each phase of the programme by sharing the task with the leadership team. For the Phase One event, he or another member of the top management team would take centre-stage at our daily live Q&A session. Each speaker would share market realities with a fresh audience of 120 staff, and outline how challenges were being addressed in their area of the business. For example, in response to changing customer expectations, HSBC successfully launched e-banking in August 2000 and as the virtual business publication *AsiaWise* noted: "HSBC has leapt from Laggardsville to Best House in the Neighbourhood." Also, as work was moved across the border to mainland China, detailed plans were put in place to provide information, support and counselling to any affected employees. Redeployment opportunities were provided to those staff who had the potential and desire to take on new roles in the bank. And in response to challenges felt by the retail bank, which included a rapid fall in mortgage rates, interest rate deregulation (which would increase the competition for deposits) and competition in the cards market (which would put pressure on fees) a drive was on to increase business volumes and find new sources of income.

Mr Or particularly liked to kick off the opening sessions of our Leadership Workshops, as this would enable him to address leaders at all levels as they gathered together. He tempered his passionate speeches with humour and often would get so involved in his delivery that he would run over time. Line managers would stand up from their seats to communicate attentiveness and the energy in the room would build in waves. It really was something to behold and I knew his efforts to motivate Team Leaders would make our job easier as the day progressed. Mr Or would detail what people could expect and when, and how the programme was helping the bank to deliver on strategies. He would explain to all why the change was happening, give the business reasons for it, define the journey and explain how we would reach our destination. He also encouraged two-way communication by asking his audience to utilise the electronic "Ask Top Management" forum to create positive discussions on change.

While a CEO will seek to establish a sense of urgency with the leadership team at the outset, I would suggest that the broad and dramatic communication of business realities is done only when the leadership team is ready to roll out a culture change programme which is learning- and development-centred. Giving staff the tools to embrace change will ensure that the resulting increase in survival anxiety across the organisation is moderated with a decrease in learning anxiety.

10.3 Core Programme Roll-Out

The actual roll out of the core programme will include a mixture of carefully coordinated communication activities which target specific parties with specific messages. The staggering of activities allowed one to cascade messages across the organization, build momentum and prepare the organization for official roll-out. Figure 40 shows the finer detail of the workforce communications plan for the roll-out of the first module of TWW! Phase Two. Having consulted with staff during the design stage and taken aboard their feedback, we would now turn to mostly one-way communication channels to impart information on the values, design process and logistics. But once the programme was launched the process would again be a lot more consultative as staff used regular team meetings to create action plans together and implement these in the workplace. Results they would feed back to line management and the programme team.

Having briefed the top team, trained Team Leaders, positioned Line Materials Coordinators to handle materials and informed staff across the organization of the upcoming launch, Team Member Packages of learning tools were distribution to every individual staff member. The wave of activities leading up to this moment generated a sense of excitement and anticipation. By blanketing the whole of the bank with a carefully structured communications campaign, we could ensure that we reached everyone in one fell swoop and that everyone received the same messages before any rumour mongering began. Everyone would know exactly what to expect and when.

Figure 40: TWW! Phase 2 Module 1 Roll-Out Communications Plan for Workforce

Group I.D.	Stakeholder Group	Outcomes Required	Key Messages	Channels	Owner/s	Date
AC01/1	**Top Team**	Understand and fully support overall roll-out plan	• Programme is strategically driven and will help deliver on strategic imperatives	Top Team Walk-Thru (1–1.5 hrs)	Programme Manager	13 Aug 2001
			• Leaders must "walk the talk"	CEO Briefing on Market Realities	Executive Sponsor	Early Sept 2001
DH01/1	**Dept Heads**	Take ownership for successful implementation of programme in local business area	• Each department head is responsible for supporting and championing programme in own business area	Dept Heads Briefing (4 x 2 hrs)	Programme Manager	Mid-Sept 2001
			• The line has ownership for the success or failure of phase two			

Group I.D.	Stakeholder Group	Outcomes Required	Key Messages	Channels	Owner/s	Date
LC01/1	**Line Champions**	Support Dept Heads and provide guidance to Team Leaders	• TWW! is a chance to take HSBC a step forward. Do everything you can to provide positive, productive support to it, participating with your teams and providing visible support and assistance to your Team Leaders and staff.	Executive Sponsor Letter (109)	Executive Sponsor	3 Oct 2001
				Communication Packages (109)	Programme Manager	8 Oct 2001
				Line Briefings	Dept Heads	By mid-Oct 2001
LMC01/1	**Line Materials Coordinators**	Efficient and effective distribution of all materials across whole bank	• Specific items and quantities to expect • Key dates for forwarding materials to Team Leaders	Email (1,400 copies)	Programme Manager	28 Sept 2001

Group I.D.	Stakeholder Group	Outcomes Required	Key Messages	Channels	Owner/s	Date
TL01/1	**Team Leaders**	Develop line managers leadership and facilitation skills Equip Team Leaders to deliver modules	• The Bank has to change • TWW! is how we are going to do it • Team Leaders have a personal responsibility towards their team members • Top management is committed to supporting TWW!	Leadership Workshop Invitation Cards (1,400) Leadership Workshops (140) Team Leader Packages of Materials (1,400)	Programme Manager	15–31 Oct 2001
TM01/1	**Team Members**	Equip Team Members to fully participate in module activities		Team Member Packages	Programme Manager	29 Oct – 2 Nov 2001

Group I.D.	Stakeholder Group	Outcomes Required	Key Messages	Channels	Owner/s	Date
GWF01/1	All	Mentally prepare for roll-out and consider logistics e.g. collecting materials, supporting one another etc.	Get ready! Phase 2 will roll out in a couple of weeks' time	TWW! Intranet News	Programme Manager & Corp. Comms.	8 Oct 2001
				TWW! Bulletin	Programme Manager	8 Oct 2001
				Posters	Programme Manager	8 Oct 2001
				Staff magazine article	Programme Manager	10 Oct 2001
				Intranet Headline News	Programme Manager & Corp. Comms.	5 Nov 2001
				Programme Website Launch	Programme Manager	5 Nov 2001

© *O'Donovan, 2006*

10.4 Control of Communications

Corporate communications usually comes under the control of the CEO during times of major cultural change but this is not always the case. For example, in HSBC Hong Kong, general communications remained under the control of the department head because there were plenty of other initiatives besides our programme, but our change management communications came under the remit of the programme team. We produced our own videos, booklets, letters, speeches, etc., and worked with corporate communications to utilise media like the internal magazine to post bi-monthly articles about the programme. The Steering Committee would review draft submissions before they were signed off by the Executive Sponsor. For best results, invite the head of communications onto the Steering Committee to ensure that the integrity of core principles and values is upheld in all media.

10.5 Chapter Summary

To communicate the vision and programme roll-out, a plethora of options are available to the strategic management team. Some mechanisms are consultative while others are one-way, and some are suitable for either internal or external use while others are transferable to both environments. We need to take these differences into account because if they are not understood, this will result in an activity-centred communications plan that does not secure buy-in, share key messages effectively or survive third-party scrutiny.

For the workforce to understand the significance of the strategic programme and why they should support it, it is essential for the leadership team to prime them by communicating the vision and market realities. The approach taken will reflect the weight of the challenges facing the organisation, the leadership style of the CEO and the level of urgency established in the upper echelons.

If the CEO and the business leaders take personal responsibility for communicating key messages, it is an indicator that they are behind the programme and understand its importance to strategy implementation. However, if the vision and market realities are not communicated in an organised fashion, and leave open the question as to whether or not the top team is "with the programme", then the workforce will dismiss the initiative before it takes its first breath. The leadership team needs to understand that the broad and dramatic communication of market realities will automatically increase survival anxiety and create a butterfly effect. To conduct this activity in a responsible fashion, give your workforce something to hold onto during scary times by providing them with both the context to embrace change and the knowledge and tools they need to do things a new way.

Successful programme roll-out will require an airtight implementation plan which staggers communication and distributions activities so that key messages are cascaded from the top team to grassroots. Have in place feedback mechanisms and, above all, recruit people across the organisation to take ownership for the successful roll-out. From now on, the success or failure of the programme is in their hands.

For best results and to reach all staff, blanket the whole organisation with a branded and carefully planned communications campaign, maximising on all communications media. Usually internal communications will come under the control of the chief executive during times of major change. If this is not the case, and the programme is generating a huge volume of communications activities, then give the programme manager the responsibility. Invite the head of corporate communications as a member of the Steering Committee as this will help ensure that messages are not altered to the detriment of the spirit intended when the programme team works cross-functionally with members of corporate communications. All drafts of articles and speeches and video rundowns should be submitted to the Steering Committee for review before being endorsed by the Executive Sponsor. And finally, as excellent communication is central to the success of a culture change programme, ensure it is not left in the hands of those who are change resistant.

11

Manage the Human Landscape

How the human landscape is managed during change can be one of the most significant and powerful determinants of whether a culture change programme is successful. In this chapter we will consider how change impacts employees differently, how to navigate the emotional dynamics and how to manage resistance.

Once the programme has been rolled out, shifts will occur on the human landscape as people demonstrate varying degrees of support and resistance to the new way of doing things. Some ten per cent will recognize the opportunities in change and quickly come onboard while, at the extreme opposite end, a hard core ten per cent will not only resist but either leave or try to hold the whole organisation back. Laggards fall in between, representing some eighty per cent of the workforce, and will have mixed feelings about the news of change. How individuals respond to change and cluster in groups will affect the dynamics across the whole organisation.

11.1 Champions, Laggards and Resistors

There are a number of factors which have a major influence on how each person responds to news of change and these factors will determine whether they cluster with the champions, the laggards or the resistors.

Figure 41: Responses to Change

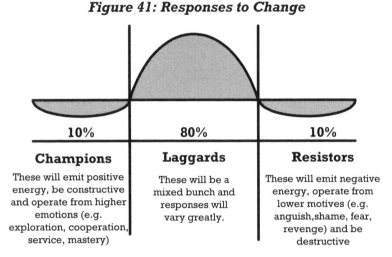

10%	80%	10%
Champions	**Laggards**	**Resistors**
These will emit positive energy, be constructive and operate from higher emotions (e.g. exploration, cooperation, service, mastery)	These will be a mixed bunch and responses will vary greatly.	These will emit negative energy, operate from lower motives (e.g. anguish,shame, fear, revenge) and be destructive

© O'Donovan, 2006

11.1.1 How News of Change is Delivered

How people perceive change at the outset is governed in no small part by how the news of change is delivered. When information is shared face-to-face by key leaders and in a timely manner, each individual has an opportunity to digest all of the implications and ask questions. Whatever conclusions the individual comes to will be their response to the full picture. In contrast, and when news is delivered prematurely, leaders will not have all the information to answer staff questions and this can raise undue anxiety and hostility. Anxious staff will fill in the blanks for themselves and some may come to the wrong conclusions. Also, when news is delivered too late, when it gets to the press before it gets to the workforce, or when it is withheld altogether, this can lead to a sense of betrayal and do irreparable damage. In March 2005, UK companies became legally responsible for communicating to all staff information which will affect them. While some organisations were not happy about this development, others embraced it quickly, as experience has taught them that it pays to be transparent with their workforce. Those who already have good practices in place will not feel the impact of this new legislation but those who have been managing internal communications badly will experience pressure to adapt as a result of this external force for change.

11.1.2 People Attach Meaning to News

When change is introduced by management each individual perceives a shift in their ability to have their needs met. Based on their own circumstances, interests and values, individuals will attach meaning to the news and the set of assumptions they arrive at will produce energy, motives and emotions, all of which can be positive, negative or fluctuating in between. Their own interpretation of the news and any conclusions they arrive at will determine whether an individual becomes a champion, laggard or resistor. So during the strategic planning stage, the top team needs to consider what meanings different stakeholder groups will attach to news of change, and how some may feel threatened. This input should be used to tailor the design of the communications plan and learning materials.

11.1.3 Line Manager Cues

During times of upheaval staff will take their cues from line managers who might have more information and a better understanding as to how change will impact staff locally. As a result of environmental shifts resources will be allocated differently and this will impact budgets, manpower deployment, the availability of overtime work, working hours, salary expectations, etc. If the boss is looking worried, this will impact team morale, so line managers need to be aware they are being watched closely for cues.

11.1.4 Political Agendas

In a highly political environment, the agendas of individuals and cliques will impact how news of change is received. If the organisation has built a complex defence mechanism against change, career politicians may well be drafted in to act as antibodies and undermine change initiatives. Often these are mediocre performers who are kept on because of their usefulness in maintaining the status quo.

11.2 Support the Cast

Asking the workforce to buy into the vision and strategies is asking for positive energy, good intentions and positive emotions. This can only come about when line managers have the knowledge, skills and attitude to manage the human landscape.

11.2.1 Give Them a Broad Metaphor

Give the workforce a broad metaphor to understand the big picture and different responses to change. To help our TWW! teams with this we designed a large learning map as the Introductory Activity for the module "Embrace Change". For the visual, we used the metaphor of a cruise liner on its journey to Treasure Island to depict HSBC implementing strategies to achieve the vision. Beyond the immediate destination lay another island further off on the skyline to illustrate that the goal posts would move further down the line. One crew member held a compass which depicted the general direction the crew would take while another held a map which represented the strategic imperatives. Staff onboard serving customers and reassuring colleagues represented those who were already with the programme — our change champions — while those delaying or falling behind depicted the laggards and resistors. For example, one lady who was tentatively boarding the cruise liner, communicated the concern "I've only worked on an-old fashioned ship." She represented those who would be worried about learning new skills and using new technology. Another, who had decided at the last moment to come aboard, was running along the pier calling "Wait for me!" He represented laggards that had become champions. In addition, a confused man stood scratching his head, asking himself "Why should I go?" (clearly messages on the value and importance of the journey had not got through to him) while a group of staff were tugging hard on the safety rope, shouting, "Don't go! It's too risky!" These resistors were trying to hold everyone else back! In the waters, competitor vessels offered competing services like jet-skiing and massage while off in the distance lay shipwrecks symbolising those firms that hadn't made it through choppy waters. The harsh winds blowing on the cruise liner represented the winds of change, while the shark-infested waters represented risks the Bank would meet along the way. To the left of the elaborate illustration was a carefully crafted list of open questions to help Team Leaders facilitate discussion amongst their staff, while to the right of the image these questions were presented in Chinese. Feedback from our teams was that this broad metaphor really helped them to understand the big picture, where they themselves were in terms of supporting change and where their colleagues were.

11.2.2 Tools and Techniques

It is not enough to raise awareness, share key messages and let them get on with it. The workforce needs tools and support to make the vision a reality. The learning packages will provide staff with a wide variety of tools which will go a long way towards decreasing learning anxiety. Teams will need the support of their Department Head to take time out of normal work activities to organise team meetings for action-planning purposes. Line managers must work together to ensure that work demands and responsibilities are covered at all times.

11.2.3 Encourage Emotional Processing

Human beings are capable of a broad range of emotions. While most are natural and valid in the greater scheme of things, the same cannot be said of any resulting behaviours. As intelligent beings, we need to equip ourselves with the knowledge and tools to process and understand our feelings so that we can take control of our emotions, question our motives and choose appropriate responses. When staff lack the tools and support to process their emotions this undermines their coping ability and there is a cost for the organisation:

❖ Low productivity;

❖ Dramatic emotional outbursts;

❖ Creates a passive-aggressive environment where people express their frustrations "sideways" through polite back-stabbing and (not so polite) harassment;

❖ Individuals get stuck, unable to move beyond shock, anger or denial because their line managers lack the knowledge and skills to help them through the upheaval;

❖ Customers can bear the brunt.

All of these scenarios result when a person's pain outweighs their ability to cope. Overwhelmed, they are likely to act on their pain.

To remove the barriers to emotional processing so that we can shift the scales, we need first to know what the barriers are on an organisational level:

❖ Thinking dominated by scientific management with executives quantitative in orientation; this creates a skills gap in executive management teams who do not have a mature understanding of how people cope with change and upheaval.

❖ Staff encouraged to demonstrate a stony stoicism, leave their emotions at home, and just bring their brain/brawn to work; alternatively, sales staff may be expected to be in a permanent state of euphoria.

❖ Some emotions are deemed socially acceptable (for example, hope, excitement) while others are frowned upon and labelled negative, a sign of weakness or dangerous (for example, fear, grief, sadness, disappointment, anger); when an emotion is judged and deemed punishable it gives way to feelings of resentment and guilt as the individual is not being validated.

❖ Where the workforce is institutionalised, the individual will have been undermined to the extent that they can't even appreciate their own emotions, let alone the emotions of others; this makes them very poor people managers.

❖ Structured forums for emotional expression are not provided for staff.

❖ From a political perspective, emotional expression is discouraged because it reveals one's hand.

On an individual level a host of other factors come into play; for example, pressures from family and national cultures where assumptions lead to specific expectations on emotional expression according to one's gender and role; a lack of the tools and resources to cope with change; and the stigma attached to using tools like counselling. To overcome barriers to emotional processing in the organisation:

❖ Nurture an appreciation for the qualitative;

❖ Challenge the assumption that some emotions are positive and others negative;

❖ Explain that all emotions are valid but not all behaviours are;

❖ Provide staff with forums for expressing emotions, such as art and drama workshops, and sports facilities to work off aggression;

❖ Allow them opportunities to progress and develop themselves with useful skills enhancement (for example, Advanced Thinking Skills and debating skills);

❖ Create communication forums so that they can challenge policies and processes (not people); and

❖ Nurture trust in the culture by encouraging people to be more open.

11.2.4 Navigate the Emotional Dynamics

When the rules of the game change, this can trigger shock, anger and denial in the workforce, with energies channelled to unproductive activities. This makes the ability to navigate the emotional challenge of organisational transformation a key skill requirement for executives.

Whether an individual perceives change as good news or bad news they will need practical support through the change process. This duty lies with their line manager and if it is done right it will help champions remain true to the cause, and bring as many laggards and resistors onboard as possible. In each of the diagrams below, the depth of the curve (amount of energy expended) and the length of the curve (the timeline) are influenced directly by the amount of help the individual gets with processing their emotions.

Managing Change Champions

Some might be surprised to learn that even champions of change need support, even when news of change is good news.

Figure 42: When Change is Good News

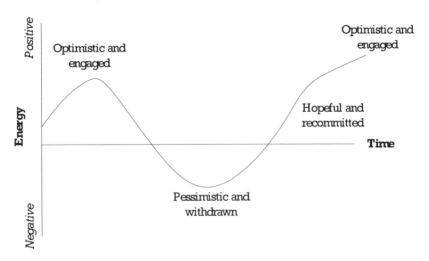

At the outset their confidence and high level of engagement may be a result of uninformed optimism. They do not have the full picture and can only see the sunny side of things. Over time, reality sets in and the reality of the situation and of what they are up against slowly dawns on them. As they lose confidence they withdraw to reconsider their assumptions and understanding. At this stage, the line manager should listen to find out what specific incidents caused the change. They should also share information and remind their change champion that during times of turmoil they will take one step forward and two steps back. If the individual is suitably encouraged and informed, they will plough back into their work encouraged by any positive signs on the horizon. Once again, they will be optimistic and engaged but this time round their optimism will be informed.

Managing Laggards and Resistors

Numerous studies have shown that people follow a reasonably predictable process when dealing with change that is imposed on them, be it the death of a loved one, the loss of a job or some other major disruption. When the individual is in shock and withdraws from the situation one can misinterpret that they are unaffected by the loss. But most likely they are in denial and have yet to start to understand the change. As the individual starts to process information, that numbness can be replaced by a mixture of grief, anger and even fear — how they channel that energy can be constructive or destructive but the very fact that they are processing their thoughts and emotions is a healthy sign. Having spent their energies, they can fall back into yearning for "the good old days", glamourising in their minds how things used to be. But the past is the past and the world around is changing with new opportunities presenting themselves. Once the individual starts to have a few wins with their new situation, this can help them to be more honest with themselves about the past, let go of the obsolete and commit to the future. The amount of energy one expends, and how long one is stuck at a particular stage will depend in no small part on the support the individual gets through the process. It can take weeks, months or even years for someone to recover and make it through to the other end of the change curve.

Figure 43: When Change is Bad News[1]

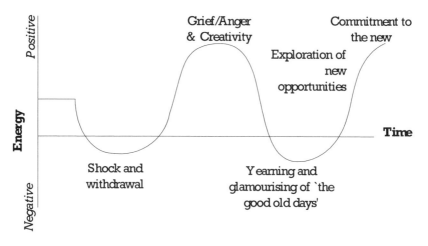

© O'Donovan, 2006

The shape of the curve will differ for each individual so a manager may have to revisit phases of the curve for a single staff member even though one may characterise the team on the whole as having moved on.

11.3 Overcoming Resistance to Change

Resistance to change can present itself on an organisational level when the culture or any element of the inert structures is limiting the organisation's ability to survive and thrive in a changing world. It can present itself on a functional or divisional level when, for example, cumbersome processes slow down customers and staff, or when the functional or divisional head is anti-change and actively discouraging staff from participating in the culture change programme. Resistance to

---

[1] Adapted from Jaffe, D. and Scott, C., *Managing Change at Work*, Thomson, 1995.

change can also present itself on an individual level. While many managers consider it with distaste, resistance to change has its value in that it may throw light on far more fundamental issues which have been ignored by those driving change. It also stimulates curiosity, allowing problems to be aired and alternative solutions discussed.

❖ *Value-adding Resistors* are genuinely fearful of the change and any perceived loss. Good communication, counselling and education can help them come on board to become change champions. They may fear that some aspects of the organisational culture have been ignored in the change process and their input can shape the change programme for the better.

❖ *Value-Destroying Resistors* undermine change initiatives to suit a hidden agenda. They are concerned with serving self-interests and protecting their own power bases.

In "Methods for Dealing with Resistance to Change" (1979) Kotter and Schlesinger identified a number of strategies for managing resistance to change. These are outlined in Figure 44 on the next page.

It is recommended that one starts with the first option and work through the alternatives in the sequence given. As the last two options can have very harmful results, they are to be avoided.

Figure 44: Methods for Dealing with Resistance to Change[2]

Approach	Commonly Used in Situations . . .	Advantages	Drawbacks
Education and Communication	Where there is a lack of information or inaccurate information and analysis	Once persuaded, people will often help with the implementation of change	Can be very time consuming if lots of people are involved
Participation and Involvement	Where the initiators do not have all the information they need to design the change, and where others have considerable power to resist	People who participate will be committed to implementing change, and any relevant information they have will be integrated into the change plan	Can be very time-consuming if participators design an inappropriate change
Facilitation and Support	Where people are resisting because of adjustment problems	No other approach works as well with adjustment problems	Can be time-consuming, expensive and still fail
Negotiation and Agreement	Where someone or some group will clearly lose out in a change, and where that group has considerable power to resist	Sometimes it is a relatively easy way to avoid major resistance	Can be too expensive in many cases if it alerts others to negotiate for compliance
Manipulation and Co-option	Where other tactics will not work, or are too expensive	It can be a relatively quick and inexpensive solution to resistance problems	Can lead to future problems if people feel manipulated
Explicit and Implicit Coercion	Where speed is essential, and the change initiators possess considerable power	It is speedy, and can overcome any kind of resistance	Can be risky if it leaves people mad at the initiators

[2] Reprinted by permission of *Harvard Business Review*. [Exhibit 1] from "Choosing Strategies for Change" by Kotter, J.P. and Schlesinger, L.A., March–April 1979. Copyright © 1979 by the Harvard Business School Publishing Corporation; all rights reserved.

Overcoming resistance to change can be a source of job-satisfaction in itself. Prior to the commencement of TWW! I met with each top team manager to gain their support for the programme. In one instance a senior executive was absolutely against the programme and for one whole hour he gave me a multitude of reasons why he did not want the programme in his major business area. As a big champion of the programme, I was taken aback by the strength of his resistance and just sat and listened, and listened some more. After the meeting, I pondered the issue and came to realise two things: firstly, that he had planned a whole range of change initiatives for his workforce; and secondly, while he is exceptionally clever he had not expressed the ability to simplify his ideas so that the most junior staff member could understand and act. Now that is something I can do. I had great difficulty arranging another meeting but eventually he relented and agreed to meet me at 7.00 one morning. I told him I would be there at 6.45. Needless to say, his secretary called to re-arrange the meeting for 7.30, a more reasonable hour. This time around I helped him see that we wanted the same thing. I would help him to implement his ideas, putting them (and other planned change initiatives) under the umbrella of the culture change programme using my budget. In essence, we would not create problems for him but rather take work off his hands. It was as simple as that. He bought in, and went on to become a major champion of the programme for its entire duration, helping in any way he could. As a team we achieved success because we were both focused on delivering value for the Bank and not caught up with self-interested motives.

11.4 Chapter Summary

Once the programme has been rolled out, each staff member will respond differently to the new way of doing things. Some ten per cent will immediately come onboard, 80 per cent will slowly find their way if given enough encouragement, while many of the remaining ten per cent may never accept the new way of doing things. On a strategic level, it is critical that the twenty per cent clustering at both ends of the curve are identified as soon as possible. The supporters can become nurtured to become champions of the culture change while the resistors, if not dealt with effectively, can completely derail the programme. Laggards represent the majority audience and the programme must be designed with them in mind.

Whether an individual becomes a change champion, a laggard or a resistor will be determined by how news of change is delivered, the meaning they attach to the news, the cues they get from line managers and any involvement they have in promoting political agendas. To support the case, give them a broad metaphor to understand the big picture, provide them with tools and techniques to decrease their learning anxiety, promote emotional processing and navigate the emotional dynamics. Resistance to change will come from two discrete groups: those who are genuinely fearful but open to guidance and committed to the organisation and those who look after their own self-interests to the detriment of the community at large. Strategies for overcoming resistance to change include education and commitment, participation and involvement, facilitation and support, negotiation and agreement, manipulation and co-option, plus implicit and explicit coercion. Leaders are encouraged to start with education and commitment and slowly work through the alternatives. The last two are to be avoided altogether because they can lead to very harmful outcomes.

12

Maintain Momentum and Solidify Ground Made

If organisations were humanised machines it would be enough to provide staff with the tools and the room to do the job and expect them to get on with it. The fact is, people have needs and expectations which must be managed so that staff are inspired and motivated for the duration of the initiative. To this end, mechanisms must be built into the programme design to maintain the momentum and anchor the new culture into everyday business practices. Once the strategic management team has done its bit, it will then be up to line management to take up the baton. Reinforcement keeps principles and values uppermost in people's hearts and minds.

12.1 Build Momentum: Phase One

12.1.1 Wow Them!

The event hall and experience are key communication vehicles for Phase One. Capture the imagination of the workforce with the environment, the activities and top management involvement.

The Environment

If the company is facing major change, a dramatically designed event hall will do much to communicate this to participants. For inspiration with the TWW! venue, which was created on-site, we

looked to the normal working environment of HSBC as our reference point. This was grey, quiet and serious. We then came
up with a dynamic design which was the complete opposite of
this in that it was fun with lots of colour, visual stimuli and background music. Our designer took the vision and ran with it and
the end product was a delightful and bold statement. Quality
meals and refreshments were provided by in-house catering
and a cleaning team descended on the venue at the end of each
day. In contrast, Cathay Pacific Airways chose a remote and
tranquil environment for their "Service Straight From The
Heart" (SSFTH) programme. They went with a beautiful hotel
resort which accommodated participants through both indoor
and outdoor activities. The retreat-like environment was inspirational and spending an afternoon in the outdoors did much to
energise teams. In this case, catering and cleaning activities
were the responsibility of hotel staff.

An excellent social environment will really complement the
physical environment. To achieve this, the programme manager must instil in the team the understanding that every day
brings new faces who are having their very first experience.
Role-modelling is the best way to set the tone. From the moment participants arrive, every individual must be treated like
a valued and respected guest. When the team delivers on this,
it builds up its own sense of professional pride and facilitators
will act as role-models to their peers. Needless to say, it will
have a positive impact on their service delivery when they return to their normal line duties.

The Activities

Experiential learning activities are both challenging and heaps
of fun. They generate all types of emotions and typically one
will hears lots of laughter from participating teams as they go
through the motions. The beauty of these activities is that they
have the appearance of games and encourage a playful approach, so we quickly put aside our "work-mode" without even
realising it. We learn best when we are having fun! During

breaks and if suitable AV equipment is available, consider showing company advertisements down the ages to encourage a sense of pride in, and identification with, the organisation.

Top Management Involvement

Top management will be involved both as regular participants and as speakers. Whether loved or otherwise, each member of this team has star value with general staff who will be excited about rubbing shoulders with them during the course of the day. As members of the top team shoulder heavy responsibilities, they will probably most appreciate a fun approach and general staff will delight in seeing this more human side.

12.1.2 Build a Critical Mass

Phase One gives the workforce a common language for change issues. As a large section of staff return from the event each day and compare their experiences with colleagues, much discussion will be generated in the workplace. Word-of mouth will help to build a critical mass. Any *lasting* impression will go beyond the superficial and will be based on the standard of the physical environment and its conduciveness to learning, the quality of learning materials and facilitator effectiveness and top management involvement, knowledge and transparency. Below I share some pointers on each:

1. The standard of the physical environment and its conduciveness to learning

❖ Each facilitator will have the responsibility for ensuring that they are well prepared each day and that they have all the tools and equipment they require to run activities

❖ Event logistics must run smoothly. Give the facilitators responsibility for ensuring that they start and end activities in a timely manner to create a seamless event. The programme manager can take turns with a deputy to oversee logistics if teams are required to move from room to room for different activities.

❖ Hygiene standards must be maintained, particularly when food is provided on-site, so arrange for a daily clean-up at the end of each day.

❖ Customer feedback must be actioned on an ongoing basis to improve newcomers' experiences and keep moral high.

❖ Any renovations or construction work being carried out nearby should be done outside of event operating hours.

2. The quality of the learning materials and facilitators' effectiveness

❖ As mentioned in an earlier chapter, the materials are the heart of the programme. A great deal of thought and effort must be put into these to ensure that they are aligned with the core principles and values of the company, as articulated in the initial proposal and other formal documents.

❖ Whatever their background, all facilitators will be put through a course on the delivery of experiential learning activities specifically.

❖ The programme team will put together a "facilitator observation rota" and disperse amongst the groups each day to provide guidance and support. Facilitators who develop exceptional facilitation skills can be kept on to help train new recruits if the event is running over an extended period.

3. Top management involvement, knowledge and transparency

❖ Speakers will need to be able to demonstrate a good understanding of different parts of the business. The programme manager can help by keeping speakers up-to-date on frequently asked questions and hot topics and also by sharing with them input from line owners of current issues so that they can answer all questions in an informed manner.

❖ Questions should be answered as honestly as possible. If the speaker is unable to answer a question, the MC can take the name and contact information of the person posing the question and ensure that they do get their answer.

❖ Speakers should share the slots fairly amongst themselves so that the burden is not left on any one individual. If the Executive Sponsor is filling most of the slots it can signal a lack of support.

❖ They can help maintain the momentum by encouraging returnees to share their insights and experiences on return to the workplace.

In the early days it is particularly important that all areas are up to par so that messages spread by word-of-mouth is positive. When participants depart, give them work-related gifts which carry the core principles and values to reinforce the language of the programme.

12.1.3 Inject New Challenges and New Blood

Inject New Challenges

To promote peak performance amongst event facilitators and keep their energy levels up, give them new challenges. For example, if ten are needed to run daily activities, have two or three extra on standby. When facilitators are attached to the event as support staff they can take turns to manage audio-visual equipment, support fellow facilitators through activities, mingle with guests and help those with special needs. They can also cover for any sick leave. Note that while most of the daily responsibilities can be delegated to facilitators over time, the same cannot be said for the speaker session. This task requires a high level of tact and the ability to handle on-the-spot situations. The programme manager or a trained deputy will retain this responsibility as part of their duties as event MC and manager.

Inject New Blood

Facilitating event activities on a daily basis is a very demanding job. Having different groups of facilitators rotate periodically will do much to inject new energy into an event which runs over an extended period. To keep the top management Q&A session fresh, employ the same tactic and rotate speakers on a daily basis. Book busy executives' time at least a month in advance so that they can keep their diaries clear. The strategic management team can consider inviting customers to share their experiences and expectations with event participants. For organisations which are seeking to reconnect with the external environment, this will help back office staff particularly to put a face on their customers.

12.2 Fan the Flames: Phase Two

Phase Two gives the workforce the tools to effect change in their day-to-day work. During Phase Two, the roll-out of each module is very much a product launch. Each set of products, or module, will be branded but will have its own identity depending on the core principle in focus. As the centralised event environment will have served its purpose and no longer operate, each roll-out will entail a company-wide communications campaign.

12.2.1 The Big Splash!

For maximum effect, use the full range of media at your disposal. If staff are spread out over a large geographical area, a road-show may be the most effective approach.

Once Phase 2 of TWW! was implemented, staff communication activities, which would become staples for each module launch included the memo to 200 Line Materials Coordinators, 1,500 posters displayed bankwide, intranet Headline News notes on the official launch date, a note from the Module Sponsor to all senior management, a note from the programme manager to Team Members and the learning materials themselves. Line management would cascade messages through briefings. During the course of the programme, we used other media to maintain the momentum. Bi-monthly double-page spreads in the internal magazine brought everyone up to speed on the latest news and line achievements and our monthly "Team Leader e-Newsletter" would serve as a useful vehicle for posting reminders about critical dates and events.

Communication is only effective when it is two-way:

❖ Our online *TWW! Customer Satisfaction Survey* gave everyone the opportunity to provide feedback on the programme and how it could be improved.

❖ Staff utilised the programme intranet to post questions to top management using "Ask Top Management" and will have experienced a sense of ownership when reviewing *TWW! Works.* This page of our intranet detailed how an ever-increasing number of company policies and processes were changing in response to staff feedback on the Q&A forum.

❖ We also set up a *TWW! LotusNotes email account* for feedback purposes but staff did not utilise this, perhaps because it was not anonymous.

❖ Team Leaders got a *module feedback questionnaire* with each rollout and this they would return to the programme team after wrapping up each of the six action-plans.

❖ As each staff member had their own copy of the *FAQ booklet* which answered 40 of the most likely questions to come up, we received few questions about the programme itself on "Ask Top Management", unless staff sought top management support in removing local obstacles.

Remember, the programme team must get official endorsement for the use of the company logo on any materials and, as with other communication activities, the Steering Committee will review drafts of articles and speeches before they are endorsed by the Executive Sponsor.

12.2.2 All Hands on Board!

The materials delivery process generates energy and keeps all eyes on the ball. As each module is launched, the focus of the workforce turns to a particular core principle. This signals closure for any preceding module and encourages all to mentally prepare for the new theme and action their "roll-out responsibilities". Allow a two-week window for the turnaround. Posters will be put up across the company public areas to create a strong visual effect. Functional heads will be considering with their local line champions the ideas put forward by the Module Sponsor on how they can make the programme come alive in the business. Line Materials Distributors will accept packages from internal and external distributions channels and advise local Team Leaders via email to collect their own set. Team Leaders will collect materials, distribute packages and inserts to their Team Members and prepare themselves to facilitate team activities. Team Members will study their own sets, review their Self-Directed Learning Plans and prepare for team meetings. When programme logistics are implemented smoothly and efficiently with the launch of each module, this does much to increase confidence and maintain momentum.

12.2.3 New Action Plans — New Goals!

There is tremendous value in having every staff member in every team action-plan on the same core principle during the same time period. As they meet for casual lunches and social activities, staff will be able to share ideas and insights, answer each other's questions and advise each other on goals formation. As a result, the social atmosphere will feel more vibrant because all minds are focused on the common purpose.

12.2.4 Share Performance Feedback

The leadership team can consider organisational performance from a number of perspectives: the customer perspective, the business process perspective, the financial perspective and the learning and growth perspective. Sharing such performance feedback keeps all eyes on the ball, encourages the sense of a shared mission and motivates the workforce. For example, when Cathay Pacific Airways was seeking to create a service culture in the late 1990s it used the "Reflex" mechanism to give regular progress reports to the workforce in terms of their shared success rate in keeping customers satisfied. In essence, a survey was designed using customer service metrics put forward by passengers themselves. At check-in, and in aircrafts, a specific number of customers would be invited to fill in the Reflex survey form and they would be rewarded for their efforts with a little gift. Completed forms were collated with data inputted onto an airline intranet site which staff could access. This happened on an ongoing basis. When feedback was positive it would create an early morning buzz because it became our habit to start the day by checking the Reflex report.

If the performance feedback related to products and services is not encouraging it may indicate the existence of unmet consumer demand. Organisations that can spot such opportunities can gain advantage over the competition by being first to capitalise on gaps in the market; for example:

❖ In the cosmetics industry, French firm L'Oreal announced in March 2006 its intention to buy the standard bearers of conscience consumption — The Body Shop.

❖ In February 2006 Sainsbury UK reported "fair trade" sales of more than €1.43 million a week, up 70 per cent on 2005.

❖ Recently, Irish rock singer Bono announced the establishment of RED, a global business initiative to channel funds from the sale of branded products into the fight against AIDS, TB and malaria in Africa. Businesses backing the venture include Amercian Express, Converse, Gap and Giorgio Armani.[1]

❖ In the US pharmaceuticals sector there is a growing market for generic drugs.

---

[1] Conor Pope, "Why Ethical Equals Profitable", *The Irish Times*, 1 May 2006, p. 33.

❖ In the fast-food industry there is a demand from providers like McDonalds for healthy foodstuffs like sandwiches and salads.

❖ In the energy industry there is a fast growing demand for cleaner fuels such as natural gas.

❖ Many investors are now demanding of financial services companies products and services which are environmentally and socially sound.

If an organisation spots such opportunities then it's back to the drawing board again to devise new strategies.

12.2.5 Celebrate Short-Term Wins

❖ A company-wide *competition* will do much to inject excitement into the initiative and generous rewards will do much to generate high-quality entries. For TWW! we held a competition which would award teams for delivering excellent service. Feedback would have to come from the customers themselves. The winning team and the partners of their choice won a trip on the "StarLeo" cruise liner together with a gold trophy and recognition in the internal magazine. Six runner-up teams won a silver trophy plus an exclusive dinner in a high-class restaurant with their functional head. Local teams would send their entries to their local Line Champions who would select the best efforts and forward these to their own Department Head. The Department Head would make the final selection for the functional area and forward entries to the programme team. We reviewed all submissions to ensure they met the entry criteria, before forwarding all to the Executive Sponsor who would make the final decision. Remember that for such a project to be successful, clear standards must be communicated to teams and a credible monitoring system must be put in place. If the focus is a service award, keep in mind that many back-office staff may not be able to put an immediate monetary value to their win. Their successes should be treated equally by reviewers. Also, if service chain members up and down the line contributed to the success, they should be named and included in the whole process.

❖ Formally recognise those who demonstrate the desired behaviours with *publicity* in the company newsletter. This may take the form of "Service Legends" where an individual went beyond the call of duty for the sake of the customer, or special features on how teams delivered in line with the programme principles and values.

❖ On a local level, I would encourage teams to *appreciate and recognise* each other with little acts of kindness like calling a team member to thank them, practising public praise and nominating colleagues for any formal awards. Such acts cost nothing and do much to improve the social environment. I would refuse any requests for a budget for such activities. If the workforce has lost sight of the fact that it costs nothing to be kind and considerate, reinforce the fact that acts of kindness can go a very long way in meeting emotional needs and improving the social environment. When staff re-learn the value of this approach, it will quickly catch on. If they are keen to communicate more formal appreciation for each others' efforts, encourage them to use any company mechanisms that are already in place.

❖ When the programme has achieved noteworthy results it may be put forward for *industry awards* in corporate governance (as evidence of delivery on operational responsibilities) people training and development, staff communications, product excellence, service excellence and of course the grand prize — corporate culture management.

Once the programme is rolled out, the functional heads will have responsibility for maintaining the momentum and celebrating wins locally. At HSBC Hong Kong, our best example of this came from a team in the Operations Department who created their own regular newsletter (see Appendix 7).

12.3 Solidify Ground Made

All the energy generated will dissipate over time if the new way of doing things is not anchored into inert structures like processes and systems. At the proposal endorsement stage, the Steering Committee will have approved a number of strategies for anchoring the new culture into everyday practices and in Chapter 9, I expanded upon some of the possibilities which can be considered during the programme design stage.

Once the strategic management team has agreed on specific measures which will support the new way of doing things, these should be actioned as soon as is feasible. Once Phase Two of the programme is up and running, conduct a review, because while some projects may have been implemented smoothly, others may be encountering difficult terrain and be in need of revisiting. This will help solidify ground made.

12.4 Chapter Summary

As corporate culture management is primarily concerned with managing the human landscape, mechanisms must be built into the programme design to maintain energy levels and celebrate wins. This will do much to maintain the momentum and solidify ground made. Line management can complement the efforts of the strategic management team by encouraging positive word-of-mouth and organising their own local initiatives to fan the flames.

During Phase One, wow the workforce with the environment, the activities and top management involvement. Create a great first impression. When participants return to the workplace and spread positive word-of-mouth, this will help to build a critical mass. Any lasting impression will go beyond the superficial and will be based on

a) The standard of the physical environment and its conduciveness to learning;

b) The quality of the learning materials and facilitators' effectiveness; and

c) Top management involvement, knowledge and transparency.

Ensure that all are up to par. To manage the energy levels of facilitators, create new challenges and inject new blood, and to keep the Q&A session fresh, rotate speakers on a regular basis. Inviting real customers to the event to share their experiences and expectations as this will expose staff to a fresh perspective.

Phase Two gives the workforce the tools to effect change in their day-to-day work. The roll-out of each module is very much a product launch and will require a company-wide communications campaign. For maximum effect, use the full range of media at your disposal. If staff are spread out over a large geographical area, a roadshow may be the most effective approach. As communication is only effective when it is two-way, create feedback forums and mechanisms to allow staff to voice their opinions. This will encourage a sense of ownership for how future modules evolve. Once the communications campaign is underway, the materials delivery process will begin. This will be a call for all hands on board as each individual actions their roll-out responsibilities. When logistical planning and implementation is smooth, this does much to increase confidence and maintain momentum. As staff review their learning materials, all eyes will turn to focus on the new action plans and goals. All minds are focused on a common purpose. This has a unifying effect on the workforce as they share insights and advise each other on goals formation. Share performance feedback as it comes through to motivate staff and capitalise on any wins.

To support staff efforts and solidify ground made, conduct a review of those cultural embedding mechanisms which have been anchored into everyday practices as part of the programme. While some might be running smoothly, others may have encountered difficult terrain and will be in need of a review.

13

MEASURE RESULTS AND PLAN FOR THE FUTURE

Every results-oriented programme will culminate with the measurement of monetary and non-monetary benefits together with the creation of a plan for the future.

While the consolidation of benefits occurs at the end of a programme, up-front identification of performance measures and targets is essential to provide credibility and focus to the initiative. In addition, and to secure the support, budget and resources at the outset, the programme manager must put together a plan on how results will be measured. This plan will be outlined in the initial proposal, and endorsed by the Steering Committee before the Executive Sponsor signs off on the whole programme. Because the environment will change as the programme is being implemented, proposals "in the works" should be revisited by the strategic management team as they may need to evolve with business requirements.

13.1 Consider the "Big Picture"

The first step towards accurate measurement is to reflect on the unique challenges the organisation faces together with the programme strategy because the choice of key measures will depend on what the organisation is seeking to achieve with the culture change initiative.

13.1.1 A Service Culture

A service culture is customer-centric and responsive to shifts in the marketplace. The organisation is structured in relation to the structure of the marketplace so that marketing and production reflect market segmentation and customer types. Different products and services are provided for different customer types and differential value is added to each. Data is managed via CRM systems and feedback centres to enhance the customer experience and call centres are managed along the same lines. People systems motivate staff and reinforce the desired knowledge, skills and attitudes while delivery systems are designed from the customer's point of view. Staff are informed, helpful and equipped to serve. They enjoy dealing with people and are constructive in the face of customer complaints.

To create a service culture one must create a service strategy that instils commitment to a service culture and to the shared philosophy of the corporate community in respect of this (beliefs, principles and values). The strategy must address customers' needs and expectations and the tracking of competitor activities.

❖ The **shared philosophy** will articulate major beliefs of the community in terms of the customer, the customer experience, the service provider, etc.

❖ **Customer needs and expectations** include *material service* and *personal service*:

   1. *"Material service"* relates to tangible goods and the systems that enable their delivery. No company can survive if its customers' product and service needs are either not fully defined or ignored when known.

   2. *"Personal service"* relates to the knowledge, skills and attitude of staff. Poor product knowledge, inadequate skills or a bad attitude can negate the value of a good service strategy.

As customer needs and expectations are forever increasing, they must be revisited periodically.

❖ An organisation seeking to gain a competitive advantage through service must gain insights into **competitors' activities**. Find out what they are doing and learn why potential customers might choose them over you.

A programme designed to create a service culture will help implement a strategy that addresses all three areas.

13.1.2 A Culture of Ethics

Citigroup's ambitious goal is to become "the world's most respected financial institution". To achieve this, CEO Chuck Prince has set about creating a culture of ethics. External forces (customer feedback, negative press and regulatory pressures) instigated the change. Already, the Chief Executive has taken steps to influence external perception and the internal way of doing things by taking high-profile steps to make the vision a reality (the dismissal of those involved in corporate governance scandals and the instigation of a bankwide culture change programme). Having conducted research to pinpoint those core principles and values which will make the vision a reality, the leadership team made sure that values like "service" and "leadership" hinged on the moral principle "integrity". They will also have identified the toxic beliefs that must be eradicated and those beliefs that will encourage the desired attitudes and behaviours. From there they will have identified how the management team can support staff in their day-to-day efforts to make the vision a reality. Internal measures of success will include evidence of a clampdown on unethical practices plus the attitudes and behaviours which support them (self-interest, collusion and other forms of toxic teamwork), the establishment *and utilisation* of internal whistle-blowing mechanisms together with the good treatment of whistleblowers, enhanced morale and trust, more support for initiatives that are for the good of the organisation (though not necessarily individuals), the retention of persons of integrity and the success of the culture change programme itself. External measures of success will include a significant improvement in press feedback, a reputation for a board culture of corporate governance based on a history of ethical conduct, increased market share and the relaxation of regulatory pressures as investor confidence increases and brand image improves. It is no surprise that Citigroup should recently find itself in trouble with the regulators again (after Citigroup Global Capital Markets was accused by the Australian Securities and Investments Commission of insider trading and unconscionable behaviour),[1] because establishing a culture of ethics is a massive undertaking and is the hardest of all cultural challenges.

13.1.3 A Culture of Innovation

In a recent Global CEO Study, four out of five CEOs pointed to revenue growth, not cost containment, as their priority for boosting financial performance. They said that the best way to drive new growth is through increasingly differentiated products and services but that this will be impossible without a renewed focus on people, because it is people who generate ideas and convert them to the tangible. Education and suitable mechanisms will create a culture of innovation and keep vital knowledge within the organisation. So what does a culture of innovation look like? It is flexible, empowering, tolerant of risks, tolerant of mistakes and strong on project management. It encourages fun, fosters synergies, allows for the free flow of information and respects the individual within the team setting. It rewards individuals *and* teams. Success translates to continuously inventing products and services that will attract consumer money and investor confidence. As pro-consumers (proactive consumers) are first to develop many industrial and commercial products, the organisation must be willing to learn from customers, competitors, general staff and even works of fiction, which are often the source of innovative and fantastic creations. Generous investment in research and development is a necessity. Internal and external

---

[1] Justin O'Brien, "Insider Trading Case to Test Chinese Walls", *The Irish Times*, 1 May 2006.

measures of success can include an increase in creative products and services, the volume of patents registered, press perception and feedback, the ability to attract and retain creative individuals, a reputation for innovation and market leadership and a workforce which reflects diversity in its psychometric profile. A number of major organisations have a successful track record in this arena and their practices are worth emulating:

❖ In Rolls-Royce, the UK aero engine group, in-depth interviews were carried out on Concorde engine designers due for retirement to ensure that knowledge, business intelligence and cultural values are preserved for future customers.

❖ BP's "expert locator system" helps employees find the right specialist within the company on a given issue (this contrasts with the attitude of some that people are deemed to be expert in the field at the instant they step into it); also, BP makes it part of a specialist's job to help a successor, rather than simply getting on with his or her job.

❖ Management innovator General Electric has benefited enormously from its careful attention to leadership development. Former CEO Jack Welch spent more than 30 per cent of his time on leadership development.

❖ Toyota's position as the world's pre-eminent carmaker is founded on its ability to exploit the problem-solving potential of rank-and-file employees.

Other best practices include the establishment of one universal intranet so all can communicate by email; the creation of an online directory of areas of expertise so that subject matter specialists can be easily sought out; having one CRM system only; and the rewarding of contributions to knowledge management (KM) and business intelligence (BI) mechanisms.[2]

---

[2] Incidentally, I see KM as the eliciting and management of both tacit and explicit knowledge while the more tangible BI is the analysis of data and information already out there.

These three challenges are not mutually exclusive but can be addressed by one culture change programme. For example, our HSBC programme focused on creating a service culture which in turn required the creation of a culture of learning. Sony now faces a similar challenge: CEO Sir Howard Stringer is seeking to reawaken the sleeping giant by renewing workforce focus on a combination of customer-centric products and services together with world-class technological innovation.

The reach of a culture change programme will be determined by the strategic goals and objectives, the choice of core principles and values, the content of learning materials and the choice of cultural embedding mechanisms. Of course, the more one tries to change, the more painful the process will be, so carefully consider the big picture challenges to prioritise, taking into consideration the degree of resistance expected towards each challenge: service, ethics and innovation. For example, as the act of serving others is honoured in Asian cultures, we did not meet significant resistance in our efforts to create a service culture. Front-line staff certainly had the right attitude — they just needed the tools, support and authority to make the corporate vision a reality. Support staff needed to be educated on the concept of the internal customer and the service chain so that they could then apply their knowledge and skills. However, a key challenge in terms of stimulating continuous learning and continuous improvement was that our local workforce believed that learning takes place in the classroom, and not in the workplace. This assumption was raised by staff a number of times during our Phase One event Q&A session, which I analysed for trends. True to Hong Kong culture, even the most junior staff member had a handful of formal qualifications under their belt and many had attended a long list of internal training courses which often were not even related to their job. We knew we had to:

1. Move learning from the centralised environment to the local workplace, giving Team Leaders the responsibility (and resources) for developing their teams; and

Culture Change Programme:
seline Measurement

		Questions
	Central Paradigm	*Community Needs:* Does the corporate community have a safe and happy work environment which is conducive to productivity and excellence? Was the workforce given the knowledge, tools and support to meet new challenges? *Organisation Needs:* Did learning anxiety decrease? Did survival anxiety increase? Did the programme meet business needs e.g. creation of service culture? Do management beliefs about people, places and things support the core principles and values on a day-to-day basis? Is the organisation's community familiar with and supportive of the programme philosophy and purpose?
EXPRESSIONS	**Attitudes**	Have targeted attitudes changed and, if so, by how much?
	Behaviours	Have targeted behaviours changed and if so, by how much?
REFLECTIONS	**Artefacts**	Are the cultural embedding mechanisms and other artefacts (e.g. emails and correspondence) congruent with the programme philosophy?
	Results	Did on-the-job application of core principles and values produce measurable results in terms of the programme goals and objectives? Did the organisation achieve alignment with the external environment? Did the organisation achieve internal integration?
	ROI	How did the financial returns from the programme relate to the costs as a percentage per dollar invested?

© O'Donovan, 2006

2. Match centralised developmental opportunities to needs.

Through their own successes with action-planning on principles and values in the workplace during Phase Two of o. programme, the workforce came to internalise the fact that learning is indeed possible every minute of the day, no matter where they are.

If an organisation is facing a two-pronged cultural challenge that includes the establishment of a culture of ethics, then this aspect must be tackled at the outset with a module focusing specifically on the all-encompassing principle "integrity". The reason is that if the culture is toxic then resistors to any change initiative have a broader range of options and resources open to them to sabotage and derail the programme. So set the standard at the outset by naming and blaming toxic beliefs, tackle any shenanigans head-on and make an example of those who engage in malpractice. Everyone will be watching from the sidelines and what is rewarded will be perpetuated. So it makes sense to do a "spring cleaning" of sorts because this will make the implementation of change efforts easier down the road.

13.2 Measurement Baseline and Approaches

Whether you are seeking to create a service culture, a culture of ethics or a culture of innovation, the programme baseline measurement will remain the same across the board (drivers, expressions and reflections). *Drivers* include needs, beliefs, principles and values, *expressions* include attitudes and behaviour and *reflections* include outcomes and results and return-on-investment. The strategic management team can use the diagram below to facilitate a discussion around possible measures.

Although the baseline will remain the same for the measurement of any culture change programme, the tactical approaches used by each organisation will vary as each corporate culture is unique, and each organisation faces unique challenges. Instruments and approaches will produce "hard" or "soft" data. Hard data is quantitative and relatively easy to measure, while soft data is qualitative, making monetary results more difficult to pin down. Before reading on to learn about instruments and approaches at each baseline level, turn to Appendix 8 to review examples of hard and soft data.

13.2.1 Drivers

Needs

Community Needs: *Does the corporate community have a safe and happy work environment which is conducive to productivity and excellence?*

I should clarify at the outset that I am not suggesting for a moment that organisations must be accountable for fulfilling all of the needs of all of their staff. Not only would this be impossible, but to do so would result in a complacent workforce which has no motivation for improving their lot. What I am proposing is that organisations recognise that their corporate community has a complex myriad of needs and will seek to have some of them met in their workplace. There will be patterns across the board in terms of their ability to have their needs met. Needs create energy and motives which, if negative and left unchecked, can have a detrimental influence on attitude, behaviour and results. If an organisation is looking to change results, it must conduct a temperature check which will provide valuable insights into the drivers of current performance. Those drivers include needs. We learnt in Part One of this book how the new CEO of a manufacturing plant found, upon investigation, that his "absentee" workforce was channelling all of their passions to outside activities where they felt that their non-material needs were being met. Wisely, he worked out an action plan with his leadership team to woo them back because he understood the relationship between happy people and high productivity. There is a lesson there for us all.

The two key internal interventions which safeguard the physical, emotional and spiritual wellbeing of staff are, firstly, the Code of Health and Safety and, secondly, the Code of Ethics.

The Code of Health and Safety

All organisations are required by law to have in place an occupational safety and health policy. The focus of such a code is on the physical environment; accident prevention, fire prevention and precautions, working environment (lighting, ventilation, seating arrangements and tidiness), hygiene in the workplace, the maintenance of first-aid boxes and the training of staff to administer first aid, and manual handling techniques for goods transportation. By tracking the health and safety record on a regular basis, one can identify if basic needs are being met in this area; sometimes breaches of the code will occur because of negligence on the part of the organisation while in other cases victims and their colleagues will have caused the problem through their own carelessness. Those who breach the code of health and safety may be prosecuted in accordance with local laws. Many organisations have a health and safety officer who is responsible for enforcing the law and supporting staff in their efforts.

The Code of Ethics

Over the past decade, there has been a significant increase in the ethical expectations of businesses by the public, who are deliberately seeking out those who articulate the basic principles which reflect how they run their operations. A well-written code goes beyond articulating common principles and values by relating these to workplace specifics. It provides a framework of decisions and actions in relation to ethical conduct in employment, setting out directives covering appropriate conduct in a variety of contexts for employees at all levels. When its integrity is upheld, it enhances the sense of community among staff, of belonging to a group with common values and purpose. When it is breached, it can result in legal action against the culprits and damage the reputation of the organisation. While having a Code of Ethics is not a legal requirement, many organisations consider it in their interest to have one in place and in the USA, the Federal Sentencing Guidelines reward companies for doing so. At its best a Core of Ethics will safeguard the emotional and spiritual wellbeing of staff and will cover all dealings. It will be upheld by all from leaders down and there will be a clearly stated policy in regard to the monitoring of the implementation of the code. At its worst, the code will refer only to money-related transactions and compliance will be determined only by how much one can get away with (the traditional Code of Conduct is not necessarily the same as a Code of Ethics as it may not be underpinned by moral principles). The availability and transparency of the Code of Ethics will vary from company to company; some might make a copy available to all staff while others will have it locked away in a human resources filing cabinet. This is a resource to protect the well-being of staff and it must be shared and upheld to protect basic human rights. The integrity of a code of ethics can be measured by:

❖ Its focus and content;

❖ Its availability;

❖ How breaches and culprits are dealt with; and

❖ How whistleblowers are treated.

Staff Survey

Below are suggestions which can provide guidance when designing a staff survey on needs. Many of the questions relate to autonomy, pay, achievement, etc. and often crop up on regular employee surveys. Using survey feedback supplemented with focus group feedback, one can glean patterns across the board in terms on staff perception of their needs and how they are being fulfilled. Often, managers are a happier lot than general staff so one should also consider how data differs for staff at different levels/grades and pinpoint the reasons for any variances. Trends can provide useful insights into current levels of commitment and productivity and can help with the design of job enrichment programmes.

❖ **Transcendence** — *to connect with something beyond the ego or to help others find fulfilment and realise their potential.* Is the corporate philosophy underpinned by moral principles and values which align with each individual's moral compass? Does the workforce have the opportunity to contribute in meaningful ways to the well-being of their internal community and their host community? Is learning and development localised in the workplace with line managers empowered to develop themselves and their staff?

❖ **Self-Actualisation** — *capacity to exercise one's fullest potential as an individual while being aware of and responsive to others; a state of well-being.* Is Self-Directed Learning and self-awareness encouraged? Are career paths clearly defined? Is the culture results-oriented? Is a sense of achievement facilitated via challenging goals? Is each individual respected for their innate uniqueness and matched with roles best suited to their talents? Is reward and recognition given where it is rightfully due? Are jobs suitably big to stretch individuals?

❖ **Cognitive** — *learning for learning alone; contributing knowledge.* Is work intellectually challenging? Are staff exposed to new ideas and best practices by working with external consultants, participating in secondments and discussing case studies? Is there a mentoring programme in place to stimulate growth and development? Do senior management staff practise continuous learning or do the mentored quickly outgrow their mentors? Are knowledge-management and business intelligence systems in place for staff to contribute to and draw from?

❖ **Aesthetic — *at peace, more curious about the inner workings of all.*** Are staff encouraged to take a holistic view of their environment to understand connections and causal relationships? Do team members share their psychometric profiles amongst themselves to enhance their understanding of each other and how they can achieve synergies as a team? (This must be voluntary because if the culture is maladapted then the information might be abused.) Is trust a part of the culture? Is emotional intelligence valued and encouraged?

❖ **Self-esteem — *Self-respect and the respect of others; to achieve, be competent, gain approval and recognition.*** Does the culture facilitate empowerment, trust, learning from mistakes, creativity and respect for the individual? Is the contribution of each individual respected in their own team? Is diversity respected and encouraged; e.g. does the *psychometric profile* of the workforce reflect diversity (think HR tools like KAI and Myers Briggs)? Is recognition given to those rightfully due it? Are staff given the training they require to perform responsibilities? Is human dignity valued?

❖ **Belonging — *to affiliate with others and be accepted.*** Do staff have a sense of belonging and pride in the organisation? Is the contribution of each individual recognized and respected by their own team through the use of processes such as Interdependent Team Learning? Are information and other resources shared? Is cooperation encouraged or do staff work alone? Are social activities organised for staff? Are minorities supported or ostracised?

❖ **Safety and Security — *stability, protection, a safe workplace, security.*** Is the Code of Health and Safety enforced to provide the corporate community with a safe physical environment? Is the Code of Ethics enforced to safeguard the emotional and spiritual well-being of staff? Does the company pay staff fairly? Are redundancy packages and the details of recruitment agencies offered to those who don't survive downsizing/turf-wars? Is it safe to argue for and sell new ideas? Is it safe to blow the whistle? Do staff trust the leadership team and if so, is this trust well placed?

❖ **Freedom — *the right to grow, the right to be true to one-self and the right to choose.*** Are staff encouraged to grow beyond their job descriptions? Are staff trusted to make the best use of their time? Are staff allowed the autonomy they require to find the best way of doing things and fulfil their responsibilities? Are crèches provided? Are flexible working hours offered? Are staff allowed freedom of association across internal subcultures and across departments? Are staff allowed freedom of thought and speech? Are staff free to stand up for their beliefs without the risk of punishment?

❖ **Fun — *pleasure and enjoyment.*** Is fun encouraged in the workplace:

a) As a stimulator of learning and creativity which will help problem-solving?

b) To promote bonding and relationship building?

c) To facilitate communication as people reveal a more approachable side?

d) To make long working hours more enjoyable?

e) As a stress reliever?

❖ **Power — *influence and authority.*** Are staff encouraged to increase their personal power through mechanisms such as Self-Directed Learning and Interdependent Teamwork? Are staff encouraged to take personal responsibility for their work? Are staff allowed the autonomy they require to get the job done? Is empire-building discouraged? Are staff given appropriate decision-making and sign-off authority? Is coercive power discouraged? Is expert power encouraged?

Community Needs: *Was the workforce given the knowledge and tools to meet new challenges?*

To determine whether the programme addressed the issues mentioned above, convene the strategic management team and the Advisory Committee to facilitate a discussion around the topics.

Leadership Focus Group

All parties can be asked to collate feedback from the line and bring it to the table. The points for discussion which I put forward below do not represent a definitive list and can be supplemented with other appropriate questions.

❖ How was the programme philosophy and strategy communicated to all staff?

❖ Was the workforce provided with learning and development tools and techniques to enable them to transfer learning to the line? Was the value "transfer learning to the workplace" included in performance management systems (e.g. Balanced Scorecard)?

❖ Did Training Department staff go out to the line to support Team Leaders in their people development responsibilities?

❖ What support courses were provided by Training to enable staff to acquire the knowledge and skills to perform new tasks and fill performance gaps?

❖ What external learning opportunities have been provided and is funding made available to staff? Are staff availing of these opportunities? If not, why not?

Organisational Needs: *Kurt Lewin identified two which are important during times of organisational change: a) an increase in survival anxiety; and b) a decrease in learning anxiety.*

a) *Did survival anxiety increase?*

❖ Have participation levels in centralised training courses (e.g. service skills) increased as staff seek to equip themselves to meet the demands of a changing workplace?

❖ If the concept of "a job for life" was done away with, how are staff coping with the changing expectations? (leaving/night-studies/sabotaging change initiatives)

❖ If "performance related pay" was introduced, how has it impacted performance levels? Is the culture now supportive of individuals with a track record for high performance or are they labelled "stars" and subjected to *Lord of the Flies* tactics?

❖ Are staff demonstrating more commitment; e.g. have staff risen to the challenge and taken on broader responsibilities as required?

b) *Did learning anxiety decrease?*

❖ Are staff (and particularly those with new roles and responsibilities) demonstrating competency and excellence?

As needs generate energy, emotions and motives, an astute leadership team will get to know their workforce and learn how to channel energies to drive high performance and productivity.

Organisational Needs: *Did the programme meet business needs e.g. creation of a culture of ethics to relax regulatory pressures and facilitate growth?*

As established earlier, a culture change programme is driven by business needs. In addition to considering if it met its objective, also consider if the programme unearthed another need related to the culture e.g. the need for more creativity and innovation to support the service culture. If so, this will need to be addressed in the next phase of the culture change cycle.

Beliefs, Core Principles and Values

Measure knowledge and support for programme philosophy, core principles and values.

e-Learning Module or Questionnaire supplemented by Focus Groups

❖ Has the programme philosophy been shared?

❖ Was staff input solicited in the creation of the statement of principles and values? Can they name the core principles and values?

❖ Do staff accept and support the core principles and values? If not, what do they think they should be and why?

❖ Have staff utilised programme design surveys to provide input on those key workplace attitudes, behaviours and outcomes that will support core principles and values?

❖ Has the entire organisation been blanketed with a communications campaign that reinforces the core principles and values?

❖ Are staff utilising communication mechanisms to ask for clarification on a) the nature of "vague" core principles and values and b) how they can implement "impractical" core principles and values in the workplace? (This should not be happening but if it is then the communications plan is lacking or the principles and values are meaningless to the workforce.)

Programme Processes and Leaders' Behaviour

Check for leadership congruency with core principles and values by reflecting on how management assumptions about people, places and things have supported the core principles and values on a day-to-day basis:

❖ Did the top team go through a workshop to explore and agree upon their philosophy about people, places and things in relation to the business? Is this philosophy principle-centred in word and spirit?

❖ Did they formally commit to and sign off on their paradigm of beliefs?

❖ During the Phase One event Q&A session, did each senior speaker demonstrate to their audience how they are supporting the principles and values in their own area of the business? Has this input been shared with the top management team for role-modelling purposes?

❖ Are top managers walking their talk? If not, are individuals being held accountable for their behaviour?

❖ What does the programme staff survey say about the congruency of department heads with the principles and values? What does it say about the support that staff are getting in different parts of the business?

13.2.2 Expressions

Attitudes

Measure attitudes to divine if targeted attitudes have changed and, if so, by how much.

Employee Attitude Surveys

The EAS can provide valuable insights into *shifts in attitude* and how the corporate community *perceives behavioural shifts* in the day-to-day business. Line staff are our eyes and our ears. For TWW! we went with the survey form already in place, using it to identify those attitudes and behaviours which aligned with our programme requirements. Of course, to get the best value from such a survey it is best to design a form which totally reflects the programme strategy and goals. Run the survey at the beginning of the programme to establish a benchmark, and again at the end of the programme to measure changes. Unless an organisation has already in place communication vehicles which are respected by the workforce and utilised on a regular basis, there is no excuse for not including everyone in the survey and allowing internal customers their voice. Large corporations can hire consultants to collate, analyse and interpret feedback.

Interactive Communication Forums

These may take the form of a series of live Q&A sessions or an electronic vehicle where staff can post questions to top management and get answers "straight from the horse's mouth". Such forums will not provide structured feedback but they will provide valuable insights into those issues which are important to staff, and staff attitudes towards those issues.

Behaviours

Measure behaviours to divine if targeted behaviours changed and, if so, by how much. Also, consider if the leadership team and the workforce at large respects the spirit intended behind the law.

In 1966, Marvin Bower told us that corporate culture is, in a nutshell, "how we do things around here". It is collective behaviour which ultimately dictates where a corporate culture takes an organisation. Behavioural changes can be tracked using a variety of approaches. For top management, the key indicator of behaviour shifts may well be the final results achieved in relation to the implementation of corporate strategies. Other measures will help track progress as the programme is implemented.

Observation/Performance Monitoring

During module activities (Phase Two meetings and action-planning) the Team Leader will observe participants and monitor how Team Members deliver in relation to their commitments. The Team Leader is responsible for ensuring that all partake in module activities, and for ensuring that individuals, pairs and the whole team cooperate to find new ways of doing things, working for their own good and the common good. The insights gleaned by the Team Leader can be used for performance management activities; e.g. matching individuals to work more suited to them, pairing colleagues who do not understand each others' roles and responsibilities, and identifying training needs.

Team Self-assessment
Self-assessments have been proven to go a longer distance in terms of motivating teams than do any assessments conducted by other parties. At the end of each Phase Two module, Team Members will gather together to track their own behaviour changes, using the Team Behavioural Outcomes provided and their action planning results. I detailed this process in Chapter 9. They will have accumulated rich data during the module implementation phase and it would be fruitful for Team Leaders to extract this data. They can ask the team what went well, when they ran into trouble and how they resolved issues, which plans needed revision and why, what new knowledge and skills they learnt, what knowledge and skills gaps have been uncovered, where they met with resistance and how they overcame it. Their feedback will guide the implementation of future action plans for individuals and the team as a whole.

Performance at Leadership Workshops
When leadership workshops are made available to all line managers, they learn what is required of them in their new role in the workplace. This knowledge they will be able to use to demonstrate new attitudes and behaviours in the workplace. Keep a record of each individual's profile and any track improvements at successive workshops. Some may have been promoted based on years of tenure and may lack the people management skills they need, while others might have superb facilitation skills and be a valuable resource for their extended team. Employee Attitude Surveys at the end of the programme will provide more feedback of perceived behavioural shifts in leadership style.

Competitions
The strategic management team can gain insights into behavioural shifts by analysing competition participation levels and the quality of entries. Such competitions can be organisation-

wide and focus on service, innovation or ethical behaviour. The idea of running a competition for staff to demonstrate ethical behaviour in the workplace will raise some eyebrows, but if the reputation of the business depends on it then I would do it without hesitation. It will build trust when staff know that they are recognised and rewarded for doing the right thing and it will put the spotlight on those who are breaching corporate policies and processes, particularly those who are abusing their position and power to get round these policies and processes.

Training

Check participation levels in support courses provided by Training. High participation levels indicate that staff consider courses helpful, that they are actively pursuing learning and skills development in line with core principles and values and that they have the support of line management. Low participation levels may indicate:

a) That courses are not, or not perceived as, useful;

b) That staff are not interested in continuous learning; or

c) That line management may not be willing or able to release staff for training.

In the latter case, Training will need to conduct a review to identify cause-and-effect relationships.

Leadership Congruency

Staff at all levels are acute observers of the extent to which top executives rhetoric and action support culture change. While leadership congruency with philosophies and strategies will make or break the programme, it is typically not easy to measure. However, the strategic nature and cross-functional design of the initiative makes it very easy for the Executive Sponsor to track congruency as, over time, a track record of behaviour will be established and reflected in the level of support the strategic management team secures from different parts of the business.

Other Measures

❖ **Service:** staff responses in mystery shopper programmes; nature of customer compliments and complaints.

❖ **Ethics:** nature of breaches of the Code of Ethics; nature of disciplinary reports; nature of lawsuits generated internally and externally; level of support for whistle-blowers; presence of an ethical approach in decisions made.

❖ **Innovation:** number of new ideas implemented; participation levels in creativity workshops; use of tools like TRIZ, SCAMPER and ASIT.

13.2.3 Reflections

Artefacts

Measure artefacts for their congruency with the programme goals and objectives.

Programme artefacts can include the policies, processes and tools used to embed the new way of doing things. The key measure of the suitability of any such mechanisms is its congruency with the programme goals and objectives (see Figure 46).

Results

Measure results for key stakeholders by considering the output resulting from on-the-job application of core principles and values.

Results achieved give different stakeholders cause to celebrate. Business leaders can demonstrate that the changed culture enabled delivery on corporate strategies. The workforce can celebrate the major role they played in making the vision a reality. Support functions can justify their existence during lean times. And last but not least, the extended programme team will enjoy a sense of satisfaction for a job well done. Results achieved will be particularly exciting for organisations which have traditionally been shy of measurement (see Figure 47).

Figure 46: Key Measures of Progress

Service Culture	Establishment of customer feedback centres in all departments, the receipt of customer feedback, customer satisfaction surveys, programme materials geared to enhance service, records kept on the number and nature of service failures, the establishment of "mystery shopper" programmes, alignment of performance management tools with strategies and core principles and values, programme communications reinforcing customer service (articles, websites, videos, intranet notices, posters, etc.), job descriptions on the role of managers written in terms of managing the customer experience, adherence to quality standards, creation of local customer-focused procedures, customer calls turned into selling opportunities, recruitment of persons with a service attitude, press reports indicating good customer service from the organisation, establishment of loyalty programmes
Culture of Ethics	Positive employee survey, programme materials geared to enhance ethics, establishment of processes to encourage and support internal whistle-blowing, quality and availability of Code of Ethics, disciplinary reports for breaches and malpractice, alignment of performance management tools with strategies and core principles and values, programme communications reinforcing ethics (articles, websites, videos, intranet notices, posters, etc.), quality and availability of Code of Health and Safety, recruitment of leaders known for their *track record of ethical conduct*, press reports indicating the organisation is honourable
Culture of Innovation	Outputs of ideas implemented (e.g. new policies, processes, products and services), programme materials geared to enhance innovation, creativity workshops, alignment of performance management tools with strategies, core principles and values, programme communications reinforcing innovation (articles, websites, videos, intranet notices, posters, etc.), patents, recruitment of the highly creative, press reports indicating the organization is an innovator

Figure 47: Key Measures of Success

Service Culture	Increased sales, increased wallet-share per customer, increased revenue, increased customer retention figures, enhanced customer satisfaction (both internal and external), more user-friendly products and services, high internal competition participation levels and results, industry awards for customer service; all of this should help increase market share
Culture of Ethics	Enhanced brand image and credibility, reduced number of lawsuits related to breaches in ethics, a reduction in turnover in different parts of the business, ability to retain persons of integrity, retention and fair treatment of whistleblowers, high internal competition participation levels and results, CSR awards for "citizen responsibilities" particularly; all of this should help increase goodwill in the community and enhance brand image
Culture of Innovation	Increased volume of patents registered, increased volume of new products and services, state-of-the-art technologies, high competition participation levels and results, industry awards for innovation, enhanced scenario planning skills, enhanced flow of information and knowledge sharing, the cultivation of an appreciation for specialist knowledge, enhanced responsiveness to changes in the marketplace; all of this should contribute to market leadership

ROI

Calculate return-on-investment by considering how the financial return from the programme relates to the costs as a percentage per dollar invested.

Later, we will look at the overall programme measurement process which will be coordinated by the programme team. Below we focus specifically on the process for calculating ROI. Team Leaders and other responsible parties can collate data pertaining to any increases in revenue as a result of programme action-planning activities, and forward relevant data to the programme team for ROI calculations.

Data Collation by line staff

❖ After each module, collect measurable results using "hard" and "soft" data.

❖ Convert any benefits to monetary units; for hard data items, such as productivity, quality and time, the conversion to monetary units is quite straightforward. As "soft data" items aren't so easy to convert, isolate how the programme activities (e.g. action-planning) may have contributed to results. Trend-line analysis, forecasting, customer feedback, expert estimation and manager estimation are some of the techniques more commonly used (for credibility reasons, ensure any estimates made are conservative).

❖ Separate monetary benefits from the non-monetary and forward all results to the programme team; Team Leaders can do so at the end of each Phase Two module while others responsible for tracking measures like customer retention figures may only be able to forward results at the end of the programme.

Consolidation of monetary results by programme manager for ROI calculation

❖ Collate monetary benefits forwarded by Team Leaders and other line parties.

❖ Total the figures to calculate increased revenue.

❖ Total the costs of the programme by referring to the programme budget and expenditure.

❖ Calculate ROI using the following calculation:

$$\frac{increased\ revenue - costs}{costs}$$

and process: i) subtract the costs of the programme from the monetary benefits and ii) divide the result by the costs. This figure represents the percentage return-on-investment per dollar invested.

❖ Compare ROI achieved to the target outlined in the programme proposal to measure overall results in this area.

Calculating ROI is a sticky process but it is doable. For many, calculating any increased revenue resulting from workplace activities will be part and parcel of the normal work duties, and if one gives adult learners the knowledge and tools to measure their results they will rise to the challenge. Will the final ROI figures be completely accurate? No, because corporate culture measurement is not an exact science, but the ROI figure will provide management with a conservative estimate (when any estimates are prudent) in terms of monetary benefits achieved in relation to programme costs. For more guidance on how to measure ROI for learning and development centred programmes, the American Society of Training and Development (ASTD)[3] has an abundance of resources to refer to.

In the preceding section I shared an array of instruments and approaches which will help measure the results of a culture change programme. Figure 48 depicts how a variety of these fit in at each baseline level of measurement.

---

[3] www.astd.org

Figure 48: Sample Approaches: Measurement at all Levels

Baseline		Measures	Instrument/Approach
REFLECTIONS	*ROI*	Final profit v cost figures	ROI Calculation: <u>benefits – costs</u> costs
	Results	External Alignment	Market share analysis; industry awards
		Internal Integration	Absence of turf wars and politicking; survival of Executive Sponsor, pro-gramme director and programme manager; feedback on service chain effectiveness
		Brand Image	Brand loyalty; press feedback; customer feedback; quality levels
		Workforce Morale	Absenteeism figures; productivity levels
		Customer Satisfaction	Customer feedback (mystery shoppers)
		Customer Retention	Benchmark against internal historical data
		Community Benefits	Staff participation in community service activities; Charity donations
	Artefacts	Congruency of cultural embedding mecha-nisms with strategy	Leaders conduct; recruitment policy; reward and recognition incentives; training course content; performance management system
EXPRESSIONS	*Behaviours*	Changes in targeted behaviours	Team Leader observation on-the-job of individuals, pairs and the whole team; action plan performance monitoring; team self-assessments; competition par-ticipation levels and the quality of en-tries; performance at leadership work-shops; participation levels in training courses; leadership congruency
	Attitudes	Changes in targeted attitudes	Employee attitude surveys; staff communication mechanisms, e.g. electronic interactive Q&A forum

DRIVERS	*Central Paradigm*	Changes in targeted beliefs	Observation; changes in corporate language and terminology
		Workforce knowledge and support of programme philosophy	CBT knowledge-based programmes (participation levels and test results) focusing on programme philosophy, knowledge and the application of knowledge; questionnaires; focus groups; programme processes
	Needs	*Community Needs:* Conduciveness of workplace to staff well-being	Code of Ethics breaches; Code of Health and Safety breaches; staff morale survey data; number of promotions or pay increases; number of training courses attended; requests for transfers; performance appraisal ratings; job enrichment opportunities; exit interviews; programme design
		Organisational Needs: Has learning anxiety decreased? Has survival anxiety increased? Did programme meet business needs?	Leadership focus group; line manager feedback during leadership workshops, e.g. confidence to take on new roles and demonstrate new skills. Increased participation in training courses and further education. Check for alignment with corporate vision and strategies and for a clearly articulated connection in programme proposal.

© O'Donovan, 2006

13.3 The Ten-Step Measurement Process

As elements of the measurement process will be kicked off as soon as the programme is launched, it is useful for the strategic management team to review the steps involved to ensure that they have a shared understanding of what the measurement process entails.

1. Programme manager conducts focus groups with key parties from the line to identify possible measures at each baseline level; select both qualitative and quantitative methods at each level where possible.

2. Once measures are pinned down, set a target for each.

3. Identify departments/individuals responsible for tracking specific measures (e.g. marketing, customer service) and identify any external parties who will be responsible for managing measures like the Employee Attitude Survey.

4. Include completed "Measurement at all Levels Chart" (Appendix 9) in programme proposal and present draft to Steering Committee for approval. Once this is given, get Executive Sponsor sign-off.

5. Design programme materials so that Team Leaders have the knowledge and tools required to measure the outputs of their action planning ("hard" and "soft" data — see Appendix 8).

6. Put in place a feedback mechanism for line teams to share their results at the end of each module.

7. Consolidate results at each baseline level; use monetary results and programme costs to calculate ROI.

8. Present all results to the Steering Committee. The programme director will present results to the broader leadership team.

9. Communicate wins across the organisation and submit the programme for industry awards.

10. Review and refine the measurement process.

The strategic management team will be able to use their knowledge of the business to identify who should be responsible for what measurement instruments and approaches.

13.4 Plan for the Future

With the completion of the programme, it can be tempting to claim success and neglect the corporate culture moving forward. To do so would undermine ground made and erode any long-term value. The change cycle is one of constant renewal.

Once the programme is completed, the process must start all over again with the questioning of the established way of doing things in relation to a changing environment. To strengthen the organisation and facilitate growth and learning a review should be conducted at the end of a culture change programme to identify successes and lessons learnt, because while most change management programmes fail flat-out, the rest can only claim partial success. Conclusions drawn can be documented and this historical data will become a valuable resource when planning for the future.

If considering a second cycle and to build on the successes of the first programme, I would again run a centralised event to share core principles and values and explore their application in an evolving workplace, particularly if the workforce runs into tens of thousands, and the first cycle took a few years. In other cases, a roadshow may achieve the same result. For the localised phase two, the workforce can build on their strong local teamwork by concentrating on cross-functional teamwork. Staff can gather firstly to share internal and external best practices and how they might be applied in the organisation, and secondly to share their knowledge through real workplace case studies. If the same CEO is in power, they will continue to be Executive Sponsor. Other key change agents (for example, programme director and programme manager) should move on to new challenges and be replaced by fresh blood. The Steering Committee and Advisory Committee will have the same make-up, but the faces will change. The Steering Committee *must* be chaired by a business leader.

This time round, and assuming the previous programme was not derailed or seriously undermined, implementation will be easier; the programme scaffolding in place, learning and development has been localised in the workplace, top management and functional management have demonstrated their support for staff efforts, the workforce have an array of reusable tools which will help them embrace change in the workplace and line wins have increased their confidence in the new way of doing things.

13.5 Chapter Summary

While results are collated at the end of a programme, the up-front identification of programme performance measures gives credibility to the initiative in the eyes of top management and helps the programme manager secure the support, budget and resources required.

To kick off the process, consider the big picture first by reflecting on the unique challenges the organisation faces together with the programme strategy. The measurement approaches selected will depend first and foremost on what outcomes the organisation is seeking to achieve with the culture change initiative. Common challenges facing organisations in this era include the creation of a service culture, a culture of ethics or a culture of innovation.

Whatever the primary focus of a culture change programme, the baseline measurement will remain the same across the board. There are three levels — drivers, expressions and reflections. *Drivers* include needs plus the shared central paradigm (beliefs and assumptions, principles and values); *expressions* include attitudes and behaviours; and *reflections* include artefacts, results and return-on-investment. Measures can include final profit v cost figures, external alignment, internal integration, brand image, community benefits, workforce morale, customer satisfaction and retention, suitability and effectiveness of cultural embedding mechanisms, shifts in targeted attitudes and behaviours, knowledge and support of core principles and values, and a safe and happy workplace which is conducive to productivity and excellence.

While the baseline measurement is the same for any culture change programme, the instruments and approaches used will differ to suit the unique corporate culture and unique organisational challenges. Instruments and approaches include return-on-investment calculations, market share analysis, line manager observation, analysis of press feedback, absenteeism figures, CBT programmes, staff surveys and focus groups, an analysis of promotions and pay increases and how they are allocated, job enrichment opportunities and industry awards.

Each instrument and approach will produce "hard" or "soft" data. "Hard data" is relatively easy to measure: internal examples include output, quality, time, cost and customer retention figures; while external examples include changes in market share and industry awards. "Soft data" is more difficult to measure but is of equal importance, because needs, beliefs and attitudes drive outcomes and results. Internal examples include the use of new skills, development and advancement opportunities and how they are allocated, and the use of initiative, workforce morale and internal integration. External examples include press feedback and customer feedback. Both qualitative and quantitative data should be used to track culture changes at each baseline level.

Once the measurement tools and approaches have been approved, targets will be set for each. Then the programme team will progress to designing and developing tools and techniques to support line teams in their efforts to measure their results at the end of each module. When the programme has been implemented, the programme manager can consolidate results for the leadership team. Any wins can be celebrated by communicating them across the organisation. This will give credibility to future culture change programmes and maintain the momentum of ground made.

During the implementation phase, the external environment will have continued to evolve and by completion of the programme a new set of external realities will be facing the organisation. The goal posts will have moved. To plan for the future, review successes and ground made together with failures and lessons learnt. Document all facts, then decide what to keep and what to let go of.

Appendix 1

TOGETHER WE WIN!
A CLOSER LOOK

Phase One: Support Activities and Projects

Together We Win! (TWW!) was a bankwide culture change programme implemented in HSBC Hong Kong plus five subsidiary companies. Figure 2 in Chapter 1 outlines all the activities and projects that supported the core programme and below are examples of what a selection of these looked like in practice.

Event Hall Development

While construction of the event hall was handled by external contractors, the programme team was responsible for the site design and development work. At the outset the 10,500 square feet of gutted space on the fourth floor of the bank looked much like a rubbish tip but it was marvellous to have a blank canvas to work with. In no time at all, and with a team of helpers, the site had been completely transformed into a purpose-built event hall. Behind the scenes activities which made this possible included the recruitment of the design contractor, the coordination of all contractors, the supervision of work-in-progress on a daily basis and the sourcing of furniture and audio-visual equipment.

Event Management

The post of Event Manager was shared by the programme manager and assistant manager, who rotated on a daily basis. Event Manager responsibilities included early arrival for set-up purposes, MC responsibilities, manpower deployment, the overseeing of logistics, live Q&A session management and facilitator coaching. Other core team members and those on attachment would take care of audio-video management and facilitator coaching during the course of the day, and gift-shop management at the end of the day. For Phase One, the team worked closely with line management to organise attendance and ensure that the make-up of any team, on any given day, reflected a good mixture of staff with different profiles. The team also worked closely with the catering staff to ensure that menus reflected staff needs, and the food delivery schedule complemented programme logistics.

Steering Committee Meetings

The strategic management team convened once every six weeks and the following process made sure the best use was made of time:

❖ Prior to a meeting the programme director would meet with the programme manager to touch base on specific issues.

❖ Then the programme manager would forward a progress report to committee members advising them of the current status, hurdles overcome, decisions made and outstanding issues in need of consensus.

❖ Committee members' responses would help further eliminate some of the outstanding issues and determine the meeting agenda to be sent out.

❖ When the team gathered the programme manager would lead the discussions by briefing all on the current status focusing on any deviations and variations to the plan.

❖ Once consensus was reached on the way forward, the meeting was adjourned and minutes were disseminated with action items and responsible parties highlighted.

Customer Feedback Focus Groups

In 2001 the programme team conducted customer feedback focus groups onsite at the event hall. The purpose of these gatherings was to solicit staff views on progress to date and the way forward. At the end of event operations, volunteers were invited to stay behind to fill in a feedback form and participate in focus groups which would be facilitated by core team members. Just as we expected, the most significant feedback from participants was that they had understood the core values but needed help transferring them to the workplace. In terms of the format, many wanted another fun event. However, this was not an option as the aim of Phase Two would be to transfer learning to the workplace to get business results. Winning acceptance for a different approach would prove challenging, but do-able. Also, and in terms of the content, many staff were thinking along the same lines as ourselves. For example, and with regard to the core value "teamwork", some expressed the view that they needed help with aspects of teamwork like "cooperating" and "respecting the contribution of the individual to the team effort". We would use this input to design Team Behavioural Outcomes for Phase Two.

Phase Two: Support Activities and Projects

Advisory Committee Meetings

When responsibility for the success or failure of the programme transferred to the line for Phase Two we established an Advisory Committee consisting of the heads of major departments: the head of financial control, the head of IT, the head of the credit cards division, the deputy head of the retail bank, the head of training and the head of operations. This group advised the strategic management team on line issues, reviewed the design of materials and ensured that these were relevant to diverse areas of the Bank. The programme manager would meet with members of each committee to address local issues, identify and overcome resistance to the programme and provide consultancy services. Meetings were held ten days prior to the gathering of the strategic management team and on one occasion, where we had to convene the Steering Committee first, the response of the Advisory Committee told us that they preferred the original process. This indicated to us a level of ownership which we had hoped for.

Materials Distribution

As the programme spanned the whole of HSBC Holdings Hong Kong plus five subsidiary companies, the localised setting called for military-type logistical planning. The programme team worked with 290 identified Line Materials Coordinators to ensure that all 1,400 Team Leaders and 13,000+ Team Members received their materials in an efficient and effective manner no matter where they were located. This would enable all parts of the business to launch each module in unison. The Line Materials Coordinators were responsible for receiving programme materials and while much of the materials were delivered to central points using internal resources, we even employed the services of DHL to deliver materials to the more remote retail outlets.

Customer Satisfaction e-Survey

By the second quarter of 2002, the sequel to Phase One was well underway so we decided to conduct a survey to solicit feedback on the first two modules and ideas on future modules. Our "Customer Satisfaction e-Survey" was conducted online via the intranet during April and May with hard copies of the form distributed for those who didn't have online access. The results provided us with a window into how change was being received in the different departments. Moreover, the comments reflected a strong correlation between staff attitude to the programme and their perception of the degree of support and encouragement they were getting from their department heads.

Electronic Q&A Forum Management

Our electronic Q&A forum "Ask Top Management" (ATM) was hosted on the programme website and launched with Phase Two of TWW! The purpose of this forum was to provide staff with an internal communication channel which they would readily utilise. This site would allow staff bankwide a communication vehicle to put to top management issues which were of general concern and in need of a top management response. A policy and a process were drawn up regarding usage, and both were posted on the programme website. Basically, any staff member could use the forum anonymously to raise a question with the top team. Questions which would not be processed included those which could be addressed by line management, derogatory questions, questions which raised personal grievances and those which included bad language. A vetting committee was established to act as forum gatekeeper and ensure that questions were answered properly. This committee included the head of the retail bank, the head of corporate and institutional banking, the head of human resources and the head of communications. The programme manager was forum administrator and for security reasons was the only individual with access to the more sensitive areas of the vehicle. This administrator role included screening questions for compliance with forum policy, collating questions and forwarding them to identified line owners for answering. Then, when draft answers came back, the programme manager would forward them to the Vetting Committee for their input and approval. Typically, some answers were accepted immediately while others were held back for further consideration. Staff who accessed the forum could read the indicator beside any one question to learn if it was still being processed. The turnaround time for any question was ten days. As each answer was approved by all members of the vetting committee the programme manager would post it live on the website for staff bankwide to read. As a result of issues raised by staff using this forum, many Bank policies changed. Also, when the ATM progress report was shared with the Asia chairman and the Asia chief executive in February 2002, it was noted that there was a degree of surprise with the huge audience the top management answers were getting. The view was taken that the vehicle was becoming an increasingly important communication vehicle for top management and the consensus was that the monthly reports would continue.

Culture Embedding Mechanisms

Allocation of Resources

How resources were allocated would indicate to the workforce what the leaders were paying attention to, measuring and controlling:

❖ *Direct*: a full-time dedicated team, the budget, a site venue for the Phase One event, the time of top management for Steering Committee Meetings and live Q&A sessions, the time of line workers to participate in the Phase One event, etc.

❖ *Indirect*: event hall overheads, the resources of cross-functional departments for support activities like modules distribution, the time of line workers to participate in Phase Two activities, etc.

Role-modelling, Teaching and Coaching

Leadership Development

Line managers became Team Leaders for their own direct and indirect reports so that we could introduce leadership at all levels across the Bank. All 1,400 Team Leaders went through our annual one-day workshops designed to develop their lead-

ership skills. The first series of workshops were held
launch of Phase Two while the second series of worksh…
tled "Leading Change with TWW!" were designed to i…
develop the facilitative style of leadership for Team Leade…
There was an increased focus on facilitation and coaching techniques so we recruited the help of Training staff to support the
programme team. With the second set of workshops, it was
clear that staff attitude towards change had improved considerably. Whereas in earlier days, more had expressed fear and
powerlessness in the face of change, expressing a strong
"blame" attitude, by the end of 2002 the general tone was a
more relaxed acceptance of the challenges the Bank faced, together with a sense of direction and the tools which could be
used to meet ongoing challenges. In September 2002, feedback
consolidated from line managers attending these workshops
was extremely positive. Many expressed that they had received
a lot of value from the "line best practices" sharing sessions
particularly. Also, the level of confidence of line managers to
facilitate team meetings and supervise staff has increased significantly, as evidenced in programme results.

Training and Development

❖ The six core values were included in all **training and development courses**.

❖ A series of **coaching workshops** were designed for Team
  Leaders to support them with their new responsibilities and
  further develop their leadership skills.

❖ New **customer service courses** were provided to train those
  who moved from the back office to the front line and anyone
  else who wished to develop in this area.

Rewards and Status

❖ Event facilitators received a **Certificate of Performance** in
  recognition of their contribution to this major programme.

rho participated in our online Customer
2001 we held a ***lucky draw***. Six individu-
a note from the programme team con-
ı their HK$250 win and this would be
personal phone call. From these six
ıanagement team chose an overall win-
.. ∪ceering Committee meeting. The winning
ıdea was for an e-Newsletter on programme progress to be
sent to every Team Leader once a month. The winner received a HK$500 shopping voucher and shared his idea in
the internal magazine.

❖ For Phase Two, teams which achieved noteworthy success
in their action-planning were profiled in the internal magazine and on the programme website, giving them ***bankwide
recognition*** for their efforts.

❖ The third key value was "Together We Delight Customers".
As Module Sponsor, the head of the retail bank decided to
introduce some extra excitement into the initiative by holding a ***bankwide competition***. For staff, the objective of the
bankwide competition was to deliver best practice examples of customer service. A key criterion was that the success had to be from the customers' viewpoint. The first prize
was a trip for the winning team members and family members on the *Super Star Leo* cruise-liner together with an engraved Gold Cup. All seven teams received an engraved
Silver Cup together with individual certificates of recognition and each Department Head rewarded the semi-finalist
team from their part of the business with dinner in a high-
class restaurant. A total of 317 team entries were received,
all showing the positive measures taken to increase the
workforce's ability to serve customers. Competition results
and winning teams were communicated bankwide in the internal "Wayfoong Magazine" and on the intranet sites. A
large number of line teams downloaded the winning team's
results from the TWW! intranet.

❖ With the introduction of **performance related pay** any individual who received an exceptional performance rating would receive

  a) A note from the Asia CEO recognising their considerable contribution to the bank;

  b) A generous bonus payment, the amount to be determined by annual profits; and

  c) The gift of share options.

❖ In 2003, and to recognise the short-term results produced by staff bankwide with TWW!, the Bank entered competitions for **industry awards**, winning both the *Best Practice Award in Training & Development* and the *Customer Service Grand Award*. In 2005, TWW! won an ASTD *Excellence in Practice Award*.

Organisational Systems and Procedures

Many **human resource policies and processes** changed at the request of line staff who called for changes via the programme e-communication vehicle "Ask Top Management". Also:

Performance Management System

❖ The six core values were included in the **competency definitions**, starting with the Competency Development Programme for retail staff.

❖ The new **performance management system** (the balanced scorecard approach) was aligned with the core values.

❖ At the request of the programme director, line managers had their role as TWW! Team Leaders reflected in their **annual objectives**.

Compensation and Benefits

With the removal of the thirteenth-month pay (a local Chinese tradition), performance-related pay was introduced and, through the performance management system, individual staff members would be rewarded for working in line with company values. This was counter-cultural in that up until this point team contribution was encouraged, but recognition often went to presiding managers. This new compensation and benefits policy was not a part of "Together, We Win!" but as the prevailing culture was not supportive of the policy, our programme materials reinforced the encouraging of respect for the individual contribution within the team setting and the giving of recognition where it was rightfully due.

Rites and Rituals

The design of the whole programme incorporated many useful *rites and rituals*. For example:

❖ The gathering of the strategic management team on a regular basis to consider aspects of the corporate culture was an invaluable practice.

❖ It became a ritual for the Advisory Committee to review learning materials and ensure that they met business needs.

❖ Also, it became a ritual for teams bankwide to align their daily activities and results with corporate strategy via action-planning. This will have done much to strengthen the organisation.

CORPORATE CULTURE: MEASUREMENT TOOLS AND TECHNIQUES

Espoused Culture	
Structured	*Unstructured*
• Induction programmes • HR Policy & Procedure manuals	• Company website • Company reports • In-house magazines • In-house intranet sites • Vision statements on board-room walls • Principles and values communicated by business leaders in public speeches and interviews
Prevailing Culture	
Structured	*Unstructured*
• Conduct large scale employee attitude surveys to encompass all • Organise smaller focus groups • Employ Change Readiness Assessment Tools (generally provided by external consultants)	• Interview business leaders • Review language and tone used in internal memos • Attend meetings and observe • Socialise with colleagues from different work groups • Attend presentations and observe • Participate in, or facilitate, training and development workshops

	<ul><li>Tour facilities</li><li>Chat with workers</li><li>Sit with your team to observe behaviour closely</li><li>Reflect on messages in public speeches and interviews of business leaders</li><li>Review communications materials (e.g. formal strategy presentations)</li><li>Review formal organisational structure and informal networks</li><li>Identify long-timers who know how things are done and also whose word carries most weight</li><li>Decipher beliefs, principles and values communicated by business leaders in public speeches and interviews</li><li>Consider local context and national culture</li></ul>Also, consider the following:<ul><li>Who are the heroes and the villains?</li><li>Do people smile and chatter at work?</li><li>Who is promoted, demoted, forced out? Why?</li><li>Regarding the make-up of executive management: is diversity encouraged?</li></ul>

Appendix 3

CHARACTERISTICS OF A "SHADES-OF-GREY" CULTURE

PEOPLE

The Individual's Locus of Control

Externally directed   Internally directed
X

Nature of Human Activity

Reactive, fatalistic   Proactive
X

The Nature of an Individual's Value

Useful to job on hand   Intrinsic to being human
X

The Nature of Corporate Culture

Dull   Intelligent
X

The Essence of Diversity

Differences in appearance   Differences in thinking
X

Subcultural Uniformity versus Diversity

High uniformity   High diversity
X

Nature of Human Nature

Humans are basically evil   Humans are basically good
X

PLACES

The Natural Environment

An externality   The centre of existence
✗

THINGS

The Organisation's Central Paradigm

Other   Principle-centred in   Principle-centred in
                            word only   word and spirit
   ✗

The Nature of Company Values

A meaningless statement   A public relations ploy   A true commitment
                              ✗

Public Image

Manufactured   Authentic
✗

The Nature of the Organisation

Inert structures   The inert and the human   An entity
                                                          ✗

Governance

Autocracy   Democracy
✗

Core Purpose

Increase shareholder value   Responsible provision of goods & services
✗

Workforce–Organisation Relationship

Human resources/Tools   Members/citizens
✗

Organisation–Stakeholder Relationship

To be manipulated   To be respected
✗

Organisation–Business Environment Relationship

Estranged   Attuned

— — — — — — — — — — — — ✕ — — — — — — — — — — — —

Bad News and Whistle-blowing

A threat   A learning opportunity

✕ —

Decision-making

Immoral   Amoral   Moral

✕ —

Ownership for Learning and Development

Centralised   Localised

✕ —

Communication

Closed   Open

✕ —

How Best Results Are Achieved

Self-interest   Altruism   Self-interest and group
                                                                       interest

— ✕ —

The Service Provider

Front-line workers   Contracted parties   All staff
✕ —

Emotional Expression

To be controlled   To be encouraged   To be encouraged
                                  and managed

— ✕ —

© *O'Donovan, 2006*

Characteristics of a "Black-and-White" Culture

PEOPLE

The Individual's Locus of Control

Externally directed   Internally directed

The Nature of an Individual's Value

Useful to job on hand   Intrinsic to being human

The Power of Mankind

A law unto himself   Subject to universal laws

The Complexity of Human Intelligence

One-dimensional   Multi-faceted

The Essence of Diversity

Differences in appearance   Differences in thinking

PLACES

The Natural Environment

An externality   The centre of existence

THINGS

The Organisation's Central Paradigm

Other	Principle-centred in word only	Principle-centred in word and spirit

✖

The Nature of Company Values

A meaningless statement	A public relations ploy	A true commitment

✖

The Nature of Reality and Truth

Moralistic Authoritative		Pragmatic

✖

Public Image

Manufactured		Authentic

✖

The Nature of the Organisation

Inert structures	The inert and the human	Human

✖

Governance

Autocracy		Democracy

✖

Core Purpose

Increase shareholder value	Responsible provision of goods & services

✖

Workforce–Organisation Relationship

Human resources/tools		Members/citizens

✖

Organisation–Stakeholder Relationship

To be manipulated		To be respected

✖

Organisation–Business Environment Relationship

Estranged   Attuned
                                                              ✖

Bad News and Whistle-blowing

A threat   A learning opportunity
✖

Decision-making

Immoral   Amoral   Moral but rigid
                                                              ✖

Ownership for Learning and Development

Centralised   Localised
✖

Communication

Closed   Open
✖

Speed of Response to Customer Demands

Low   Medium   High
✖

The Service Provider

Front-line workers   Contracted parties   All staff
                                                              ✖

Emotional Expression

Unacceptable   To be encouraged   To be encouraged
                          and managed
                              ✖

© O'Donovan, 2006

APPENDIX 5: TRACKING MY DECISION MAKING PROCESS

Situation/Issue: _____

My Decision: _____

Stakeholders	Pressures	My Deciding Factors	Consequences for Me	Consequences for each other Stakeholder	Repercussions (if any)	Moving Forward
		Self Interest? or Self interest & group interest? or Moral Laws? Does this reflect – a short v long term perspective? – self-interest or moral integrity?				Lessons learnt: What I would do differently if presented with same situation/ issue again:

Appendix 6

ETHICAL DECISION-MAKING TOOL

Everything we do, or don't do, is a choice that can affect the course of our lives and the lives of others. Change, whether or not for the advancement of good, is always just a decision away. Therefore, we need to take personal responsibility for making decisions which are ethical and empowering.

	Items	Action Steps
P R O C E S S	1. Clarify	• Determine precisely what must be decided. • Formulate and devise the full range of things you could do. • Eliminate impractical, illegal and improper alternatives. • Force yourself to develop at least three ethically justifiable options. • Examine each option to determine which ethical principles and values are involved.
	2. Evaluate	• If any of the options require the sacrifice of any ethical principle, evaluate the facts and assumptions carefully. • Distinguish solid facts from beliefs, desires, theories, suppositions, unsupported conclusions and opinions that might generate rationalisations. • Take into account the credibility of the sources of information and the fact that self-interest, bias and ideological commitments tend to obscure objectivity and affect perceptions about what is true. • With regard to each alternative, carefully consider the benefits, burdens and risks to each stakeholder.

	Items	Action Steps
↑ S S E C O R P ↓	**3. Decide**	• Make a judgement about what is or is not true and about what consequences are most likely to occur.
		• If there is an ethical problem, evaluate the viable alternatives according to personal conscience, prioritise the values so that you can choose which values to advance and which to subordinate and determine who will be helped the most and harmed the least.
		• It is sometimes helpful to consider the worst case scenario.
		• In addition, consider whether ethically questionable conduct can be avoided by modifying goals or methods or by consulting with those likely to be affected in order to get their input or consent.
		• Finally, you may want to rely on three "ethics guides": *Golden Rule*: Are you treating others as you would want to be treated? *Publicity*: Would you be comfortable if your reasoning and decision were to be publicised? How would feel about seeing it on the front page of tomorrow's papers? *Kid-on-your-Shoulder*: Would you be comfortable if your children were observing you? Are you practising what you preach?
	4. Implement	• Develop a plan to implement the decision in a way that maximises the benefits and minimises the costs and risks.
		• Remember that any decision or act, however ethical, is bound to be weakened by a sanctimonious, pious, judgemental or self-righteous attitude.
	5. Monitor and Modify	• An ethical decision-maker should monitor the effects of decisions and be prepared and willing to revise a plan, or take a different course of action, based on new information.
		• Since most decisions are based on imperfect information and "best effect" predictions, it is inevitable that some will be wrong. Those decisions will either fail to produce the consequences anticipated or they will produce unintended and/or unforeseen consequences.
		• The ethical decision-maker is willing to adjust to new information.

This tool was developed from "The Seven-Step Path to Better Decisions" found in *Making Ethical Decisions* by Michael Josephson, president and founder of the Josephson Institute of Ethics. *Making Ethical Decisions* is available at www.josephsoninstitute.org

Common Rationalisations

People are especially vulnerable to rationalisations when they seek to advance a cause. Here are some of the most common:

❖ **If it's necessary, it's ethical.** This approach often leads to ends-justify-the-means reasoning.

❖ **The false necessity trap.** We sometimes over-estimate the cost of doing the right thing and understimate the cost of not doing it.

❖ **If it's legal and permissible, it's proper.** This substitutes legal requirements for personal moral judgement.

❖ **I was just doing it for you.** This is the primary justification for withholding important information in personal and professional relationships.

❖ **I'm just fighting fire with fire.** The reasoning here is that if everyone is doing it, it is OK.

❖ **It doesn't hurt anyone.** The reasoning is that we can violate ethical principles so long as there is no clear and immediate harm to others.

❖ **Everyone's doing it.** This is a false "safety in numbers" rationale which uncritically treats cultural and organisational norms as ethical norms.

❖ **It's okay if I don't benefit personally.** This justifies improper conduct done for others or for institutional purposes.

❖ **"I deserve additional perks."** People who feel they are over-worked or underpaid rationalise that minor "perks" are fair compensation.

❖ **"I can still be objective."** This rationalisation ignores the fact that a loss of objectivity always prevents perception of the loss of objectivity.

❖ **"It falls into a grey area."** Shades-of-grey reasoning can be helpful for seeing a broad range of perspectives. However, this reasoning allows more scope for improper behaviour if the decision-maker does not have clear ethical standards.

Reprinted from *Making Ethical Decisions* with permission of The Josephson Institute of Ethics; © 2006 www.josephsoninstitute.org

Appendix 7

OPERATIONS NEWSLETTER

The figure below shares an overview of a newletter which HSBC Hong Kong operations staff designed themselves to share wins and maintain momentum in the face of change.

Newsletter Content May '02

A Note from the Manager

Feedback on business activity, the ability to meet all targets (including service lead time, cost and productivity), the importance of designing new workflows and procedures, the benefits of physically relocating office.

Customer Service Corner

Number of commendations, number of complaints, Customer Contact Briefings conducted in response to line action planning needs with Module Three of TWW!

Chat Room

A new chatroom which complemented the "Ask Top Management" communication forum for staff bankwide; this new forum would allow staff to raise issues locally and anonymously.

Operational Risk Measurement and Management

Staff given specific measures in terms of "People", "Systems", "Processes" and "External" risk; they were advised that an action plan had been drawn up to measure and monitor risks and that they would be briefed by individual Section Managers on this.

Briefing Session

44 compliance briefings were held recently; 2 demonstrations were held on the operation and workflow of payment processing.

Activity

Information on office relocation and opening ceremony; tournament win for bowling team.

Liaision Group Meeting

Feedback on how ideas raised over the past two months were actioned locally.

Service Performance

Feedback on changes in the Productivity Index and Commendation.

Staff Recognition

1) Photos and names of six staff who received most appreciation from their supervisors in 1Q02.

2) Photos and names of ten staff for effective Fraud Prevention including case information.

Appendix 8

HARD AND SOFT DATA

Internal Measures

Hard Data

❖ **Output:** number of new customers, items assembled, forms processed, units produced, jobs completed, items sold, increased revenue.

❖ **Time:** projects overrunning, employee overtime, training and development costs, computers down.

❖ **Quality:** product defects, defects in services, rework, scrap and wastage, service failures.

❖ **Cost:** cost of settling lawsuits generated internally for ethics failures or for health and safety failures, cost of replacing knowledge workers who depart, overheads, variable costs, sales expenses.

Soft Data

❖ **Social Climate:** job satisfaction, no. of grievances, no. of discrimination cases, atmosphere, staff turnover figures, internal customer compliments and complaints.

❖ **Conduct:** visits to the doctor, tardiness, Code of Safety Violations, Code of Ethics violations.

❖ **Attitude:** staff trust in leadership team, staff perceptions of employer, staff perceptions of work environment, staff perceptions of own job.

❖ **Adaptability:** staff use of new knowledge, skills and attitude (e.g. service attitude).

❖ **Skills:** crisis managed effectively, conflict situations resolved peacefully, problems solved, quality of decisions made.

❖ **Development and Advancement:** number of pay rises and pay cuts, number of promotions and demotions, number of transfers, number of training courses attended, number of high performers, number of low performers.

External Measures

Hard Data

❖ **A Service Culture:** increased marketshare, changes in track record for taking care of customers; decreases in quality-related complaints.

❖ **A Culture of Ethics:** relaxation of regulatory pressures, increased marketshare, number (and costs of settling) lawsuits generated from outside for ethics breaches or for health and safety violations, track record for the responsible provision of goods and services.

❖ **Culture of Innovation:** number of patents and their utilisation, market leadership, track record for product and service innovation.

Soft Data

❖ **A Service Culture:** reputation for service quality, press feedback, customer feedback, ability to attract "service stars", service awards.

❖ **A Culture of Ethics:** reputation for integrity based on a track record of ethical conduct, press feedback, customer feedback, ability to attract persons of stellar character, corporate governance awards.

❖ **A Culture of Innovation:** reputation for innovation, press feedback, customer feedback, ability to attract and retain innovators, awards for innovation.

Appendix 9

Measurement at all Levels Chart

Measurement at All Levels			
	Baseline	**Instrument and Approach**	**Target**
Reflections	*ROI* *Results* *Artefacts*		
Expressions	*Behaviours* *Attitudes*		
Drivers	*Central Paradigm* *Needs*		

BIBLIOGRAPHY

Bach, Richard, *Jonathan Livingstone Seagull*, Turnstone Press, 1972.

Bakan, Joe, *The Corporation*, Constable & Robinson Ltd., 2005.

Bower, Marvin, *The Will to Manage*, McGraw-Hill, 1966.

Brassard, M. and Ritter, D., *Memory Jogger*, GOAL/QPC, 1994.

Coelho, Paulo, *The Alchemist*, Harper Collins, 1995.

Collins, J.C., *Good to Great*, Harper Collins, 2001.

Collins, J.C. and Porras, J.I., *Built to Last*, Harper Business Essentials, 2002.

Connor, Daryl, *Managing the Human Aspects of CRM Projects*, Headstrong, 2000.

Covey, Stephen, *The 7 Habits of Highly Effective People*, Fireside, 1990.

Covey, Stephen, *Principle-Centered Leadership*, FreePress, 1990.

Deal, Terence E. and Kennedy, Allan A., *Corporate Cultures*, Perseus Publishing, 1982.

Deal, Terence E. and Kennedy, Allan A., *The New Corporate Cultures*, Perseus Publishing, 1999.

Duck, Jeanie, "Managing Change", *Harvard Business Review*, November 1993.

Gerstner, Louis V. Jr., *Who Says Elephants Can't Dance?* Harper Business, 2002.

Glasser, William, *Control Theory*, Harper and Row, 2004.

GlobeScan, *Corporate Social Responsibility Monitor*, 2005.

Handy, Charles, "Democracy's New Frontier", *The Economist*, January 2005.

Handy, Charles, *The New Alchemists*, Hutchison, 1999.

Hickman, Craig and Silva, Michael, *Creating Excellence*, George Allen and Unwin, 1985.

International Survey Research, *Ethics and Organizational Culture: How Corporate Culture Impacts Shareholder Security*, September 2002.

Jaffe, D., and Scott C., *Managing Change at Work*, Thomson, 1995.

Johnson, Spencer Dr., *Who Moved My Cheese?* Vermillion, 2000.

Katzenbach, J.R., *Peak Performance*, Harvard Business School Press, 2000.

Kirton, M.J. DSc., *Kirton Adaption-Innovation Inventory Tool*, 1985.

Ley Toffler, Barbara, *Final Accounting*, Doubleday, 2002.

O'Brien, Justin, "Insider Trading Case To Test Chinese Walls", *The Irish Times*, 1 May 2006.

O'Donovan, Gabrielle, "A Board Culture of Corporate Governance", *Corporate Governance International*, September 2003.

Pope, Conor, "Why Ethical Equals Profitable", *The Irish Times*, 1 May 2006.

Prokesch, Steven, "Remaking the American CEO", *New York Times*, 15 January 1987.

Pfeffer, J. and O'Reilly, C.A., *Hidden Principle*, Harvard Business School Press, 2000.

Richards, Louise, *Financial Times*, 25 February 2005, p. 12.

Rudinow, Barry, *Critical Thinking*, Harcourt Brace, 1994.

Schaef, Anne Wilson, and Fassel, Diane, *The Addictive Organisation*, Harper Collins, 1990.

Schaffer, R.H. and Thomson, H.A. "Successful Change Efforts Begin With Results", *Harvard Business Review*, January–February 1998.

Schein, Edgar, *Organizational Cultures and Leadership*, Third Edition, Jossey-Bass, 2004.

Schneider, B., "The People Make the Place", *Personnel Psychology*, 1987.

Schwartz, Peter and Gibb, Blair, *When Good Companies Do Bad Things*, John Wiley & Sons, 1999.

Senge, Peter, *The Dance of Change*, Currency Doubleday, 1999.

Senge, Peter, *The Fifth Discipline*, Bantam Dell Publishing Group, 1990.

Serwer Andy, "Wall Street Comes to Main Street", *Fortune Magazine*, May 2004, p. 88.

Singer, Peter, *The President of Good and Evil*, Granta, 2004.

Stewart, Jim. *Managing Change Through Training and Development*, Kogan Page, 1996.

Sullivan, Andrew, *Time Magazine*, 26 April 2004.

Thaler, David, "The Role of Industrial Relations in the Structural Change of Organizations", *European Industrial Relations Observatory* online, 2002.

The Christian Science Monitor, 2004.

Tichy, Noel, *The Leadership Engine*, Harper Business, 2002.

Tuckman, B.W. and Jensen, M.A.C., Stages of Small Group Development, *Group and Organizational Studies*, 2, p. 419-427, 1977

Zohar, Danah and Marshall, Ian, *Spiritual Capital*, Bloomsbury Publishing, 2004.

Other Books That Have Influenced My Work

Annas, Julia, *Ancient Philosophy*, Oxford University Press, 2000.

Axelrod, Alan, *Patton on Leadership*, Prentice Hall Press, 1999.

Benton, D.A., *How To Think Like a CEO*, Warner Books, 1999.

Drucker, Michael, *Managing in Turbulent Times*, Pan Books Ltd., 1980.

Duck, Jeanie Daniel, *The Change Monster*, Crown Business, 2001.

Hammer, Michael and Champy, James, *Reengineering the Corporation*, Nicholas Brealey Publishing Ltd., 1994.

Handy, Charles, *The Gods of Management*, Arrow Books Ltd, 1991.

Johnson, Gerry, *Strategic Change and the Management Process*, 1987.

Johnson, Kevan and Scholes, Gerry, *Exploring Corporate Strategy*, Prentice Hall International, 1984.

Lundin, Paul and Christensen, John, *Fish*, Hodder and Stoughton, 2000.

Magee, Bryan, *The Story of Philosophy*, Dorling Press, 2001.

McConnell, Carmel, *Change Activist*, Pearson Education Ltd., 2001.

Moore, Thomas, *The Original Self*, Harper Collins, 2000.

O'Donovan, Gabrielle, "Is Corporate Culture Important?" *Mondaq Legal & Financial*, May 2003.

O'Donovan, Gabrielle, "Change Management: The Whole Equation", *Banking Today*, April 2003.

Orwell, George, *Animal Farm*, Longman Group, 1983.

Peck, M. Scott, *The Road Less Travelled*, Hutchison & Co., 1983.

Roberts, Wess, *Leadership Secrets of Attila the Hun*, Warner Books, 1987.

Staub de Laszlo, Violet, *The Basic Writings of C.G. Jung*, Modern Library, 1993.

Townsend, Robert, *Up The Organisation*, Coronet, 1971.

Watzlawick, Paul, Weakland, John and Fisch, Richard, *Change*, W.W. Norton and Co, 1974.

INDEX